COUNTRY COOKING
FROM FARTHINGHOE

Also by Nicola Cox

GOOD FOOD FROM FARTHINGHOE

COUNTRY COOKING FROM FARTHINGHOE

A Calendar of Recipes

by

Nicola Cox

with line illustrations by
David Green

London
Victor Gollancz Ltd
in association with Peter Crawley
1984

*I dedicate this book to my mother
who really can cook.*

© Nicola Cox 1984

British Library Cataloguing in Publication Data
Cox, Nicola
  Country cooking from Farthinghoe.
  1. Cookery, English
  I. Title
  641.5942   TX717

  ISBN 0-575-03504-8

Typeset in Great Britain by
Rowland Phototypesetting Limited
and printed in Great Britain
by R. J. Acford Limited
Chichester, Sussex

CONTENTS

ACKNOWLEDGEMENTS

Without Simon this book might never have reached the publishers; his encouragement, expertise and hard work throughout the tasting, testing and typing stages has helped produce what is, I hope, a really good book and for which I would like to say 'Thank you, darling'.

My thanks to Mrs James our secretary for her untiring good humour and good typing, to my students who have tested and tried the recipes endlessly and to David Green whose pen has captured much of the spirit of Farthinghoe.

Peter Crawley and Stephen Bray with the Gollancz team have been wonderful in their encouragement and forbearance with my endless niggling changes in our endeavours to get everything just right.

It has been a pleasure to work again with Sheila Bush whose clear and discerning editorial eye has helped eliminate confusing points and has smoothed away the rough edges.

As with so many things, it is team work that counts and my heartfelt thanks go to the whole team who have helped to bring out this book.

Nicola Cox
July 1984

INTRODUCTION

Nowadays it's an art to eat in season because the deep freezer and fresh food flown in from foreign fields blur the seasonal edges or even swallow them up completely. In the past, the constraints of primitive storage, lack of winter feeding for animals and absence of high speed transport forced everyone to eat what was naturally to hand. We are lucky today to have such a wide choice but, on the other hand, it's easy to end up with tired beans from the other side of the world rather than waiting to appreciate the first little ones of summer. And who remembers the months when fresh young lamb is at its best, or in what months the milk is best for us to turn our hand to making cheese?

Country cooking is the name I use for the best of English cooking. It's emphatically not just for those who live in the country, but for all who appreciate and want to use ingredients at their seasonal best and probably also at their cheapest. It incorporates all the best that has been handed down to us over the generations, together with all the most exciting innovations and ideas of today.

English country cooking has evolved from the English climate and seasons and from many historic influences. The Romans brought us many new ingredients such as onion and garlic, mint and savory; the Normans introduced their style of made-up dishes and names; while the Crusaders brought back new ingredients, new ideas of how to use them and the exotic spices of the East. The Renaissance contributed, for some, a new awareness of the civilised pleasures of life, and increasing trade made it possible to get new and exciting ingredients. The printed word meant that recipes could be handed on to a wider audience than one's family; widespread use of coal and the arrival of the cooking range changed cooking methods and the Indian Empire left some of its flavour. All these influences caused gradual evolution, one being absorbed to enrich our tradition before the next one came along.

But from the beginning of this century changes in the kitchen have been as revolutionary as elsewhere and the pace fast and furious. Storage and transportation methods, production and breeding techniques, the universal experience of travel, the lack of help and time but the availability of machines to take much of the drudgery from the kitchen—all these and more besides have brought their influences to bear on the food we use and how we cook it. Our cuisine has not been able to assimilate each innovation gradually, and has been all but bowled over by so many new elements and changes. But not quite. I do not believe that the fast food, freezer and microwave scene will overwhelm us, but rather will be tamed and put to good use, while the flavour of real food will again come to be appreciated. The seasons will remain constant (or inconstant in this country!), time is available to some, and the pleasures of cooking, rather than just coping, are beginning to reassert themselves.

The 'experts' have just discovered that we all need to be involved in 'time-intensive products', which to you and me means that we need plenty of time to get on with what we enjoy! Cooking is certainly one way of indulging this but, to me at any rate, indulgence simply means doing things when you want to do them. For instance, make bread when you feel like it but freeze a couple of loaves because you probably won't have the urge to do it again next week. Make jelly when you have enough red currants, pick vegetables a little too young—a waste, perhaps, but a lovely extravagance all the same—and make a game pie when you notice the pheasant has been hung for long enough.

I hate many of the unnecessary additives now used in food, and don't like to rely, more than I need, on processed or convenience foods. But I will certainly use a freezer and a simplified cooking style wherever possible, for there is no quicker way of killing the pleasure of cooking than with an endless cycle of meals without time to cope. Today's English cooking is struggling to emerge from this welter of change, and is showing signs of being as virile as ever. Look around you, and you will find home-produced honey, real eggs (remember them?) and someone in the village with a few spare lettuces or beetroot he'd love you to buy. Search out a small butcher who really knows his meat and hasn't got a huge freezer room; I have one I use just for beef, attracted initially by his beautifully polished brass plate and well hung sides of beef. The beef really is in prime condition, and you can tell this by the yellowish fat and the deep red meat, both sure signs of maturity and flavour. Ask him for some real hill lamb or a proper bit of mutton and, if that's not his speciality, find another one who can get it for you. Try a piece of pork from a real fat porker, and you'll never go back to the fatless watery things that so many of us have become accustomed to putting up with.

There is taste and flavour to be found, if we'll only look for it, and these ideas will only spread again if we encourage them. Use natural products wherever possible. It's not faddy to use sea salt or cold pressed oils, wholemeal and health bread, proper natural yoghurt, brown rice, muesli and granary flour pastry. Not only do they have more flavour but their vitamins and trace elements haven't been bludgeoned out of them, and they can help us to the truly balanced diet so essential for our health and humour.

This is not going to be a scholarly or academic work, but one in which I hope to lead you through this modern labyrinth. I want to rescue some of our tradition and heritage that we are in danger of losing, to incorporate all that is modern in machinery, ingredients and style and to absorb all this into my interpretation of country cooking today. I shall be drawing from my experience of living in the rural village of Farthinghoe with my developing garden and a large family, using what is available because I'm usually much too mean to buy things out of season. I also rely on the sounding board of demonstrating and talking to thousands of people every year, getting to know that they like our Farthinghoe style of cooking and food and feel that it's right in modern Britain today.

Before I had a garden of my own it was easy to fail to appreciate the changing seasons, to rush through life, head down, looking inwards and not noticing the differences in the culinary year as they came. But now, more and more, I find myself guided by the country year; in this book I shall be dealing with everything in its season, so I hope to be able to give you a warning order, as it were, to look out for such and such, for some things have no sooner come than they have gone again. In the country year there always seems to be too much or too little of everything. I know we can use the freezer to put things up for winter, but personally I don't do this more often than I need. Apart from usually preferring to eat in season, I don't like to spend much of my summer blanching over a hot stove when I could be getting brown in the sun. I find I need lots of recipes for, say, rhubarb, which is very prolific in early spring when I'm really pleased to see it. It's wonderful to have courgettes and French beans in plenty and to eat them nearly every day, but I need so many ways of using them. What to do with courgettes when you have been away and they have grown too big? Apples, apples, apples in the autumn; of course they're lovely, but what can we do with them all? We shall start with recipes using the first handful of tiny baby beans from the garden or shops and end up with those that accommodate the plenty of autumn.

Herbs are one of the joys of cooking. They are superb when fresh, and I now have some fifty or sixty in my own garden. But as a travelling army wife for some years, I know what it is to have to rely on dried herbs, and recently I have experimented to decide which freeze well or can be preserved in other ways. So, should you be holidaying in Italy and see great mouth-watering bunches of basil, buy a bottle or two of vinegar and stuff the basil in, to be brought home in your suitcase; then you will not only have basil-flavoured vinegar for your salads but can also fish out the basil, which will have retained much of its wonderful flavour.

Salad herbs are for everyone with even the tiniest plot of garden, a roof garden or even a wide windowsill. One sorrel plant and one of salad burnet look pretty against each other anyway with their different colours and varying shaped leaves; add a row of rocket, and you will be able to ring the changes and give all your salads that little bit of extra something.

Our festivals and moments for celebration crop up throughout the year, and one needs the best of plum pudding recipes, hot cross buns that really work, a spring stuffing for that Easter bird or an alternative for the Christmas bird. I've taken a long time to acquire some of these, so if you haven't already your own favourite, maybe mine will be a help.

I love many of the best recipes of the past and using all that the country can offer. The pleasure of sipping a thimbleful of home-made sloe gin outside in the winter is enhanced by recalling the brilliant October day when we gathered the sloes. Another home-made favourite is orange brandy, made from great-great-grandmama's 17th Lancers recipe, delicious and much cheaper and drier than Grand Marnier. But how many of these good things from past generations are in danger of being lost? When did you last have boiled leg of mutton and caper sauce? I'm ashamed to say that, till recently, I had never had it since childhood days with granny; but get your butcher to hang you a really good leg of two to three year old mutton and remind yourself what food can really taste of.

The country way is 'everything in its own time and time for everything' but, my goodness, how difficult it is these days to follow this old maxim. To me, this means time to pod the beans (how I hated this job as a child, it seemed such a waste of the holidays and my children still think so!); now I find it wonderfully soothing to sit in the sun with the pods popping between my fingers and the tiny jade beans trickling into the colander. Time to pickle vegetables, time to try out an elderflower sorbet or to gather violets to crystallise. These are fun to do if hardly essential, but it takes an age to thumb through innumerable old books to find a recipe to adapt and play about with. So I've done a bit of the leg work and testing, and you may be interested or amused to try some of these rather more unusual ideas. Some of the cooks from the past can tell us so much if we read their books carefully. Hanna Glasse from the 18th century and Meg Dods from the early 19th century are two of my favourites; they write from long experience, and let drop those little tips that ensure success. You know from reading their recipes that their food was tasty and good; they had intimate knowledge of their ingredients and métier and knew how to bring out the best from their raw materials. I often turn to them and some of the dishes in this book are based on their original recipes.

There is a great vogue for chefs and their recipes and the pleasures and beauty of the *nouvelle cuisine*. I find that restaurant food ill lends itself to the home cook because chefs don't want to cook until the client has sat down, whereas the home cook is loath to cook once the guests have arrived. I try to think out all my cooking with the unaided cook in mind, and so I ponder on the difficulties, when entertaining, of last-minute vegetables, sauces and carving, and try to work out how we can have really good food and yet not be a slave to the kitchen.

Much as I admire the true philosophy of the *nouvelle cuisine*, the only facets of it that I find suit most hostesses are its use of top quality ingredients, treated very simply, already in the best English tradition, and its lightness of style. The beautifully decorated and arranged plates, done with the chef's deft fingers and constant practice, will drive most housewives mad and end up with guests belatedly eating tepid food.

I was brought up in the country on top-quality meat, vegetables and fruit picked from the garden half-an-hour before the meal and our own Jersey cows producing the milk, cream, butter and cheese. I swear this produced some of the greatest food in the world, and although now I may not have bright golden cream in which the spoon gets stuck, or my own home-made butter, and may not be able to afford great roasts of beef or saddles of lamb, I can still cook good seasonal food in an interesting way with the care and love that good ingredients deserve.

HOW TO READ THE RECIPES

I have used the same star system as in *Good Food from Farthinghoe* to show how simple, or complicated, a dish is, though this is very subjective and depends on the cook's experience and kitchen equipment.

* Easy   ** Straightforward   *** More complicated

P   This symbol warns you if *Pre-preparation* or *Planning* are necessary because it is disheartening to get half way through a recipe before discovering that the chicken should have been marinading since yesterday!

F   Dishes which freeze successfully are marked with an *F*. It is one thing to freeze a dish for a few days or a week or so ahead for a party, and quite another to dig out something which has been in the freezer for months. I must say I prefer to cook things fresh wherever possible, and rarely serve anything from the freezer for special occasions. But all possible left-overs from our demonstrations are carefully frozen to finish up later, and I am often very pleasantly surprised by their storing qualities.

I don't propose to repeat here all my ideas on equipment, ingredients and basic recipes that I talked about in *Good Food from Farthinghoe*, although it all still applies, as indeed do my thoughts on the store cupboard.

Measurements and Sizes. All the recipes have been based on imperial measurements (for until we can buy meat and vegetables in metric quantities there is not much point in thinking metric), though metric equivalents are shown. It is important to cook each complete recipe either in imperial or metric and not in a mixture of both. Most of the recipes are for 4–6 people, giving 4 generous or 6 smallish portions.

13

Quantities for large parties. Many people have said how useful they found the Buffet Section in *Good Food from Farthinghoe* because it gave the quantities for 25 people as well as for 4–6. Therefore in this book I have picked out various recipes which I find particularly useful for large parties, and have again given the quantities for 25, because it is often so difficult to know which ingredients to double up and which only need to be increased slightly. They are marked in the index thus ●

Eggs, Flour, Sugar and Cream. Eggs are No. 3, flour is plain, sugar is granulated and cream is whipping unless otherwise stated.

Butter. I use Anchor butter for cooking because, although salty, it is firm, without a lot of the milky residue which can make a butter difficult to use in pastry and liable to burn when frying. Where Anchor butter would be too salty, I use lightly salted or unsalted butter, which is becoming easier to buy.

I cook on an Aga and have a convectionaire electric oven (which has the advantage of cooking evenly with its all-round heat, allowing, for example, the pastry on the bottom of flans to cook as fast as the top). But all these recipes have been well tested and can be cooked in a standard gas or electric oven.

Salt. I use sea-salt in all my recipes, coarse for boiling potatoes, pasta, etc., and fine for seasoning. I have always preferred the natural, less chemical flavour of sea-salt, but have only recently discovered what processes refined salt goes through. Intensive heating and flash cooling remove the important trace minerals: the added iodine causes discoloration so it is bleached, and coated with a substance to make it free-flowing. So sea-salt it is for me, though Lane's herbal salt also makes a tasty addition to cooking and dressings.

DEEP MIDWINTER

Winter draws out what Summer laid in

—Thomas Fuller

DEEP MIDWINTER

A year really has no beginning, and it's partly the fact that it is an everlasting cycle with no beginning, middle or end that makes it so fascinating. But books have to start somewhere, as no one has yet produced a book in the round, and publishers, being eminently logical people, feel that the beginning of the calendar year must be the place to start!

I feel, however, that so much of the Christmas and New Year season carry on into the new year that our overwhelming feeling in early January can be one of exhaustion, excess and ennui. We have coped with Christmas, fought our way through the children's holidays, been to too many parties and got over the excitements of New Year's Eve, and the first of January probably begins with a hangover. The turkey carcass sits like a beached hulk, balefully demanding some sort of attention (be it only the dustbin if we have really given up), and there may be the naked knuckle of ham, a drooping mound of Christmas pudding and a tired rind of Stilton. What a way to start the year, and what a moment to start a book! But on the assumption that we are, as usual, full of New Year resolutions, let's get rid of last year's debris and resolve to make this the year in which we eat what is in prime season, catch everything exactly at its best, and probably at its cheapest, and don't miss the few vital weeks of the marmalade oranges or the asparagus. With this resolve and a few recipes to clear up the remnants of Saturnalia we can launch ourselves into the New Year, knowing we have several months before the growing year begins seriously and we have any excuse for panic.

For gardeners, this allows us time to plan and think out what we will grow and what new varieties we may wish to try, and time to send for unusual but worthwhile seeds. Thompson and Morgan and Suttons have seed catalogues to set one dreaming, while John and Caroline Stevens of Suffolk Herbs (*see page 279*) have an amazing range of herb, vegetable and wild flower seed to offer. On a cold January evening I sit by the fire and see, in my mind's eye, row upon row of perfectly grown vegetables in an immaculate kitchen garden, whereas I know perfectly well that the reality will probably be a missed sowing date, the greenhouse unwatered and the vegetable beds pillaged by wood pigeon and alive with cabbage whites. But whatever the mortality rate, those that make it through to the plate will at least have a good taste. Lashings of dung is the answer, with close planting as well as firm planting, and as few chemicals as possible. If you are interested in organic gardening, do contact the Henry Doubleday Research Association (*see page 279*). I have used biological control with the greatest success for whitefly in the greenhouse; you hang up tobacco leaves with parasitic wasps' eggs which hatch and live on the white fly all summer. No more spraying or inhaling beastly chemicals, no more wondering if the cucumber or tomatoes are really safe to eat.

Recommending varieties is a dangerous game, but I must just mention one or two that I have tried and found particularly good. The red Brunswick onion set produces a sweet-fleshed onion which can be eaten raw, looks pretty sliced, or will keep well into winter with a fine flavour. Sutton's Ishikura is a tall, straight, very long-standing spring onion, ideal for Chinese dishes, and a spring planting stands throughout the summer and following winter. Yellow courgettes, especially Thompson and Morgan's Burpee Golden Zucchini, make a nice variation and are easier to see to pick than the green. Sutton's tall curled green kale is a gem, and I would hate to be without the cabbage 'April'. Golden Wonder Turnips have a lovely flavour and colour, and the pumpkin Sutton's Table Ace, although a smallish, acorn shape, has a dark green skin and fine, firm-tasting orange flesh that keeps well into winter. The Florence fennel from Suffolk Herbs, Zefa Fino, has produced the fleshiest roots for me without bolting, while their Italian Lettuce, *Lattuga Meraviglia delle 4 Stagioni*, produces its red-tinted leaves all the year round. Salad Bowl, the non-hearting lettuce, is useful as decoration and an all-purpose lettuce which lasts well, but I love Sutton's Lobjoits Green Cos because hasn't a good cos lettuce got a lovely flavour?

But, back to reality and with or without a garden, town or country, now is the time to use all those winter vegetables which suit the season so well. It's also a chance to cook some good winter food that only tastes right in these chilly months, before we are confronted with the new season's produce and spring delicacies.

This is the blowy time of year when I will make any excuse to tuck myself up in the warmth and welcome of my kitchen. The pungent smell of oranges and rows of gold and amber pots seem a worthwhile result from an afternoon spent marmalade making. Pounding dough and making cakes is more fun than shovelling snow, and the rich-smelling hot food will be greatly appreciated by the family coming in from the cold. Of course, unless we live in the country with an outdoor job, or unless we keep our house particularly cold, we simply don't need the steaming platefuls of rich fatty meat, mounds of potatoes and huge suet puddings which used to be necessary to fuel the inner central heating system, preferring to heat the air around us, pleasant but a much more wasteful and more expensive way of using energy! But even now, though few of us need to live on a constant high calory diet, there is no denying that after a cold morning spent playing or watching rugger, battling our way to work, toiling in the garden or just tramping the country to work up an appetite, a steaming bowl of Kidney Soup, followed by Lancashire Hot Pot and an Orange and Date Steamed Pudding, can seem mighty good.

One way of getting round the calory problem is to produce just one warming winter course and balance the rest of our meal with lighter salads or fruit. This seems the right approach to me; don't let us forego these beautiful dishes which are so much part of our cooking heritage, but let us temper them with a balance of light and simple dishes. Let's combine simple, healthy, everyday food which we can prepare quickly with other dishes that take a bit of time and trouble, and in which we can express and enjoy ourselves, the latter produced for entertaining, for weekends or just when the mood takes us and time allows.

I try to feed my family on good natural food in season, because, without being at all faddy, human beings, like racehorses, look better, work better and *are* better when fed on a balanced, fresh wholesome diet. Try a slice of Knibbed Wheat Health Loaf, spread with some Miso-Soya, that fermented soya spread not unlike marmite and full of health-giving properties; top it with some Yoghurt Cream Cheese, Pickled Vegetables and salad leaves or sprouted seeds, and you've got a really good, nourishing plateful.

Make the most of your winter cooking while it's nice to be warm and snug in the kitchen, mixing traditional dishes and your new ideas and making use of whatever is at its seasonal best. Before you know where you are, spring will be upon you.

DEEP MIDWINTER

First Courses and Supper Dishes

Smoked Cod's Roe Special
Smoked Cod's Roe Mousseline
Chicken Liver Scalpicon
The End of the Ham
Hambone and Bean Soup
Haricot Bean Salad
Farthinghoe Country Quiche
Chicken and Mushroom Pancakes

Soups

Kidney Soup
Mulligatawny Soup
Artichoke Soup
Publisher's Leek Soup

Fish

Soft Herring Roes Meunière
Kedgeree
Fish Cakes
Fish Steaks and Shallot Mousseline

Main Courses

Ham and Banana Rolls au Gratin
Baked Brown Rice and Ham
Toad in the Hole
● Spiced Sausage Turnover
Braised Lambs' Hearts with Apricots
Stuffed Cabbage Leaves
Liver with Raisins and Port
Marinated Pork with Crackling
   Fingers and Baked Apples
Boiled Leg of Mutton and Caper
   Sauce
Lancashire Hot Pot
● Boned Shoulder of Lamb with Dried
   Pear and Nut Stuffing
Steak and Kidney Pie with Flaky
   Pastry
Steak and Kidney Pudding

Vegetables

Leeks au Gratin
Gratin of Cauliflower in Mushroom
   Sauce
● Onions in Béchamel Sauce
Stovie Potatoes
Bacon Stovies
Hot Beetroot with Oil and Vinegar
Steamed Savoy Cabbage with
   Buttered Breadcrumbs
Braised Curly Kale
Braised Jerusalem Artichokes
Healthy Winter Salad with Yoghurt
   and Olive Oil Dressing
● Flageolets aux Herbes

Puddings

Marlborough Tart
Lemon Meringue Pie
Orange Crêpes
Orange and Date Steamed Pudding
● Winter Fruit Salad
● Snow Cream with Rosemary
Hot Apricot Soufflé
Orange and Ratafia Creams
Whipped Syllabub

Miscellaneous

Potted Stilton
Stilton Cream
Home-Made Sausages
Knibbed Wheat Health Loaf
Oatcakes
Flap Jacks
Everlasting Cake
Creamy Marmalade Sauce
Dark Seville Marmalade
Ginger Marmalade
17th Lancers Orange Brandy
Orange Brandy Marmalade

● Also quantities for 25 persons

First Courses and Supper Dishes

** Smoked Cod's Roe Special and Smoked Cod's Roe Mousseline

January and February are the months when smoked cod's roe is plentiful and at its best. In large cities you will probably find it at any time, but it is not always distributed to the country, so now is the moment to use it and to lay in a little stock for the freezer. I prefer not to freeze anything salty for more than a few months, but it should see you through the summer.

I love the Greek taramasalata, but that is not the only way to use smoked cod's roe. My mother does this delicious English version, and the spread keeps well in the fridge to dig into for several weeks. The Cod's Roe Mousseline is not meant to be a long keeper but is excellent and delicate, just right for a party.

Smoked Cod's Roe Special

Ingredients
4–6 people

8 oz (225g) smoked cod's roe
3–4 oz (75–100g) soft butter
½ clove garlic (optional)
juice of ½–1 lemon (approx)
shake of tabasco sauce to taste
1 tbs chopped parsley
2–4 tbs cream (optional)
pepper
salt only if necessary

If the cod's roe is rather hard and dry, soak it in hot water for a few minutes to make it easier to skin. Smoked cod's roe can vary from the very dry and salty to quite soft and delicate, so use your discretion, and don't hesitate to add more butter or cream if it needs it. Peel the smoked roe. Cream the butter until really soft, or process in a food processor, then add the roe and crushed garlic, if used, and beat together until light. Add lemon juice to taste and season with tabasco and pepper. Add the parsley and, depending on how strongly flavoured it is, a little cream to soften the flavour. Pack into pots and serve with hot melba toast or bread as a starter or on biscuits or packed into sticks of celery to go with drinks.

Smoked Cod's Roe Mousseline

Follow the recipe above but use only half the amount of butter; then whip about 4–6 fl oz (100–175ml) of cream until softly flowing and gradually whisk this (by hand) into the creamed smoked roe, with lemon juice to taste, to make a very light mixture. The cream must not be fully whipped or the mixture will be cotton woolly, and the creamed roe and whipped cream must be at the same temperature when they are combined.

Chicken Liver Scalpicon

Here we lightly sauté chicken livers and serve them in a tasty sauce. They can be served in little cocottes on their own, with rice, or on toast, or can be used to fill vol-au-vents, pastry shells and pancakes.

Ingredients
4–6 people

¾–1 lb (350–450g) chicken or duck livers
2 oz (50g) butter
1 finely chopped onion
4 oz (100g) mushrooms or
    1 tbs mushroom ketchup (optional)
¾ oz (20g) plain flour
5 fl oz (150ml) red wine or 2–3 tbs
    Madeira or sherry   } to make up to 15 fl oz (450 ml)
10 fl oz (300ml) good stock
1 teasp tomato purée
1 tbs finely chopped parsley
salt, pepper and cayenne

Pick the chicken livers over, carefully removing threads and green-tinged flesh which can be bitter. Cut into generous pieces.

Melt the butter and gently fry the onion. When soft but not brown, turn up the heat and fry the chicken livers and mushrooms (if used), halved or quartered if large, until the livers are sealed and lightly browned but still rosy inside. Remove from the pan and add the flour to the butter in the pan. Cook gently for 2–3 minutes, remove from the heat, wait for the sizzling to cease and add the wine (or Madeira or sherry), stock and tomato purée (and the mushroom ketchup if used). Bring to the boil, whisking, and simmer for 10–20 minutes until reduced and rich looking. Season and return the chicken livers and mushrooms to the sauce, together with the chopped parsley. Serve on toast, in cocottes or how you will.

The End of the Ham

The invaluable Christmas ham has furnished us with many good meals and dishes. We have had plates of ham with soft boiled or poached eggs, toasted ham and chutney sandwiches for impromptu suppers, ham sandwiches galore for energetic walkers and sportsmen, elegant dishes of Ham and Banana Rolls and homely dishes of Baked Brown Rice and Ham.

Baked Ham and Eggs on a Plate. The dwindling ham can now only offer us some final, wafer-thin slices which can be heated in a very hot oven (450°F/230°C/Gas 8) on a generously buttered plate for a few moments before breaking an egg or two over it. Top with a little grated cheese, a spoonful or so of cream and a generous grind of pepper and return to the oven for a few moments until the egg is lightly baked; it will continue to cook on the plate, so remove it early. It makes a good supper with a slice of toast.

Potted Ham. Now the very last chunks and scraps can be removed and potted; you need half the weight of the ham in soft butter, and a little cayenne pepper and mace. Chop the ham in a food processor, add the butter and seasoning and process until not too smooth. Pack into a pot and use for sandwiches or with hot toast. Now only the meaty bone remains forlorn on the plate. This will make Hambone and Bean Soup, and I usually cook extra beans to make Haricot Bean Salad.

P F ** Hambone and Bean Soup

A tasty soup or a meal in itself if you leave more beans in or add some sliced smoked sausage and serve it with croûtons. You can take out some of the cooked beans to make Haricot Bean Salad.

Ingredients
4–6 people

1 lb (450g) haricot beans (this is enough for soup and salad or you can add more if a thicker soup or larger salad is required)
1 oz (25g) ham fat or butter
4 oz (100g) diced onion
4 oz (100g) diced carrot
2 oz (50g) diced turnip or parsnip (optional)
½ stick diced celery
slices smoked sausage (optional)
a little finely chopped parsley
fried croûtons (optional)
salt and pepper if necessary

Hambone Stock
1 meaty hambone
1 onion
1 large carrot
1 stick celery
½–1 small turnip or parsnip
1 flattened clove garlic
1 bay leaf
a few parsley stalks
1 sprig thyme
2 cloves
6–8 peppercorns
1 ham or beef stock cube
4–4½ pts (2.8–3.1l) water

Soak the beans in plenty of cold water for 5–6 hours or overnight.

Hambone Stock. Place all the ingredients for the hambone stock into a large pan and bring to the boil; skim if necessary, then simmer, covered, for 5–6 hours or cook in a low oven (or overnight in the Aga). Strain off the stock and return to the pan with the soaked and drained beans; simmer gently for about 1½–2½ hours until the beans are tender. Remove 1 lb (450g) of the cooked beans and set aside for a salad if you wish. You may like to simmer the remainder until a little more cooked and mushy. Process the beans briefly until they are not too smooth or press some of them through a sieve and return to the pan with their stock.

Melt the butter in a small pan and add the diced vegetables; sweat gently without browning for 20–30 minutes until tender and butter-flavoured, then add to the soup with sliced smoked sausage, if used. Correct the seasoning, heat and serve scattered with parsley, handing fried croûtons if you wish.

F *   Haricot Bean Salad

Make this when you are making Hambone and Bean Soup, and you will have a lovely dish to eat as part of a mixed hors d'oeuvre, on its own as a first course, or as a vegetable.

Ingredients

**1 lb (450g) cooked beans from Hambone
and Bean Soup** (*see p22*)

Dressing
**4 tbs fruity olive oil
lemon juice or vinegar to taste
chopped parsley or chervil
salt and pepper**

While the beans are still hot, dress them with salt and pepper to taste. Add the oil and lemon juice or vinegar to taste and serve, preferably still luke-warm, scattered with parsley or chervil.

𝓕 ✷✷   Farthinghoe Country Quiche

I don't know many recipes for wholemeal pastry that I find work very well. This one does, and I use healthy granary flour to give it taste and texture and a good nutty crunch. The filling is a country mixture of smoked bacon, cheese and mushrooms, but vary this as the spirit moves you. You can also use it to make cooked tartlets filled subsequently, perhaps with cold chicken and vegetables in mayonnaise.

Should you wish to make the pastry with a soft, sunflower oil margarine you must use it really well chilled or frozen so that you don't make too soft a dough, for this pastry needs to include enough water so that it won't be crumbly when cooked.

Ingredients
4–6 people

Pastry
3½ oz (85g) firm butter or margarine
6 oz (175g) granary flour
½ teasp salt
4 tbs cold water

Filling
3–4 oz (75–100g) smoked streaky bacon, cut thick
½ oz (12g) butter or margarine
4 oz (100g) mushrooms (optional)
3 eggs *or* 2 eggs and 2 yolks
6 fl oz (175ml) milk and 4 fl oz (100 ml) cream *or* use all milk
3–4 oz (75–100g) Cheddar cheese
1–2 tomatoes (optional)
salt, pepper and nutmeg

Pastry. If using soft margarine and a food processor, cube the margarine and chill in the freezer until firm. If you are making the pastry by hand, freeze the margarine, then grate into the flour quickly.

Place the flour and salt in a bowl, or in the food processor with metal blade, and add firm butter or frozen margarine in cubes or grated. Rub in or process, adding the water at once, until a dough forms; knead briefly until smooth, then form into a flat disc and chill for ½–2 hours until firm. Roll very thinly and line a 9" (24cm) flan tin; prick the base and line with tinfoil and baking beans. Bake in a hot oven (425°F/220°C/Gas 7) for 8–12 minutes until set; then remove tinfoil and beans and continue to bake in a moderately hot oven (375°F/190°C/Gas 5) for a further 10–15 minutes until firm but not too brown. Fill with the filling and continue to bake for about 20–30 minutes until the filling is just firm and golden brown. Serve at once, while the pastry is crisp. The quiche is also nice warm or cold, and it freezes very well.

Filling. Cut the bacon into large dice and fry in the butter until lightly browned. Add the mushrooms, if used, and sauté lightly. Beat together the eggs, milk and cream, seasoning and three-quarters of the cheese, add the bacon and mushrooms and pour into the quiche. Top with sliced tomato, if used, and sprinkle over remaining cheese.

$\mathcal{F}$ **   Chicken and Mushroom Pancakes

Plain pancakes that can be filled with a variety of fillings or with left overs are not only very practical but also very popular. The unfilled pancakes can be kept in the freezer ready for filling with left-over turkey, ham, chicken, or whatever, and after Christmas (or at any time) will be a great boon. Filled pancakes can be frozen individually wrapped.

Ingredients
12 people as a first course
4–6 people as a main course

20 Pancakes
3 eggs
15 fl oz (450ml) milk and water mixed
    half-and-half
8 oz (225g) plain flour
5–6 tbs sunflower or light oil
½ teasp salt

Filling for 12 Pancakes
1–1½ lb (450–675g) cooked diced
    chicken or turkey
8 oz (225g) button mushrooms
2 tbs oil

Filling Sauce
2½ oz (65g) butter
1 chopped onion
2½ oz (65g) plain flour
15 fl oz (450ml) chicken stock
12 fl oz (350ml) milk
1 tbs Dijon mustard
pinch ground mace
salt and pepper

Topping Sauce (optional)
¾ oz (20g) butter
¾ oz (20g) plain flour
1 pt (600ml) milk
salt and pepper

To Assemble
4–6 tbs grated cheese or breadcrumbs
    and few flakes butter

Pancakes. Break the eggs into the food processor or liquidiser and add half the milk and water mixture, the flour and salt. Process until smooth, adding the remaining liquid and finally the oil. Rest the mixture for 10–15 minutes, or about 1–2 hours if you have made it by hand.

Heat and lightly grease a heavy flat-based 8″ (20cm) frying pan with lard or oil. Pour in about half a coffee cup (2–3 tbs) of the mixture and swirl around the pan. Cook until lightly brown, turn, and cook the second side. Turn out and pile up ready to use, remembering to cool the base of the pan in cold water before making the next pancake. You should not need to grease the pan after the first time as there is enough oil in the mixture to keep it greased. Should your first pancake stick, scrape it out, clean the pan with salt and kitchen paper but do not wash it. Heat it, grease it and try again; after 2–3 tries the most stubborn pan should comply!

Stack the pancakes with a sheet of kitchen paper between every six or so. Keep in a plastic bag or damp cloth until ready to use. (To freeze, put cling film between each pancake and freeze in a plastic bag.)

Filling. Slice the mushrooms and sauté in the oil in a frying pan. Dice up the chicken or turkey into generous cubes.

Filling Sauce. Melt the butter in a saucepan, add the onion and fry gently until golden, then add the flour and cook, stirring, over moderate heat for 2–3 minutes. Draw the pan off the heat, wait for the sizzling to cease, then add the chicken stock and milk. Return the pan to the heat and bring to the boil, whisking. Simmer for 2–3 minutes and add the mustard and seasoning. Fold in the mushrooms and chicken and keep warm.

Topping sauce. Make in exactly the same way as the filling sauce, but it will be of a coating consistency.

To Assemble. Place a generous spoonful of the mixture on each pancake, fold in the edges and roll up. Place quite close together in a well-greased gratin dish and top with the topping sauce and grated cheese or breadcrumbs and flakes of butter. Alternatively (especially if the pancakes have just been filled with the hot filling and you are ready to serve them), top with grated cheese and a few breadcrumbs and flakes of butter. Pop in a hot oven (400°F/200°C/Gas 6) for just a few minutes until hot through and the cheese has melted.

To heat through from cold, allow 40–50 minutes for the sauced version in a moderately hot oven (375°F/190°C/Gas 5) until brown and bubbling. The unsauced version will need a dribble or two of cream and to be tightly covered until hot.

Soups

F * **Kidney Soup**

This used to be a winter favourite, but seems to be rather forgotten nowadays. I find it very popular and think it's well worth reviving, especially as kidneys are not at all expensive.

Ingredients
4–6 people

8 oz (225g) lambs' kidneys
1½ oz (35g) butter
1 finely chopped stick celery
1 finely chopped large onion
1 finely chopped carrot
1½ oz (35g) flour
2 pts (1.2l) good stock
1 tbs tomato purée
1 bay leaf
1 sprig fresh or pinch dried thyme
salt and pepper

To Garnish
fresh chopped parsley
fried croûtons

Dice a quarter of the kidneys for garnish and mince or chop the remainder finely. Melt nearly all the butter in a saucepan and gently soften the onion, celery and carrot for 5–10 minutes; add the chopped kidney and fry for 2–3 minutes; sprinkle on the flour and cook, stirring, for 2–3 minutes longer. Draw the pan off the stove and wait for the sizzling to cease. Pour on the stock, add the tomato purée, bay leaf, thyme and seasoning and bring to the boil whilst whisking. Simmer gently, covered, for 1–1½ hours and then liquidise. Sieve and correct the seasoning.

Fry the remaining kidney briefly in the rest of the butter and add. Serve with a dusting of chopped parsley and fried croûtons.

F ✳✳ Mulligatawny Soup

One of India's dishes which has taken a permanent place in our cookbooks. We may not serve it at breakfast, as it is served in India, but it makes a good soup for any other time!

Ingredients
4–6 people

1–2 tbs dripping or oil
1 large finely chopped onion
2 finely chopped carrots
1 small finely chopped parsnip or turnip
1 small peeled and finely chopped
   cooking apple
1–2 teasp curry powder
2 teasp flour
2½–3 pts (1.5–1.8l) good stock or stock
   cubes and water
1 teasp lime or lemon pickle (optional)
lime or lemon juice to taste
salt
pepper if necessary

Spice Bag
½ teasp whole coriander
2 cardamom pods or ¼ teasp ground
   cardamom
6 peppercorns
2–3 parsley stalks
1 bay leaf
1 sprig thyme
strip thinly pared lime or lemon rind

Garnish
2–3 oz (50–75g) cooked, dry rice

Melt the dripping in a large pan and add the onion, carrot, parsnip and apple. Fry gently for 10–15 minutes while you prepare the spice bag.

Sprinkle the curry powder and flour over the vegetables and fry for several minutes before drawing off the stove and adding the stock, salt and bag of spice. Bring to the simmer, whisking, then simmer for 45–60 minutes until well flavoured. Remove the spice bag, squeeze well, and add the lime or lemon pickle. Purée and sieve the soup. Check the seasoning and add a squeeze of lime or lemon juice if necessary. Hand a bowl of dry cooked rice to sprinkle over the soup.

Spice Bag. Bruise the coriander, cardamom and peppercorns in a mortar and tie in muslin with the parsley stalks, thyme, bayleaf and strip of lime or lemon rind.

F * ## Artichoke Soup

Winter and early spring are the time for these delicately flavoured but knobbly tubers. When in a hurry, I have been known not to peel them but just scrub them really well, though the finished soup will be a little greyish. If you want to peel them ahead, leave them in a little water to which you have added a 50mg vitamin C tablet (from the chemist). This is useful for any fruit or vegetable which discolours once peeled, like apples, pears, etc. I put them into a plastic bag with this acidulated water excluding all the air. If you freeze this soup, either add the egg yolks and cream on reheating, or reheat very carefully in a *bain marie*.

Ingredients
4–6 people

1 lb (450g) scrubbed and peeled
    artichokes
2 oz (50g) butter
2 finely chopped onions
2 peeled and diced potatoes
1½ pts (900ml) good chicken stock
5 fl oz (150ml) milk
2 egg yolks
5 fl oz (150ml) cream
some finely chopped parsley
salt and pepper

Melt the butter in a saucepan and gently cook the onion until tender. Cut up and add the artichokes and the potatoes. Stir until coated in butter, press a butter paper down on the vegetables, cover with a lid and cook very gently for 10–15 minutes; do not fry or brown. In this way the vegetables absorb the butter and have a wonderful flavour. Add the stock, season and simmer for about 15–20 minutes, until completely tender.

Liquidise or sieve, return to the rinsed-out pan, add the milk and correct the seasoning. Heat. Whisk the egg yolks well to prepare them for the hot soup, add the cream and whisk again. Very slowly, in a fine thread, add the soup to the yolks, whisking well; when about 10 fl oz (300ml) has been added, return the mixture to the saucepan. Heat through but *do not boil* or the yolks will curdle. Serve sprinkled with chopped parsley.

F * Publisher's Leek Soup

We are rather inclined to make smooth soup with our modern machinery. This simple soup, for which I have to thank my publisher Peter Crawley, has generous bits of leek in it, and makes a really comforting soup. It provides a cosy supper dish if you cube and dry some stale brown bread, preferably home-made, in the oven. Put in the bottom of the soup bowl with a handful of grated cheese, and ladle over the soup.

Ingredients
4–6 people

¾–1 lb (350–450g) white and tender
   green leeks
1½ oz (35g) butter
1½ oz (35g) flour
2 pts (1.2l) good stock
¼ pt (150ml) milk
½ chicken stock cube

1 bay leaf
good pinch mace
salt and pepper

To Serve
croûtons
a little grated cheese (optional)
chopped parsley (optional)

Wash the leeks well and cut them in half lengthways so that you can rinse the mud from between the leaves. Cut them into slices between ½"–1" (1–2cm) thick, thinner for elegant soup or thicker for a more rustic character. Melt the butter in a heavy pan or casserole (earthenware gives a good flavour) and fry gently, covered, without browning to sweat the leeks for about 20–30 minutes. Remove the pan from the heat and stir in the flour. Add the stock and milk and return to the stove. Add a pinch of mace, the bay leaf and stock cube and bring to the boil whilst stirring. Simmer for 20 minutes before serving. Serve with croûtons, a little grated cheese or some chopped parsley if you wish.

Fish

* Soft Herring Roes Meunière

From January onwards the herring is at its best and you should be able to buy the soft roes separately. They are delicious when very lightly cooked and served on toast as a supper dish or savoury.

Ingredients
2 people for supper
4–6 people for a savoury

½–¾ lb (225–350g) soft herring roes
a little milk
a little plain flour
2–3 oz (50–75g) butter (more if you have to fry 4–6 croûtes of bread)

2–6 thickish slices stale white bread, cut into 2½″–3″ (5–6cm) circles if for a savoury
juice ½ lemon
parsley to garnish
salt, pepper and cayenne

Soak the picked-over roes in a little milk for 5–10 minutes.

Season a little flour on a plate with salt, pepper and cayenne pepper. Heat about 1 oz (25g) of the butter and, when hot, fry the bread croûtes until crisp and golden on both sides. Drain on kitchen paper and keep warm.

Melt and heat about 1 oz (25g) more of the butter in the frying pan. Take the roes out of the milk, dip each in the seasoned flour and fry them all gently, turning once until just cooked but still very pale and soft. Remove from the butter and set on the croûtes. Add a little bit more fresh butter to the pan, and when it froths add a good squeeze or two of lemon juice. Pour this over the roes, give a light dusting of salt and cayenne pepper and serve with a nice sprig of curly parsley.

* Kedgeree

Whether it is for breakfast or for supper, made with salmon or smoked haddock, kedgeree is a firm favourite. It is one of those dishes adopted from India which has really stuck, even if it has lost its original spices and is now made with fish rather than lentils. The quantities don't have to be too precise so long as the rice does not swamp the fish and you are generous with the butter.

It might be useful to know that 1 lb (450g) of raw fillet gives you about 9 oz (250g) of cooked, flaked fish. Each ounce of uncooked rice will weigh about 2½ oz (65g) when cooked, so use about 7½ oz (210g) of uncooked rice for this recipe.

Ingredients
4–6 people

9 oz (250g) cooked flaked salmon or smoked haddock	2–3 hard boiled or soft boiled eggs
1¼ lb (550g) cooked rice	1 egg
3–4 oz (75–100g) butter	2–3 tbs finely chopped parsley
	salt and cayenne pepper

Melt the butter in a large frying pan and, when hot, add the rice, flaked fish and roughly chopped eggs. Toss and turn until hot through, seasoning with salt and cayenne to taste; it should be fairly highly seasoned. Then toss in most of the parsley. Make a little nest and break in the egg; cover it with the hot rice and leave to cook gently for about half a minute. Stir the semi-cooked egg right through the kedgeree and serve at once whilst moist, sprinkled with the reserved parsley.

Chopped onion fried in the butter, chives, curry powder or a little cream can all be added with advantage to vary the kedgeree.

ℱ ** Fish Cakes

Salmon, haddock, cod or coley all make good fish-cakes. They are lovely for breakfast, and rather a treat these days, or good for lunch or supper. It is worth making them in quantity and freezing. The balance of fish, potato and seasoning is the important thing.

Ingredients
10–12 fishcakes

1–1½ lb (450–675g) raw or ¾ lb (350g) cooked and flaked salmon, haddock, cod or coley	seasoned flour
	2–3 drops oil
	approx 3–4 oz (75–100g) dried breadcrumbs
¾ lb (350g) mashed potato	salt and pepper
3 tbs mixed chopped chives and parsley	fat or oil for frying
2–3 eggs	

Cook the fish in a little seasoned milk if raw; skin and flake.

Mix the flaked fish and mashed potato, add seasoning and herbs and bind with one of the eggs. Form into cakes with floured hands and pat with seasoned flour. (The fish cakes can be fried just like this if time is short, but they won't be so crisp.) Whisk the remaining eggs with a few drops of oil to help give a crisp crust, and a pinch of salt to break down the egg. First dip the fish cakes into the egg, then roll them in breadcrumbs until well coated.

Heat about ¼″–½″ (½–1cm) fat or oil in a frying pan and, when hot, fry the fish cakes briskly on each side to a nice brown. Drain on kitchen paper and serve.

Having formed the cakes, I often chill them until firm in the freezer because they are then easier to dip in the egg and breadcrumbs.

✱✱ Fish Steaks and Shallot Mousseline Sauce

Fresh fish deserves poaching in this way (and there is nothing really better than North Sea cod or haddock) and serving with this delicate shallot and butter mousseline. The sauce can be prepared in two parts beforehand, then heated and combined on serving. The fish is never boiled but is just left sitting on the side of the stove to poach. The cooking liquid, though a little salty, is tasty and can be used to make a potato or fish soup.

Ingredients
4–6 people

4–6×8 oz (225g) fish steaks, cod or
    haddock, or slightly smaller steaks of
    the richer salmon, turbot or halibut
1½ pts (900ml) water
½ pt (300ml) milk
2 slices lemon
6–8 peppercorns
2 teasp salt

Shallot Mousseline Sauce
3 tbs very finely chopped shallots
2 fl oz (50ml) water
1–2 tbs lemon juice
1 egg yolk
1 tbs cold water
4 oz (100g) lightly salted butter
salt and pepper

Bring the water and milk to the boil in a heavy pan, add the lemon, peppercorns and salt and the fish steaks. Bring the water just back to the simmer, then cover and leave in a warm place on the side of the stove for about 10 minutes. Lift out the cooked steaks, drain carefully and lay on a warm serving dish. Serve as they are or coated with a little sauce, the rest in a sauce boat.

Shallot Mousseline Sauce. Put the shallots, water and lemon juice in a small heavy pan (not aluminium, which reacts with lemon) and simmer until the shallot is tender and the liquid reduced by half.

While it simmers, you can make the egg yolk mousse over it in a small bowl. Place the egg yolk and cold water in a small bowl and whisk over gentle heat until the yolk thickens and the mixture greatly increases in volume. Set aside.

To the reduced shallot liquid, add the diced butter and keep whisking and boiling the mixture. The butter will melt and foam, thickening the mixture into a light sauce. Either immediately whisk into the egg mousseline, season and serve, or set aside and, on serving, bring back to the boil, season and whisk into the egg mousseline.

Main Courses

** Ham and Banana Rolls au Gratin

This is one of my mother-in-law's special dishes. Try it while you can still carve decent slices from the ham to wrap around the bananas. I have also made it most successfully with cubed ham and cut-up banana for a buffet supper. The flavour of rosemary marries the ham with the banana.

Ingredients
4–6 people

8 slices ham
2 large bananas
10 fl oz (300ml) milk, heated with 1 slice
   onion and several sprigs rosemary
1 oz (25g) butter
1 oz (25g) plain flour
5 fl oz (150ml) whipping cream
1 teasp Dijon mustard
squeeze lemon juice
1–2 oz (25–50g) grated cheese
salt and pepper

Heat the milk with the onion and rosemary and leave, covered, to infuse for about 10 minutes.

Melt the butter in a saucepan, add the flour and cook, stirring, over moderate heat for 1–2 minutes. Draw the pan off the heat, wait for the sizzling to cease, then add the strained, flavoured milk. Bring to the boil, whisking well, and simmer for 1–2 minutes. Thin with the cream, add mustard, very little salt but plenty of pepper and a squeeze of lemon juice.

Cut the peeled bananas in half lengthways and again in half cross-ways; wrap each slice of ham round a piece of banana and place in a well-greased gratin dish. Cover with the sauce and scatter with the cheese. Bake in a moderately hot oven (375°F/190°C/Gas 5) for 25–35 minutes until bubbling and golden.

* Baked Brown Rice and Ham

Once the ham starts to look a bit of a has-been and everyone has seen it in various guises, try using some of it in this comfortable risotto of brown rice, which is so enjoyed and appreciated after the rich food of Christmas. Brown rice is much better for us than white, and its nutty flavour and chewy texture make it far more interesting to eat. I like to serve it frequently, and of course you can adapt this recipe either to make a plain risotto or to use up various other meats.

Ingredients
4–6 people

8–12 oz (225–350g) diced ham (or other cooked meat)
10–12 oz (275–350g) long grain brown rice
2 tbs rendered ham fat, dripping, oil or butter

1 finely chopped onion
1 teasp curry powder
1 tbs currants
about 1 pt (600ml) stock or ½ ham stock cube (Knorr) and water
a little salt and plenty of pepper

Fry the onion in the fat in a casserole until softened, then add the curry powder and rice. Fry for another 2–3 minutes to seal the starch on to the grains of rice before adding the ham, currants and hot stock. Season lightly, especially with salt, for the ham may be salty, stir once, cover closely and cook in a slow oven (300°F/150°C/Gas 2) for about 1½–2 hours, or simmer very gently until tender. Taste a few grains of rice taken from the middle to see if they are tender but still a bit chewy. If all the stock has not gone, boil fast for a moment, or, if the mixture is dry before the rice is tender, add a little more boiling stock or water.

This dish will keep warm in a very slow oven.

* Toad in the Hole

This is always a great stand-by and favourite for a simple lunch at any time of year. In the old days, it was often made with pieces of steak, but now is invariably made with sausages. You can add some chopped herbs to the batter, but if the sausages are really good and spicy it's not necessary. You need really hot smoking fat when you pour in the batter, and a large enough tin to make a thin, crisp, puffed layer.

Ingredients
4–6 people

Batter
6 oz (175g) plain flour
2 eggs
10 fl oz (300ml) milk
up to 5 fl oz (150ml) cold water
½ teasp salt
pepper

1–1½ lb (425–650g) best pork sausages
2–3 tbs pork fat or dripping

Batter. Sift the flour and seasoning into a bowl, make a hole in the middle and break in the eggs. Stir with a whisk or wooden spoon, gradually incorporating the flour and adding the milk. Beat really well, then thin to cream consistency with the water. Rest for 1–2 hours before cooking. The batter can also be made in a food processor or liquidiser, breaking the eggs in first, in which case it will only need a 10–20 minute rest.

Cook the sausages for about 5–10 minutes, until just colouring, in the fat in a 10″ × 12″ (25cm × 30cm) roasting pan in a hot oven (425°F/220°C/Gas 7). Then remove to a plate while you reheat the pan in the oven with a ⅛″ (2mm) layer of fat left in it. Heat until the fat is smoking, then quickly arrange the sausages in the pan, pour over the batter and return to the oven to cook for 35–45 minutes, until the batter is well risen and golden brown. Do not open the oven door for at least the first 20 minutes. Serve at once.

F **   Spiced Sausage Turnover

This will keep hot, wrapped in many layers of newspaper and tinfoil, for 3–4 hours, and is a great favourite for shooting and winter picnics. It can be prepared and left ready to cook for a large party, and is especially popular with teenagers. If you want to freeze it, use fresh sausage-meat and fresh pastry and omit the hard-boiled egg. Freeze uncooked and allow a little longer cooking time.

Ingredients *4–6 people*	*To Glaze (optional)* **egg wash**
½ lb (225g) pkt puff pastry	*3 turnovers for 25 people*
1 lb (450g) best pork sausage-meat	3 × ½ lb (225g) pkt puff pastry
½ oz (12g) dripping or oil	3½ lb (1.6kg) best pork sausage-meat
1 finely chopped onion	1 oz (25g) dripping or oil
2–3 oz (50–75g) mushrooms (optional)	3 finely chopped onions
2 peeled, de-seeded and diced tomatoes	8 oz (225g) mushrooms (optional)
1 tbs chopped fresh or ¼ teasp dried herbs	6 peeled, de-seeded and diced tomatoes
1–2 hard-boiled eggs	3 tbs fresh or ¾ teasp dried herbs
1 egg	6 hard-boiled eggs
salt, pepper and ground mace	2–3 eggs
	¼ teasp ground mace
	salt and pepper

Melt the dripping or oil in a small frying pan and soften the onion in it. Halve or quarter the mushrooms (if used), add, and fry for 3–4 minutes. Add the mixture to the sausage-meat with the tomatoes, chopped herbs and roughly cut up hard-boiled eggs. Mix well together, binding with an egg and seasoning with salt, pepper and mace.

Roll the packet of pastry thinly to a square of approximately 12″ × 12″ (30cm × 30cm). Trim off the edges with a sharp knife and cut off a ½″ (1cm) strip for decoration. Set on a greased baking sheet and place the sausage-meat mixture down the centre; fold up both sides of the pastry and seal with water in a zig-zag crest along the top. Decorate with pastry trimmings, cut 1–2 slits to let the steam out and brush with egg wash. Bake in a hot oven (425°F/220°C/Gas 7) for 30 minutes or so until well risen, crisp and golden. Serve at once, cut into generous slices, or wrap up for a picnic.

Variation for 25 people. Roll each packet of pastry into an oblong approximately 12″ × 14″ (30cm × 35cm). If cooking 3 in the oven at once, allow about 45 minutes.

PF ✳✳   # Braised Lambs' Hearts with Apricots

Hearts, like some game, seem to benefit from a touch of sweetness, and this delicious, slow-cooked dish with its apricots and hint of cinnamon is such a good, cheap winter dish.

Ingredients
4–6 people

4–6 good lambs' hearts (about 1–1½ lb
   (450–675g) weight in all)
2 oz (50g) dried apricots
2 onions
1 carrot
1 stick celery
¾ oz (20g) dripping
3–4 rashers diced streaky bacon
1 oz (25g) plain flour
¾ pt (450ml) stock or stock cube and
   water
½ stick cinnamon
bouquet garni
a little potato or cornflour if necessary
salt and pepper

Soak the apricots for about 30 minutes in the minimum of warm water. Rinse the hearts under the cold tap to get rid of any blood, then leave to soak in cold salted water for 15–30 minutes. Cut the top flaps and tubes off each heart and discard; then cut each heart into about 4–6 pieces and pat dry with kitchen paper.

Chop the onions and dice the carrot and celery. Heat the dripping in a casserole or frying pan and gently fry the bacon, onion, carrot and celery for 5–10 minutes until soft and golden. Add the bits of heart to the pan and toss over heat until they just stiffen. Sprinkle over the flour and mix in, then, off the stove, stir in the apricots and their water, the stock, cinnamon stick and bouquet garni. Season lightly and cover closely (transfer to a casserole if you have used a frying pan so far). Cook in a slow oven (250°F/130°C/Gas 1) for about 3 hours or until tender.

De-grease the pan, and if necessary thicken with a little potato flour or cornflour, mixed with a little cold water. Correct the seasoning, remove the bouquet garni and cinnamon stick and serve.

This dish is nice served with mashed potatoes, and it keeps warm or reheats beautifully and also freezes well.

$\mathcal{F}$ **   **Stuffed Cabbage Leaves**

Use either mince or left-over cold meat for these cabbage-leaf parcels. They are braised with a little smoked bacon for flavour, and finished with soured cream.

Ingredients
4–6 people

8 good cabbage leaves
8 oz (225g) minced meat
5 fl oz (150ml) double or whipping cream
good squeeze lemon juice
½ teasp potato flour or cornflour
½ oz (12g) dripping or 1 tbs oil
6–8 rashers streaky bacon, smoked for
    choice
1 finely chopped onion
4 oz (100g) sliced mushrooms (optional)
2 oz (50g) rice
½ clove crushed or finely chopped garlic
a little finely chopped fresh thyme
1 tbs finely chopped parsley
8–10 fl oz (225–300ml) stock
1 egg
1 teasp paprika
salt and pepper

Add a good squeeze of lemon and the potato flour or cornflour to the cream and leave aside to 'sour' and thicken.

Blanch the cabbage leaves in plenty of boiling salt water until they are pliable. Drain well and remove the hard stalk.

Melt the dripping in a saucepan, dice 2 rashers of the bacon and gently fry with the onion and sliced mushrooms (if used) until the bacon is browned and the onion softened. Add the rice and garlic and fry briefly to seal on the starch, then add 4 fl oz (100ml) of the stock and the herbs. Cover and boil for 6–8 minutes until the stock has gone. Mix the minced meat with the rice mixture, bind with the egg and season with paprika and salt and pepper. Divide the mixture into eight. Place one portion on each cabbage leaf, turn the edges in and roll into a neat parcel. Squeeze together in your hand and pack fairly tightly together in one layer in the base of a greased ovenproof dish or casserole. Cover with the remaining slices of bacon.

Mix half the soured cream with the remaining stock and pour over nearly to cover the parcels. Cover with a lid and bake in a moderate oven (350°F/180°C/Gas 4) for 1 hour. Remove the lid, pour over the remaining soured cream and cook uncovered for a further 10–15 minutes. Serve sprinkled with paprika, and perhaps with Stovie Potatoes (*see page 48*).

✳✳ Liver with Raisins and Port

A delicious way of doing liver, which so many people overcook. But it does really need last minute cooking, as it should be served as soon as the butter is added to the sauce.

Ingredients
4–6 people

1–1½ lbs (450–657g) calves' or lambs'
   liver, cut in ½" (1cm) thick slices
a little milk
1 large or 2 small oranges
2 tbs raisins
1 large onion
1 clove garlic
1 tbs olive oil
3 oz (75g) butter
seasoned flour
4–6 tbs port or red wine
4–6 tbs stock
salt and pepper

Steep the slices of liver in a little milk for half-an-hour or so if possible. Soak the raisins in hot water so that they plump up. Cut 4–6 wafer thin slices from the centre of the orange and set aside for garnish. Take julienne strips of peel from the remaining orange and blanch in boiling water for about 5 minutes, then refresh under the cold tap to set the colour. Squeeze the juice from the ends of the orange.

Finely chop the onion and garlic. Heat the olive oil and ½ oz (12g) of the butter in a large frying pan and gently fry the onion and garlic until soft and golden. Remove from the pan. Drain the liver and pat dry, dip in seasoned flour and shake off excess. Fry the liver in a little more butter in the pan over moderate heat, turning when the blood rises and removing when just done (not quite firm when pressed with a finger). Keep warm in a serving dish. Return the onion and garlic to the pan, add the orange juice, port, stock and drained raisins and boil hard to reduce until syrupy. Add the orange julienne and, off the stove, the remaining butter in little pieces, shaking the pan to amalgamate the butter with the sauce and so thicken it. Do not allow to boil or the butter may separate. Correct seasoning and pour over the liver. Serve at once.

P ✳✳   Marinated Pork with Crackling Fingers and Baked Apples

A nice roast of pork, tasty and succulent from a spicy marinade, and with really crisp crackling removed and cooked separately, makes a good Sunday lunch or an elegant dinner dish. Small apples baked separately, especially the vivid red and gold crab John Downie, make an attractive garnish, and Risotto Doré (*see page 204*) accompanies it well. Other less expensive joints of pork, like spare-rib and blade-bone, are also nice cooked this way.

Ingredients
4–6 people

2½–3 lb (1.15–1.35kg) boned, skinned
   and rolled loin of pork
bones from the pork
2 crushed cloves garlic
1 small fresh red or green chilli (or use
   dried)
8 fl oz (225ml) dry white wine
1 bay leaf
1 tbs chopped parsley
2–3 tbs olive oil
the skin from the pork
4–6 eating apples
1 oz (25g) butter
1–2 tbs water
a little stock, wine or water for gravy
1–1½ teasp salt
bunch of watercress

You can get the butcher to prepare the meat, but be sure to take the skin and bones as well. Rub the meat well with the salt, pounded with the garlic cloves and the de-seeded, finely chopped chilli. Marinate for 12–24 hours with the wine, bay, parsley and oil.

   Cut the skin into fingers and rub with salt and pepper. Set aside.

   Take the meat from the marinade, pat dry, and set in a roasting pan with the bones around it. Roast in a moderately hot oven (375°F/190°C/Gas 5) for 1–1½ hours, basting with several spoonfuls of the marinade from time to time, letting the pan juices brown but not burn.

   Meanwhile, core the apples and score through the skin only in a circle around their upper halves; set them in a roasting dish with a dab of butter in each core hole and 1–2 tbs water in the dish. Bake for about ½ hour with the pork until fluffy and done but keeping their shape. Place the salted pork skin fingers on a baking sheet and put them in a hot oven (425°F/220°C/Gas 7) for about 5–12 minutes until bubbled crisp and golden; keep warm.

To Serve. Set the pork on a serving dish and surround with the apples, each with a sprig of watercress for garnish, and piles of crackling fingers. Deglaze the pan with any remaining marinade and stock, wine or water to make a rich gravy. Boil down, skim, correct seasoning and serve separately.

**   Boiled Leg of Mutton and Caper Sauce

Mutton—the meat of 2–7 year-old sheep—is not readily available, but anyone who has ever enjoyed its succulent flavour and distinctive texture will probably hanker to try it again. It is quite strong and gamey, and almost like venison.

A good butcher, whom you can trust, will find it for you, and hill mutton, probably the best, can be collected or sent out by rail from Mr Roley Fraser of MacDonald Fraser (*see page 279*). Strangely enough, mutton would be no more expensive to produce than lamb, were there only more demand for it, because the sheep could feed at negligible cost on the hill from the lamb to the mutton stage.

It should be hung for a couple of weeks, and then is excellent used in the usual way for roasts, braises and stews, or boiled and served with caper sauce or on a bed of 'bashed neeps' or with a cauliflower sauce. Of course, hogget (lamb that is approaching one year old) can also be boiled and is very good but without such a flavour.

Ingredients
10–15 people

9 lb (45kg) leg of mutton
2 onions
12 cloves
4 large carrots
4 turnips (optional)
large bouquet of parsley, thyme and
    winter savory
1–2 tbs salt

Caper Sauce
6 oz (175g) butter
4 fl oz (100ml) cooking liquid from the
    mutton or milk or water
1½ teasp plain flour
4 tbs capers and a little of their juice
1–2 teasp wine vinegar
salt and pepper

Trim off excess fat and wipe the leg well. You may need to trim the shank, but don't cut it too high or you may lose juices from the meat. Fit it snugly into a pan, preferably oval. Cover with boiling water or add the leg to boiling water in the pan and bring back to the boil. Then salt and skim thoroughly, allowing 15–30 minutes, adding a cupful of cold water and shaking the pan to help bring up the scum. Skim again, until the liquor is clear. Now adjust the heat so that the water simmers gently at approx (200–205°F/95–98°C) on a thermometer. Add the vegetables, the onions stuck with the cloves, and the herbs. Simmer for about 2½ hours. The lamb can stand in the hot water until ready to serve, but make sure not to spike it with a knife or a fork prong at any stage, as this would let out the meat juices. Remove to a hot serving dish and carve. It can be served on a bed of turnip purée (bashed neeps) into which the juices run when the meat is cut.

Caper Sauce. Cut the butter up small and place it in a saucepan with the cooled cooking liquid or milk. Sift over the flour and heat gently, whisking and shaking all the time. Once the butter has melted and amalgamated with the liquid, bring to the boil once but no more, or a floury flavour will develop or the butter might separate; the sauce should be the consistency of thick cream. Finely chop half the capers, then, whilst whisking, add both chopped and whole capers to the sauce with a little of their liquid and a little vinegar. Season and heat, stirring all the time.

Serve in a sauceboat.

ℱ **   Lancashire Hot Pot

Behind the neck and rather under the shoulder are the middle neck chops, and these are just right for a classic Lancashire Hot Pot with onion and carrot and topped with sliced potatoes. Pop in a lamb's kidney in the traditional way, and try adding the anchovy essence and mushroom ketchup, for they give such a good flavour.

Ingredients
4–6 people

8 or so middle neck chops (trimmed of
   excess fat)
1 lamb's kidney
1 oz (25g) plain flour
1½ oz (35g) dripping, lard or oil
12 oz (350g) sliced onions
8 oz (225g) or more sliced carrots
10–15 fl oz (300–450ml) stock
1 teasp anchovy essence (optional)
1 tbs mushroom ketchup (optional)
1¼–2 lb (600–900g) sliced potatoes
a little melted dripping or oil
salt, pepper and paprika

Season the flour with salt, pepper and paprika. Roll the chops in the seasoned flour, shaking excess back on to the plate. Heat the dripping and brown the chops on both sides; remove them and fry the onions until golden; remove them and fry the carrots until softened. Add the remaining flour to the fat in the pan and cook for several moments; then add the stock, anchovy essence and mushroom ketchup to make a gravy.

Take a wide, deep casserole, preferably earthenware, and put in it a layer of thickly sliced potatoes. Lay the lamb on this and mix in the lamb's kidney, cored and sliced. Top this with the carrots and then the onions, and pour over the prepared gravy. Cover with another thick layer of potatoes and put on the lid. Cook in a moderately hot oven (375°F/190°C/Gas 5) for about 1¾ hours. Remove the lid, paint the potatoes with a little melted dripping or oil and continue to cook for a further ½–¾ hour until browned on top.

This is an ideal dish to re-heat. In this case cook for the first 1¾ hours and then cool. Re-heat for 1 hour at the same temperature, removing the lid for the last ½–¾ hour.

$\mathcal{P}$ ** Boned Shoulder of Lamb with Dried Pear and Nut Stuffing

As it is otherwise rather difficult to carve, I often bone out a shoulder of lamb or get the butcher to do it for me; with an interesting stuffing it will go quite a long way. It is delicious if the roasting is finished on a bed of Flageolets aux Herbes (*see page 53*), the beans absorbing the fat and juices from the lamb. Cold it is rather nice for a large buffet party.

Ingredients

6–8 people	*25 people*
4 lb (1.8kg) approx shoulder of lamb	2 large shoulders lamb
6–8 oz (175–225g) best pork sausage-meat	1 lb (450g) best pork sausage-meat
3 oz (75g) dried pears or apricots	6 oz (175g) dried pears or apricots
1½ oz (35g) whole hazelnuts	3 oz (75g) whole hazelnuts
1 very finely chopped shallot or very small onion	1–2 very finely chopped shallots or small onion
½ stick very finely chopped celery	1 stick very finely chopped celery
1 tbs chopped parsley	2 tbs chopped parsley
¼–½ teasp pounded coriander seeds (optional)	¾–1 teasp pounded coriander seeds (optional)
½ beaten egg	1 egg
salt and pepper	salt and pepper

Cut up the pears or apricots and soak them in a little warm water until soft.

Roast the whole hazelnuts until brown, rub off the skins on a tea towel and chop or crush very roughly. Combine the sausage-meat with the hazelnuts, very finely chopped onion and celery, the parsley and coriander. Stir in the drained pears or apricots, add seasoning, and bind with beaten egg.

Bone out the shoulder of lamb and lay the stuffing in it. Form into a neat long roll and sew up with a large darning needle and heavy button thread. Tie in 2–3 places with string, then roast in a moderately hot oven (375°F/190°C/Gas 5) for about 1¼–1¾ hours. Shoulder of lamb is best rather well-cooked, so that the excess fat can drain from it. Finish roasting on top of the flageolets for the last ½–¾ hour. Draw out the thread before carving.

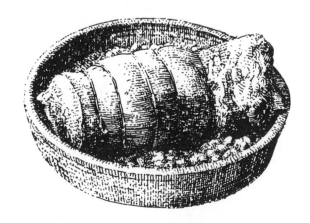

P F ✳✳   **Steak and Kidney Pie with Flaky Pastry**

Flaky pastry makes a lovely crust for this pie, but it must be thinly rolled so that it cooks and crisps right through. The filling needs cooking well ahead so that it is completely cold when the pastry goes on.

Ingredients
4–6 people

1½–2 lb (675–900g) rump or best braising steak	*Flaky Pastry*
6–8 oz (175–225g) beef kidney	5 oz (125g) 'strong' flour
a little flour	squeeze lemon juice
4 oz (100g) mushrooms	3½ oz (90g) butter
bouquet garni	2–3 fl oz (50–75ml) iced water
1 pt (600ml) beef stock	pinch salt
egg wash	
salt, pepper and cayenne	

Pastry. Sieve the flour and salt into a bowl or food processor with metal blade and add a squeeze of lemon juice. Divide the firm but malleable butter into quarters. Rub in or process in one quarter until the mixture is like breadcrumbs, then add enough iced water to form a medium firm dough. Knead briefly until smooth and roll into an oblong ¼" (½cm) thick. Take the next quarter of butter, and with the point of a knife place dabs of butter on the top two-thirds of the pastry, leaving an inch margin all round. Sprinkle with flour and fold the bottom third up and the top third down, then press the edges together to seal. Turn the pastry one turn to your right. Repeat the process with the remaining portions of butter. Refrigerate if the pastry becomes too soft. Rest in the fridge for 1–2 hours or overnight before using.

Cut the steak into 1½" (3cm) cubes and the skinned and cored kidney into rather smaller pieces. Toss the meat in a little flour, seasoned with salt, pepper and a trace of cayenne pepper. Pack the meat with the whole or quartered mushrooms into a casserole, add the bouquet garni and the stock. Cover closely and cook gently in a very moderate oven (325°F/170°C/Gas 3) for 1½–2½ hours until the meat is just tender. Turn into a pie dish with a pie funnel, set in place in the middle and leave until cold. Then remove any fat from the top of the pie.

Roll the pastry a little larger than the pie top and cut off a ½" (1cm) strip from the edge of the pastry to fit round the pie dish rim. Moisten the rim with cold water and fit on the strip. Moisten it with cold water and lay on the pastry cover but do not stretch. Press in place, trim and decorate, make a hole in the crust and brush with egg wash. Bake in a hot oven (425°F/220°C/Gas 7) for 10–15 minutes until a good brown, then turn down to moderate (350°F/180°C/Gas 4) and continue to cook for 30–40 minutes until the pie is heated through and the pastry is a good crisp brown. Serve at once, for if the pastry rests the steam inside tends to make it soggy.

F **   Steak and Kidney Pudding

Suet crust needs delicate handling, like scone dough, to be tender and light, and the filling needs careful seasoning, with the gravy neither too thin nor too floury, neither too much nor too little. Long cooking is also important, so that the crust is light golden for this much-loved winter dish. You can, if you wish, cook the steak and kidney as a casserole the day before, then pack it into the suet crust, which you would then boil for only about 2½ hours.

Ingredients
4–6 people

1½–2 lb (675–900g) lean braising beef
6–8 oz (175–225g) beef kidney
4 oz (100g) mushrooms or 1 tbs
   mushroom ketchup
1–2 tbs plain flour
1 bay leaf
a little fresh chopped or pinch dried
   thyme and parsley
10–15 fl oz (300–450ml) approx beef
   stock
salt, pepper and paprika

Suet Crust
6 oz (175g) chopped best beef suet
12 oz (350g) self-raising flour
8 fl oz (225ml) cold water approx
½ teasp salt

Cut the beef into ¾"–1" (1cm–2cm) chunks. Skin, core and slice the kidney, and slice or quarter the mushrooms, if used. Toss the meat lightly with the flour, seasoned with salt, pepper and paprika.

Grease a 3–4pt (1.7–2.25kg) basin well and line with the pastry, leaving the excess hanging over the top rim. Pack the filling loosely into the bowl; add the mushrooms or mushroom ketchup, chopped herbs and bay leaf. Add stock to three-quarter fill the bowl. Moisten the edges of the pastry with water, roll the remaining quarter of pastry for a lid and fit into place. Cover with greased paper and tinfoil or a securely tied cloth. Place bowl in a steamer or on a saucer in a saucepan with boiling water to come halfway up. Cover closely and boil or steam for 3½–4 hours. Top up with boiling water when necessary.

Suet Crust. If you are using real suet, not a packet, pull it apart, discarding the membranes and thready bits, then chop finely and weigh. Sift the flour and salt into a mixing bowl, stir in the finely chopped suet and mix to a medium soft dough with the water, using a knife (like a scone mix). Knead briefly into one lump, cut off a quarter of the pastry and set aside. Roll the remainder on a well floured board into a round of 9" (23cm) diameter and thicker in the middle than round the edges. Sprinkle well with flour and fold in half with the fold away from you. Draw the edges towards you a little and carefully roll out the centre to form the pastry into a bag which will fit the pudding basin.

To Serve. Remove the cloth or tinfoil and paper and carefully run a knife between pastry and bowl. Place a deep serving plate on top of the bowl and invert. Remove the bowl and serve.

Vegetables

*   Leeks au Gratin

Leeks are a wonderful winter vegetable, standing for long months in the garden or readily available in the shops. They need careful cleaning as there is nothing worse than crunching on grit as you eat them; if you slit them down one side, cutting part way through, you can run them under the tap, washing earth and grit out from between each half. Sliced and braised gently in a little butter until meltingly tender, they can be served just like that, or turned into a fashionable purée with a little cream or *beurre noisette*. You can also bind them with a little potato flour and milk and serve them almost as a leek porridge. My mother uses a slab of bread as a sponge, or the up-side-down saucer technique to drain off unwanted liquid which tends to gather under leeks; the leeks are laid over the saucer in a dish, and the moisture gathers in the bottom. Whole or cut up and carefully cooked and drained, leeks are nice in a white sauce; topped with cheese and breadcrumbs and browned, they become one of those superb simple dishes so much enjoyed by gourmets.

Ingredients
4–6 people

1½–2 lb (675–900g) prepared leeks,
   white and tender green
4 oz (100g) grated Cheddar or Gruyère
   cheese
3–4 tbs breadcrumbs
a few flakes butter
salt and pepper

Sauce
1½ oz (35g) butter
1 oz (25g) plain flour
15 fl oz (450g) milk
salt, pepper and nutmeg

Carefully wash the leeks and cook in boiling salted water for about 10–20 minutes until just tender. Drain well and lay them neatly in a buttered gratin dish, season with salt and pepper and pour over the sauce. Sprinkle with cheese and breadcrumbs, top with a few flakes of butter and brown under the grill.

Sauce. Melt the butter in a saucepan, add the flour and cook, stirring, over moderate heat for 2–3 minutes; then draw the pan off the heat, wait for the sizzling to cease and add the milk. Bring to the boil, whisking well, season and simmer very gently until of good coating consistency.

**   Gratin of Cauliflower in Mushroom Sauce

Vegetables for entertaining are always a problem, but a carefully prepared gratin, either left keeping warm or ready to re-heat, is often a good answer. This mushroom sauce, very delicately flavoured with Gruyère cheese, enhances the flavour of winter and spring cauliflower. The mushroom flavour improves with keeping, so it is almost better re-heated.

Ingredients
4–6 people

1 medium cauliflower
½ oz (12g) butter
3–4 tbs breadcrumbs
little flakes butter
salt and pepper

Mushroom Sauce
4 oz (100g) button mushrooms
2 oz (50g) butter
squeeze lemon juice (optional)
1 oz (25g) plain flour
15 fl oz (450ml) milk or half-and-half
   milk and cauliflower water
2–3 tbs grated Gruyère or rather more
   Cheddar cheese
¼ teasp mustard
salt and pepper

Wash the cauliflower and break into generous florets. Cook these for about 8–12 minutes until just cooked in plenty of boiling salted water, or steam them if you prefer. Drain, reserving about 8 fl oz (225ml) of the cauliflower water if you want to use it for the sauce. Refresh the cauliflower briefly under the cold tap. Drain again and pack into a buttered, shallow ovenproof gratin dish. Season with salt and pepper and pour over the sauce. Top with breadcrumbs and flakes of butter and either bake in a hot over (400°F/200°C/Gas 5) for 20–30 minutes or leave aside to re-heat later in a hot oven for about 45–50 minutes.

Mushroom Sauce. Wash and dice the mushrooms, then add them to ½ oz (12g) of melted butter in a small pan with a squeeze of lemon juice. Cook them gently without browning until tender but crisp. Set aside.

   Melt the remaining butter, add the flour and cook for 2–3 minutes over moderate heat, stirring. Draw off the stove, wait for the sizzling to cease, then add the milk, or milk and cauliflower water, and bring to the boil, whisking. Simmer for 1–2 minutes and add the mushrooms and their liquid, cheese, mustard and seasoning. Pour the sauce, which should be of coating consistency, over the cauliflower.

$\mathcal{F}$ ✳✳   Onions in Béchamel Sauce

This is a lovely vegetable; serve it with roast pork or a mature leg of lamb in place of onion sauce. If you process and thin down any that's left over with stock or reserved onion water, you have a simple good soup. Or you can make it with carrots and onions, add cheese to the sauce, put cheese and breadcrumbs on top and bake it for supper, with or without added hard boiled eggs.

Ingredients
4–6 people

1½ lb (675g) onions
2 cloves
½ teasp sugar
salt and pepper

Béchamel Sauce
15 fl oz (450ml) milk infused with 1 sprig
   thyme, ¼ bay leaf, scrap of mace or
   grated nutmeg and 4 peppercorns
1 oz (25g) butter
1 oz (25g) plain flour
salt and pepper

25 people

8–10 lb (3½–4½kg) onions
6 cloves
1 tbs sugar
salt and pepper

Béchamel Sauce
3 pts (1.7l) milk infused with 4 sprigs
   thyme 1 bay leaf, 2 blades mace or
   some grated nutmeg and 12 pepper
   corns
4 oz (100g) butter
4 oz (100g) plain flour
salt and pepper

Peel and quarter or halve the onions, according to size, and boil for 20–30 minutes in water to cover, until tender, with the cloves, sugar, salt and pepper added. Drain the onions, reserving their liquid for soup if you wish, and discard the cloves. Add the onions to the béchamel sauce and stir together. Turn into a dish and serve.

Béchamel Sauce. Heat the milk with thyme, bay, mace and peppercorns. When hot, cover and leave it to infuse for 10 minutes or so. Alternatively, make the sauce with the flavouring ingredients in and strain when it has finished simmering. Melt the butter in a heavy pan, add the flour and cook, stirring, for 2–3 minutes; then draw the pan off the heat and add the strained infused milk (or milk and flavourings). Return to the stove, season, and bring to the boil, whisking. Simmer gently for about 20 minutes (up to 50 minutes for the larger quantity), until reduced and thick enough for the onions. Strain out the flavourings if they are still in.

*   Stovie Potatoes

This is a Scots dish and the Scots know about potatoes. In the North, the potato grows with less chance of being affected by the dreaded blight, that aphid-borne scourge that can decimate a crop. You used to be able to buy lots of different kinds of potato, each with its individual character and flavour. Nowadays, though potatoes are meant to be sold by name, like Desirée and Vanessa, both good all-rounders, it is more often a case of 'reds' or 'whites', although you can still get a few of the old varieties from some specialist growers.

You can still buy Golden Wonders in Scotland, a potato of unsurpassed flavour and quality. It has a soft floury texture and a nutty flavour akin to chestnut or artichoke, and is well worth growing if you can. It was the use of seaweed to manure the Ayrshire fields and those in the Western Isles which gave their potatoes such a marvellous flavour and made Ayrshires so popular. We are now rather inclined to think of potatoes as a bit boring, and that only new potoates have a special flavour, but we should also look for positive flavours in maincrop potatoes. Certainly in Stovie or Stoved Potatoes (*étuvé* from the French) you will get the full flavour, and it's a great winter way of cooking them. You must have a heavy pan with a close fitting lid, and the simplest version is really the best (I believe it often used to be served just with oatcakes and a bowl of milk). You can jazz it up a bit with onion, bacon, diced ham, cold meat or even cheese to make a simple, good supper dish.

Ingredients
4–6 people

1–1½ lb (450–675g) even, medium sized
   potatoes (5–8)
5 fl oz (150ml) water
½–1 oz (12–25g) butter, dripping or tasty
   fat
salt and pepper

Peel the potatoes and put them, with the water, in a heavy pan in one layer (a cast iron casserole is good); scatter with little bits of butter or fat and salt lightly. Cover closely and cook gently, shaking from time to time, for 30–40 minutes, by which time the potatoes should be tender, buttery and breaking up slightly, and the water should have all gone. If you cook them too fast and the water has gone before they are cooked, add a little more. Grind a little pepper over them on serving. They are delicious served with something like finnan haddock cooked in milk or Stuffed Cabbage Leaves (*see page 37*).

* ## Bacon Stovies

A slightly more elaborate version which can be used as a supper dish, especially nice if you can get some proper old-fashioned cured and smoked bacon. Meat or ham in larger quantities or grated cheese can be layered with sliced potatoes and fried onion for endless variations; the important things are the heavy tightly-lidded pan (some say it should be iron) and gentle heat.

Ingredients
4–6 people

1½–2 lb (675–900g) peeled even-sized
   potatoes
4 oz (100g) thick cut smoked bacon
2 tbs dripping, fat or oil

2 large sliced onions
4 fl oz (100ml) water
finely chopped parsley
salt and pepper

Dice the bacon and melt the dripping in a heavy casserole; add the bacon and onion and cook until the onion softens and the bacon browns a little. Cut the potatoes into generous chunks or leave them whole. Add them to the pan, mix them in, season and add the water. Cover closely and cook over very gentle heat for 30–40 minutes, until the potatoes are soft and tender and probably rather broken up, and the liquid has gone. Sprinkle with parsley and serve from the pan.

F * ## Hot Beetroot with Oil and Vinegar

This is my mother's own way with beetroot, and it is quite delicious. Now it's easy with a food processor, but in my childhood it involved putting hot cooked beetroot through the mincer with awful looking trickles of beetroot juice dripping on to the stone floor.

Ingredients
4–6 people

2–2½ lb (900g–1.15kg) beetroot
1 tbs sugar
4–5 tbs wine vinegar (shallot flavoured is
   nice)
2–3 tbs oil
¾–1 teasp salt
plenty of pepper

Boil the beetroot until tender, drain, and rub off the skins with your thumb under the cold tap. Mince or process in a food processor to a minced consistency (not so far as a purée), add the sugar and season generously with salt and pepper. Stir in oil and vinegar to taste. Re-heat and serve with with cold meat, liver or game dishes.

Steamed Savoy Cabbage with Buttered Breadcrumbs

Crinkly leafed savoy cabbage with its dark green outer leaves and golden yellow middle is at its best after New Year, once it has had some sharp frosts on it. It's so pretty that I like to cook it cut into segments like a cake and steam it. This is one of the hardiest cabbages, for the deeply veined leaves allow the winter rains to drain away and the hearts never become soggy and spoilt.

Ingredients
4–6 people

1 head medium sized savoy cabbage
good squeeze lemon juice
salt and pepper

Buttered Breadcrumbs
3–4 oz (75–100g) butter
3–4 tbs breadcrumbs

Remove the outer leaves, wash the cabbage well and cut into about eight segments. Lay these in a steamer (I use a three-tiered Chinese bamboo one), salt lightly and steam over boiling water for about 12–20 minutes until the cabbage is cooked but still crisp. While it cooks, prepare the breadcrumbs. Then set the cabbage on a serving dish and season with salt and pepper. Squeeze over a little lemon juice, dribble over the butter and scatter some browned crumbs over each segment. Serve at once or the crumbs go soggy.

Buttered Breadcrumbs. Heat the butter, add the breadcrumbs and keep stirring over moderate heat until they are crisp and golden brown and the butter has come out of them again, adding a little more if they absorb it all.

Variation. Steam the cabbage, set it in a serving dish and pour over it Old English Butter Sauce (*see page 148*). It is quite delicious like that, or you can sprinkle over dry toasted sesame seeds for added nutty crunch.

F ** Braised Curly Kale

We love this vegetable, but it has to be blanched to remove its strong flavour and gently braised until tender. We serve it with venison or beef for dinner parties, and nearly everyone wonders what it is and asks for more. It is such a useful winter standby, very hardy and available all winter, right through till the spring, and so easy to grow. I should hate a winter without it to turn to.

Ingredients
4–6 people

2–3 lb (900g–1.35kg) prepared curly kale
2–3 oz (50–75g) smoked thick-cut streaky
    bacon
1 large onion
2 oz (50g) goosefat, duck fat, pork
    dripping or lard
freshly grated nutmeg
salt and pepper

Pull the curly leaves off the tough stems and discard the stems. Blanch the kale for 2–3 minutes in plenty of boiling salt water. Drain and refresh under the cold tap and squeeze lightly. Chop the onion fine, dice the bacon and fry together in the fat until softened and the fat runs from the bacon. Chop the kale roughly and add it to the pan with a seasoning of salt and pepper. Cover and braise in a slow oven (300°F/150°C/Gas 2) for 1–2 hours until tender. Serve like that, or process in the food processor until finely chopped but not a purée. Correct the seasoning and add a little nutmeg.

*   Braised Jerusalem Artichokes

All winter these knobbly roots will wait underground (or in the shops) for you. Their lovely smoky flavour and soft texture seem to be brought out best by braising gently in this way with a little bacon.

Ingredients
4–6 people

1–1½ lb (450–675g) peeled artichokes
1 oz (25g) butter
1 finely chopped onion
1–2 rashers bacon
salt and pepper

Melt the butter in a heavy bottomed casserole. Dice the bacon and add, together with the onion, and cook gently until the onion softens before adding the artichokes, cut into even sized pieces. Season and fry gently for about 5 minutes, then cover and cook very gently either on the stove or in a slow oven (300°F/150°C/Gas 2) for about 15–30 minutes until tender. If there is too much liquid, reduce fast, uncovered, until just a little syrupy juice remains.

* Healthy Winter Salad with Yoghurt and Olive Oil Dressing

I think we all long for really healthy winter salads, and it is amazing how, even in the depths of winter, there are still quite a lot of fresh vegetables in the garden or the shops if you look. Everything in this salad is good for us, and the varying flavours blend to a pleasing whole; the dressing is healthy too; but be generous with the pine nuts, or sunflower seeds, if you can, for their soft richness mellows the crisp freshness of the salad. I find that chillis grown in the greenhouse last deep into the winter and add a healthy zest to the salad. Of course, you will want to vary and change the ingredients to suit your taste, and to make use of what is available at the time. The fresher picked or dug the better.

Ingredients

A mixture of any, or all, of the following:

white winter cabbage
thinly sliced sprouts
sliced Chinese leaves
chopped watercress
grated raw celeriac
grated or matchstick-cut raw carrot
thinly sliced celery
peeled raw Jerusalem artichoke,
    matchstick-cut
peeled, grated or matchstick-cut raw
    turnip
chopped heads and stalks of broccoli
sliced raw mushrooms
diced boiled potatoes (optional, but they
    soften the texture a little)
shredded radicchio
sliced blanched chicory
shredded sorrel

torn salad burnet
a little chopped shallot, Welsh onion or
    leek
plenty of chopped parsley
chopped chervil
a few leaves of thyme
sprouted seeds of alfalfa or the like
mustard and cress
2–3 tbs pine nuts or sunflower seeds

Dressing
5 fl oz (150ml) plain yoghurt
a little finely chopped fresh chilli
    (optional)
¼ teasp Dijon mustard
1 tbs herb vinegar
3–4 tbs best cold pressed olive oil
¼ teasp Lane's Herb Salt or sea-salt

Prepare all the vegetables and toss with the dressing in a salad bowl. Toast and toss the pine nuts or sunflower seeds in a dry heavy pan (omelette pan) over moderate heat until browned, add to the salad and serve.

Dressing. Drain the yoghurt for 10–15 minutes in a muslin-lined sieve to get rid of the whey and to thicken it.

Mix the very finely chopped chilli (without seeds), salt, mustard and vinegar in a bowl, add in the drained yoghurt and whisk in the olive oil.

$\mathcal{P}$ *   # Flageolets aux Herbes

The slim, sage green coloured dried beans, known as *flageolets*, make a good winter vegetable, though I have frequently served them in summer with a wider variety of chopped herbs. They go particularly well with roast or braised lamb. They are good for a large party as they re-heat well or can be frozen.

Ingredients

4–6 people	*25 people*
½ lb (225g) dried green flageolets or haricot beans	2 lb (900g) dried green flageolets or haricot beans
1 oz (25g) butter	4 oz (100g) butter
¾–1 pt (450–600ml) stock (or to cover)	2½–3½ pts (1.5–2l) stock (or to cover)
½ oz (12g) soft butter	1½ oz (35g) soft butter
½ oz (12g) plain flour	1½ oz (35g) plain flour
2–3 tbs fresh chopped parsley and chervil	8–10 tbs fresh chopped parsley and chervil
salt and pepper	salt and pepper

Soak the beans for several hours, or overnight, in tepid water and then drain (a pinch of bicarbonate of soda will help to soften hard water and ease the soaking). Place the beans in a pan with the butter and stock just to cover and cook gently for 1½–2½ hours until tender. Reduce the stock by fast boiling if it seems excessive and season with plenty of salt and pepper. Cream the butter and flour together into *beurre manié* and add in little pieces to thicken the bean sauce; bring to the simmer for a few moments and stir in the herbs before serving.

The beans will keep warm or reheat well.

Puddings

$\mathcal{F}$ **   Marlborough Tart

Not very many old books have a recipe for this quite delicious tart, though sometimes you will find it under the name of Duke of Cambridge Tart. In fact, many people who serve it and guard their recipe may not be pleased with me for bringing it to your attention. It seems to come from Scotland and may be derived from Queen Mary's Tart, brought to Edinburgh by Mary of Guise. Some versions spread the pastry with apricot jam before pouring in the filling but either way it is scrumptious – but very wicked!

Ingredients
4–6 people

Pastry	*Filling*
6 oz (175g) plain flour	**6 oz (175g) butter**
2 tbs icing sugar	**6 oz (175g) soft brown sugar**
4 oz (100g) firm butter	**4 egg yolks**
1 egg yolk	**a little grated lemon rind**
1–2 tbs iced water	**squeeze lemon juice**
pinch salt	
2 oz (50g) mixed cut peel	
3–4 tbs apricot jam (optional)	

Pastry. Sieve the flour, salt and icing sugar into a bowl or the food processor. Add the firm butter cut up into hazelnut-sized pieces and rub in or process to the breadcrumb stage. Bind with the yolk and a very little cold water. Form into a flat disc and rest for 1–2 hours in the fridge in a plastic bag.

    Roll the pastry to fit a 9″ (24cm) removable base flan tin. Prick the pastry, line with tinfoil and baking beans and bake in a hot oven (400°F/200°C/Gas 6) for 8–10 minutes until the pastry is set. Remove the tinfoil and return to a moderately hot oven (375°F/190°C/Gas 5) for a further 10–15 minutes until the pastry is nearly cooked before lowering the oven temperature to moderate (350°F/180°C/Gas 4). Spread the apricot jam, if used, over the base of the pastry and scatter with the peel. Pour the filling into the pastry shell and return to the moderate oven for about 30 minutes. Serve hot, or—even better—warm or cold.

Filling. Melt the butter in a heavy saucepan, add the sugar, egg yolks, some grated lemon rind and a good squeeze of juice. Heat gently to simmering point, stirring all the time, for it can catch rather easily, and then boil for one minute (contrary to what you would expect, the egg yolks will not curdle). Pour over the peel in the pastry shell.

✱✱   Lemon Meringue Pie

This classic pudding is a great favourite with its crisp pastry, sharp but creamy filling and slow cooked crunchy meringue on top.

Ingredients
4–6 people

Pastry
6 oz (175g) plain flour
2 tbs icing sugar
4 oz (100g) firm butter
1 egg yolk
1–2 tbs iced water
pinch salt

Meringue
3 egg whites
6 oz (175g) castor sugar

Lemon Filling
5 tbs (1¾ oz (45g)) cornflour
12 fl oz (350ml) water
4 oz (100g) sugar
1 oz (25g) butter
grated rind 1 lemon
6 tbs lemon juice (1½–2 lemons)
3 egg yolks
½ teasp salt

Pastry. Sift the flour, salt, and icing sugar into a bowl or the food processor with a metal blade and add the butter in hazelnut-sized pieces. Rub in or process to the breadcrumb stage, then bind with the egg yolk and cold water. Form into a flat disc and rest the pastry in the fridge for ½–2 hours.

To Bake Blind. Roll and line a 9″ (24cm) removable base flan tin. Prick, line with tinfoil and baking beans and bake blind in a hot oven (400°F/200°C/Gas 6) for 10–12 minutes until the pastry is set. Remove the foil and beans and continue to bake in a moderately hot oven (375°F/190°C/Gas 5) for about 15–20 minutes until light golden. Fill with lemon filling and bake in a moderate oven (350°F/180°C/Gas 4) for about 20 minutes until just set. Remove from the tart tin and set on an ovenproof plate.

Lemon Filling. Mix the cornflour and salt with a little of the cold water. Heat the rest of the water with the sugar, and when nearly boiling stir in the cornflour and bring to the boil, whisking hard. Simmer for 2 minutes, remove from the stove and add the lemon rind and juice and the butter. Cool a little before whisking in the egg yolks, then turn into the pastry case to cook.

Meringue. Whisk the egg whites until just holding a peak, then gradually whisk in 2 oz (50g) of the sugar. Whisk until very stiff indeed before folding in the remaining sugar and piling the meringue on top of the pie. Bake in a slow oven (300°F/150°C/Gas 2) for ¾ hour or more for a good crisp meringue top. Serve hot, warm or cold.

ℱ ∗   Orange Crêpes

A really delicate and rich pancake spread with marmalade, Grand Marnier and butter and served hot. It makes a wonderful end to a winter dinner party.

Ingredients
4–6 people

2 oz (50g) plain flour
2 eggs
8 fl oz (225ml) single cream
2 tbs Grand Marnier
2 oz (50g) melted butter
grated rind ½ orange
½ teasp vanilla essence
¼ teasp salt

4 tbs orange marmalade
1 tbs melted butter
1 tbs Grand Marnier
icing sugar

Sift the flour and salt into a bowl, make a hole in the middle and break in the eggs; whisk, gradually incorporating the flour and cream, beat well and add the Grand Marnier, melted butter, orange rind and vanilla essence. Rest for one hour. Or make in a food processor or liquidiser and only rest for a few minutes.

Heat an 8″ (20cm) frying pan or pancake pan and rub with a bit of butter, pour in just enough batter to cover the pan, brown on one side and turn over to brown on the second side. Remove. Make 8–12 pancakes.

Combine the chopped marmalade, butter and Grand Marnier and spread over the crêpes, fold into four and lay overlapping in a buttered shallow ovenproof dish. Sprinkle heavily with icing sugar and heat in a hot oven (425°F/220°C/Gas 7) for 5–7 minutes, or a little longer from cold. Serve at once, perhaps with Crème Chantilly (*see page 265*) or Crème Fraîche (*see page 170*), though they don't really need it.

ℱ ∗∗   Orange and Date Steamed Pudding

A light-as-air sponge makes one of the best Sunday puddings. Serve it up with Creamy Marmalade Sauce (*see page 66*) or thick cream, and old men will remember their childhood while children will be glad they are children. It's so easy for the cook, too. Leave the butter out to soften overnight, whip the mixture up in the morning by hand for a superlative pudding or by food processor for speed, then leave it to steam for 1½–2 hours until you are ready to eat. The same mixture can be used to make castle puddings, which only take 30–40 minutes' steaming.

Ingredients
4–6 people

3 eggs and their weight in both very soft
   butter and castor sugar
grated rind of 1 orange
the weight of 2 eggs in self-raising flour
2–3 tbs orange juice
4 oz (100g) succulent dates
pinch salt

Place the eggs in a bowl of tap-warm water before you start so that they warm a little and will then combine with the butter and sugar more easily.

   Cream the butter until very soft, then cream in the castor sugar and grated orange rind. There is still nothing better than using your hand to cream butter and sugar in a wide bowl. Once well creamed, turn to the eggs and whisk them to a froth. Gradually beat them into the creamed butter and sugar with a wire whisk or wooden spoon; the mixture should remain thick and it should not curdle (if it looks like curdling, fold in a little sifted flour). Finally fold in the sifted flour and salt and mix to a dropping consistency with orange juice.

   Grease a 2 pt (1.2l) pudding basin and decorate with halved, stoned dates. Turn the mixture into the prepared basin, cover with buttered paper and tinfoil or a cloth tied on with string. Place in a steamer or saucepan with boiling water to come halfway up the bowl, cover tightly and steam or boil for 1½–2 hours. Replenish the pan with boiling water, if necessary, and keep boiling all the time. Turn out and serve with Creamy Marmalade Sauce or thick cream.

Castle Puddings. Grease some castle pudding moulds, or deep coffee cups, and fill ⅔ full. Cover with tinfoil, boil or steam for 20–30 minutes, turn out and serve.

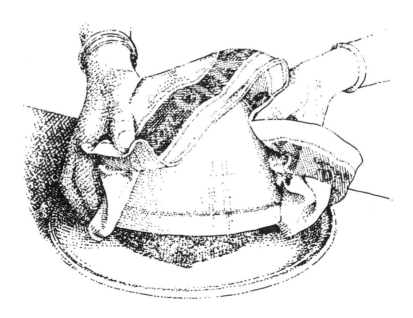

$P\,\mathcal{F}$ ** Winter Fruit Salad

Sun-dried mixed fruit is steeped in china tea and flavoured with lemon and cinnamon. It's a nice winter dish, not quite as exotic as Koshaf* but nevertheless extremely useful, and it goes well with old fashioned Snow Cream with Rosemary (*see below*).

Ingredients

4–6 people	*25 people*
1 lb (450g) mixed dried fruit (peaches, apricots, pears, prunes, raisins and apples)	3–3½ lb (1.35–1.6kg) mixed dried fruit (peaches, apricots, pears, prunes, raisins and apples)
1½ pts (900ml) china tea or water (2 teasp tea leaves)	4–5 pts (2.25–2.8l) china tea (2–3 tbs tea leaves)
1 lemon	3–4 lemons
6 oz (175g) sugar or to taste	1 lb (450g) sugar or to taste
2″ (5cm) stick cinnamon	6″ (15cm) stick cinnamon

Soak the dried fruit for at least 12 hours in the cold tea or water. Take julienne strips from the lemon, blanch in boiling water for 5 minutes or until tender, then drain and refresh under the cold tap.

Drain the fruit, measure the liquid, and make up to 1½ pts (900ml) again with water. Place in a pan with sugar, cinnamon stick and lemon julienne and heat gently until the sugar has dissolved. Add the fruit to the syrup and simmer gently until tender. Remove the fruit and boil down the syrup for about 5–10 minutes until heavier. Add the lemon juice, pour over the fruit and chill before serving.

This will keep for a week in the fridge and is lovely for breakfast with muesli or yoghurt.

Variation for 25 people. After the dried fruit has been soaking in the cold tea or water, the drained liquid should be made up to 4–5 pts (2.25–2.8l) with water.

P * Snow Cream with Rosemary

This lightly whipped and flavoured cream is almost a syllabub and should be made 12 hrs ahead. It can be served with Winter Fruit Salad or on its own in small glasses accompanied by Little Almond Fingers (*see page 170*).

Ingredients

4–6 people	*25 people*
8 fl oz (225ml) whipping cream	1¼–1½ pts (750–900ml) whipping cream
⅛ teasp fresh rosemary approx	1 teasp very finely chopped rosemary
1 lemon	3 lemons
2 tbs sherry	3 fl oz (75ml) sherry
2 egg whites	6 egg whites
2–3 tbs castor sugar	4 oz (100g) castor sugar or to taste

* *Good Food from Farthinghoe*

Combine the cream with the very finely chopped rosemary, the grated rind and juice of the lemon and the sherry, and whisk until stiff. Whip the whites of egg until just holding a peak, then whisk in the sugar until stiff. Fold the whites into the cream and turn into a bowl or little glasses. Serve chilled.

** Hot Apricot Soufflé

Diced apricots and Grand Marnier or 17th Lancers Orange Brandy give this soufflé its character. Don't forget that all the inside of the soufflé dish needs generously buttering with soft butter and heavily sprinkling with sugar to give that caramelised outer crust which really makes a sweet soufflé.

Ingredients
4–6 people

1 lb (450g) fresh apricots or 14 oz (400g)
   tin drained apricot halves or 8 oz
   (225g) cooked dried apricots
½ oz (12g) butter (to cook fresh apricots)
a little soft butter and castor sugar to
   prepare the soufflé dish
5 fl oz (150ml) milk
3 tbs castor sugar
good pinch salt
1½ oz (35g) flour mixed with 6 tbs cold
   apricot juice or milk
¾ oz (20g) butter
4 egg yolks
4 tbs Grand Marnier, orange or apricot
   brandy or other liqueur
a few drops almond essence
6 egg whites

Generously butter a 2 pt (1.2l) Soufflé dish (especially around the rim) and sprinkle heavily with castor sugar. Place the milk, sugar and salt in a small pan and bring to the boil, dissolving the sugar. Off the stove, stir in the mixed flour and apricot juice or milk. Boil, whisking hard, for 2–3 minutes until smooth and thick. Set aside covered.

Dice the stoned fresh apricots and sauté briskly in ½ oz (12g) hot butter. Tinned or cooked dried apricots just need draining and dicing.

When ready to cook the soufflé, re-warm the sauce, beat in the butter, egg yolks, Grand Marnier and almond essence; then fold in the diced apricots, followed by the egg whites, whisked until they just hold a peak. Turn into the prepared soufflé dish and smooth the surface of the soufflé. Cook in a hot oven (400°F/200°C/Gas 6) for about 20–25 minutes, until well risen, golden and just trembling when you move the dish. Serve *at once*. Like all soufflés it should still be a little runny in the middle.

$\mathcal{PF}$ *   Orange and Ratafia Creams

Try this while the Seville oranges are in. They have a very short season, so you may feel inclined to freeze a few for making this pudding later (grate them whilst frozen, then thaw and squeeze the juice). This is very quick to make; it needs to be made a day or so ahead and can also be frozen.

Ingredients
4–6 people

15 fl oz (450ml) double cream
4–5 oz (100–125g) castor sugar
2 small oranges (preferably Seville oranges)

2 tbs Grand Marnier
1 packet ratafia macaroons

Combine the cream, grated orange rind and sugar in a saucepan. Stir whilst heating for about 10 minutes, just bringing to the boil. Cool, stirring from time to time so that a skin does not form. When almost cold (if it's still warm the cream may curdle), add the strained orange juice and Grand Marnier. Distribute the ratafias between 4–6 glasses or little pots (or use one dish) and pour the cream over them. Cover and leave in a cool place for 24 hours.

    If you want to freeze this dish, let it stand for 24 hours then freeze. Thaw well before serving.

$\mathcal{P}$ **   Whipped Syllabub

This is another rich cream pudding which is useful because it can be made quickly and well ahead—but don't let it pick up fridgy smells. I have taken my recipe from Mrs Beeton, added a little grated lemon rind and more juice and reduced the brandy a little. It really needs to sit for 24 hours and will keep for several days, but it has been known to get eaten almost immediately!

Ingredients
4–6 people

½ pt (300ml) thick double cream
4 fl oz (100ml) sherry or white wine
2–3 tbs brandy
little grated lemon rind

juice ½–1 lemon
little grated nutmeg
3 oz (75g) castor sugar

Place the cream and nutmeg in a large cold bowl and beat slowly with a balloon whisk. Mix the sherry or white wine, brandy, lemon rind and juice and nutmeg in a jug, and as the cream thickens add the liquid, whisking all the time, and sprinkle on the sugar. When the cream has absorbed all the liquid and will hold its shape, spoon into pretty glasses and preferably leave for 24 hours before serving. A cool larder is better than the fridge.

Miscellaneous

ℱ * Potted Stilton

The Christmas Stilton gradually degenerates into an unappetising dry rind and no longer looks enticing. But plenty of value can still be had from it if potted up like this or turned into Stilton Cream.

Ingredients

6 oz (175g) Stilton without rind
4–6 oz (100–175g) soft butter
3 tbs white wine, beer or milk

Cream the butter and sieve the Stilton. Add the Stilton to the butter and cream well together, gradually adding in the wine (if it's warmed a little, it will be absorbed more easily).

In a food processor, cream the butter before adding in the unsieved cheese and, once amalgamated and creamy, drip in the wine.

Turn into a pot, keep in the cool and serve with sticks of field celery and oatcakes.

* Stilton Cream

This is another way of using up Stilton, though of course it can be made with any other blue cheese such as blue Cheshire, Roquefort, Bleu d'Auvergne or Gorgonzola. And at any time of year.

Ingredients

4 oz (100g) Stilton (best not cold from the
   fridge)
4 oz (100g) cream cheese (Eden Vale
   Somerset soft cream cheese)
1–2 tbs cream
1½ teasp brandy
chopped chives, Welsh onion or celery
   leaves

Sieve the Stilton and cream cheese together, adding the cream, brandy and chopped herbs.

In a food processor, process the Stilton until smooth before adding the cream cheese and flavourings. Be careful not to over-process and turn the cream cheese to butter.

F ✱✱　　Home-Made Sausages

Real meaty and spicy sausages are not so easy to come by now. Where is the Oxford sausage, the Epping sausage or the celebrated Fetter Lane sausage which owed much of its favour and fame to sweet basil? I don't know—but I do know that when we made 100% pure pork sausages and sold them from our freezers, they were exceedingly popular. An old butcher called Alf, aged 80, taught me to make them and I thought you might like the recipe, though perhaps not for 50 lb at a time!

Skins may be got from your butcher (*or see page 279*). They will keep for a very long time in a plastic bag with some coarse salt, and I have had some in the larder for two years. Soak well before using. If you don't have a Kenwood sausage filling attachment, but still want to put them into skins (they are distinctly better and more rewarding to make in skins), this can be done with a plastic funnel, large forcing bag and two pairs of hands.

Ingredients
Approx 6 lb (2.7kg)

4 lb (1.8kg) lean pork cut from the throat
　or shoulder
2–2½ lb (900g–1.15kg) back pork fat
1½ oz (35g) salt
1½ teasp *quatre épice*　　⎫
½ teasp ground mace　　　⎬ mixed and sifted together
scant ¼ oz (6g) ground black pepper ⎭
1½ teasp dried basil
2–3 oz (50–75g) breadcrumbs (optional)
1–2 eggs (optional if making in skins but
　necessary if making skinless sausages)
a little water
8–10 yds sausage skins in salt

First wash the skins in a sink of cold water (but don't lose them down the plug hole!) and run the tap through them to remove the salt.

Cut up the meat and fat into cubes, removing gristle, then scatter with the well pounded seasoning and a few shakes of cold water from your fingers and mix well. Pass through the coarse plate of the mincer and mix thoroughly with your hands (adding in breadcrumbs and eggs if used).

To Fill the Skins. Place the sausage filling attachment on the Kenwood and work a length of skin on to the plastic filler nozzle. Pass the sausage meat through the mincer, with the large or medium cutting plate in place, and into the skins. Work the skins off the filler tube as they fill with sausage meat but do not have them too tightly packed. When the skins are full, form into links.

To Form Links. Pinch the skin to form one sausage and let it hang down; then a second of the same size also hanging down over your finger; pinch a third and bring it up to form a third, then pass sufficient filled skin over the top and through the loop made by the second and third sausage to form the next two sausages, progressing up to make a new link. Bring another sausage up to the link and again pass sufficient over the top and through the link to make two more sausages, all rather like crochet and much easier when shown rather than explained! When you are practised, eight sausages should make 1 lb give or take an ounce. Leave for 12 hours, then divide and freeze. Fry them gently without pricking so that the succulent juices are kept within the skins.

They have no preservative, so do not expect them to keep too long, 4–5 days in the fridge or 3–6 months in the freezer.

To Make Skinless Sausages. Knead the mixture, including egg and breadcrumbs to help it hold together (some sources enjoin breadcrumbs in all sausages to help them bind, but I prefer them crumbly but pure meat). Form into cakes or rolls with wet hands and fry in hot fat, rolling them round to brown lightly on all sides, then lower the heat until they are cooked.

Keep the uncooked mixture packed tight in a bowl until you are ready to use it, up to 3–4 days, or freeze.

To Make and Use a Sausage Filling Bag. Get a plastic funnel which has a diameter of roughly ¾–1" (2–3cm). You can cut the spout off at the right width, leaving only 2–3" (5–8cm) length. Then cut off most of the bowl part, leaving just enough to hold it in place inside a large forcing bag. Set the funnel in place, fill the bag with sausage meat and twist the end really tight to seal. Work the sausage skin on to the nozzle, then, with someone holding the bag tightly closed, squeeze the sausage meat into the skins but don't let the skins come off the nozzle too fast. Squeeze with a milking action close to the funnel.

F * Knibbed Wheat Health Loaf

Having given our standard week-by-week brown bread recipe in *Good Food from Farthinghoe*, I am now including a loaf that is very quick to make, with bran added for roughage and knibbed wheat for texture (in autumn I throw in a handful of freshly harvested wheat). Do make sure that wheat germ, bran and flour are fresh, for they get a bitter taste when stale.

Ingredients
1 loaf

8 oz (225g) 100% wholemeal 'strong'
   bread flour
6 oz (175g) knibbed wheat
2 oz (50g) bran
2 tbs wheat germ
1 tbs malt or honey
1 oz (25g) fresh yeast
15 fl oz (450ml) tepid water
1½ teasp salt

Mix the flour, knibbed wheat, bran and wheat germ with the salt in a large mixing bowl. Cream together the malt or honey and yeast and add the tepid water. Combine with the flour and mix to a soft dough; knead in the bowl (for it is a very soft dough) for 5–10 minutes. Alternatively, tip all the ingredients except for the water, into the food processor; switch on, trickle in the water to make a moist dough and process for about 45 seconds.

Turn into a greased 1½–2 lb (675–900g) loaf tin, level the top and leave to rise for about ¾–1½ hours inside a plastic bag, in a warm place, until doubled in size. Bake in a moderately hot oven (375°F/190°C/Gas 5) for about 35–40 minutes until cooked. Cool on a rack.

This loaf will cut into thin slices without crumbling, and has something of the texture of a nutty, moist German bread.

* Oatcakes

They are so easy to make (especially with a food processor) taking only fifteen minutes from weighing out to cooling rack. You can either roll each half of the mixture into a 7½" (18cm) circle and cut it into eight segments, or roll all the mixture out and cut into rounds. This is a bit more wasteful as it is difficult to get a second rolling, for the mixture becomes too firm and crumbly to re-form and roll again. So I usually form it into segments for the family and only cut rounds when I want the oatcakes neat for a picnic or to accompany a cheese board. These oatcakes are good natural healthy food—and so cheap.

Ingredients
16 oatcakes

8 oz (225g) medium oatmeal
½ teasp bicarbonate of soda
1 tbs melted or soft dripping, duck,
   goose, chicken or pork fat, or butter
3–4 fl oz (75–100ml) boiling water
¼ teasp salt

Place the oatmeal, salt and bicarbonate of soda in a bowl or the food processor with metal blade; trickle over the melted fat and rub or process in. Then add the boiling water and knead, or process, to a sticky dough. I use a deep bowl and the back of my knuckles and stir round and round until it forms a dough. Don't have it too dry or the oatcakes will be rather crumbly.

Take half the mixture (keeping the other half warm), form it into a ball and roll out on a liberally oatmealed board, using lots of oatmeal so that it does not stick. Roll to ⅛″ (⅓cm) thick, making a 7½″ (18cm) circle, and pressing the edges in where it tends to crumble. To make the oatcakes nice and white, rub the rolled surface with dry oatmeal. Slide the disc on to a baking sheet and cut across and across to make 8 segments or 4 farles. Pop into the oven while you quickly roll the second ball. If you wish, you can roll all the dough at once to ⅛″ (⅓cm) thickness and cut circles using a 2″–2½″ (6cm) cutter.

Either way, bake in a moderately hot oven (375°F/190°C/Gas 5) for 10 minutes or so until firm and very lightly coloured. Sometimes I turn them over if the bottom sides look a bit damp. Cool on a rack and store in an airtight tin. Serve with marmalade for breakfast or with cheese; they also make a nice accompaniment to many first courses.

F * Flap Jacks

These crunchy oat fingers must be one of Britain's favourite teatime biscuits. They are crisp and short when fully cooked, or you can cook them a little less if you like them chewy.

Ingredients
approx 28 flap jacks

2 tbs golden syrup
6 oz (175g) butter or margarine
6 oz (175g) Demerara sugar

8 oz (225g) rolled oats
½–1 teasp ground ginger (optional)
pinch of salt

Melt the butter and golden syrup gently in a saucepan. Mix the sugar, oats, ground ginger and salt, pour on the melted butter and syrup and mix well. Turn into a greased 8″ × 12″ (20cm × 30cm) tin and bake in a moderate oven (350°F/180°C/Gas 4) for about 30–35 minutes until golden brown. Leave to cool in the tin for a while, then cut into fingers and finish cooling on a rack. When quite cold, store in an airtight tin.

F ∗ Everlasting cake

This is a large, economical cake that is easy enough for the children to make themselves. It takes a week or so to mature but will then keep for ages. Square or oblong, it cuts easily into non-crumbly slices, is nice enough plain, but even better spread with butter or jam.

Ingredients
a roughly 8" × 9" (24cm × 24cm) cake

1 lb (450g) plain flour
1½ teasp mixed spice
8 oz (225g) butter
12 oz (350g) soft dark brown sugar
grated rind of 1 lemon
4 eggs
10 fl oz (300ml) beer or lager
1 teasp bicarbonate of soda
8 oz (225g) sultanas } *or* use 1 lb (450g)
8 oz (225g) raisins } mixed fruit
½ teasp salt

Prepare a roughly 8" × 9" × 3" deep (20cm × 24cm × 7cm) tin by lining with Bakewell or greased greaseproof paper. Use two strips; one goes down one side, across the bottom and up the other side; the other goes down one end, across the bottom and up the other.

Sift the flour with the salt and mixed spice, cut the margarine into dice and rub in until the mixture resembles breadcrumbs (a large food processor will cope with this amount). Add the sugar and grated lemon rind and stir together. Whisk the eggs, add the beer and bicarbonate of soda and whisk again. Add to the dry mixture and beat well before stirring in the fruit and turning into the prepared tin. Bake in a very moderate oven (325°F/170°C/ Gas 3) for 1½–2 hours until a skewer inserted in the centre of the cake comes out clean.

Leave to cool in the tin and keep in an airtight tin for about 1 week before eating.

∗ Creamy Marmalade Sauce

This sauce, or variations of it, can be used with steamed or baked puddings, tarts and even ice cream.

Ingredients

6 tbs orange marmalade (try the Orange Brandy Marmalade for this—*see page 68*)
5 fl oz (150ml) water
1½ teasp cornflour
squeeze lemon juice
1 egg
2 oz (50g) soft butter
2 tbs orange brandy or brandy (optional)

Chop up any large bits of peel in the marmalade, then mix it with most of the water and bring to the boil. Mix the cornflour with the rest of the water and add with a good squeeze of lemon juice; bring to the boil again and simmer for 2–3 minutes. Whisk the egg to a froth in a bowl before gradually pouring on the hot sauce while you go on whisking. Return to the pan and whisk in the butter, cut into little pieces, and the orange brandy, if used. Heat gently without boiling, stirring all the time until the sauce thickens, then keep warm over very low heat or in a *bain marie*.

Dark Seville Marmalade

A dark, rather bitter marmalade, reminiscent of Cooper's Oxford Marmalade (but rather better); we usually make a big batch every January.

Ingredients
approx 18 lbs

4 lb (1.8kg) Seville oranges

8 lemons
12 pts (5.8l) water
8 lb (3.6kg) granulated sugar
2 lb (900g) soft dark brown sugar

Wash and dry the fruit. Quarter the oranges and lemons lengthways and pull out all the pulp and flesh, catching all the juice. Remove all the pips from the flesh (you can do this in a sieve, set over a bowl), tie up the pips in a bit of muslin and chop all the flesh. *Using a food processor*. Stack the peel tightly upright and slice thinly. *Cutting by hand*. Place the unsliced peel, chopped pulp, fruit juices and bag of pips in a bowl with the water and leave in a warm room for 12–24 hours. Then slice the peel thinly. (You can soak the processor sliced peel as well).

Turn into a wide jam pan and simmer for 3–4 hours until the water has reduced by about half and the peel is absolutely tender; remove the bag of pips and squeeze well. The marmalade should have boiled down to about 7 pts (4l) by now. While it is simmering, look out the jars and wash, dry and warm them ready for use.

Warm the sugars in a low oven, add to the pan and stir over gentle heat until the sugar has completely dissolved. Now boil fast for 10–20 minutes until a set is reached (a little marmalade cooled in a saucer will wrinkle when pushed with a finger, *see page 168*). Remove the marmalade from the heat and leave for 10–15 minutes for the peel to settle and a thin skin to form before stirring gently to distribute the peel evenly.

Pot in clean, warm jars, cover with waxed discs and airtight covers and label at once. For one of the simplest but greatest pleasures in life, try a batch of home-made oatcakes with your freshly made marmalade.

Ginger Marmalade

I like to make a small batch of this fresh gingery marmalade to use as a change from Dark Seville Marmalade. You can include some finely chopped stem ginger in syrup or crystallised ginger, quite a useful way to get rid of those last few bits that are sometimes left after Christmas.

Ingredients
approx 4 lbs (1.8kg)

3 Seville oranges
2 lemons

4 pts (2.25l) water
1½ oz (35g) fresh root ginger
2–3 oz (50–75g) stem or crystallised ginger (optional)
2½ lbs (1.15kg) granulated sugar

Wash the fruit and cut into quarters, then into thin slices; remove all the pips and tie them into a bit of muslin. Put the fruit, water and the bag of pips into a jam pan and simmer gently for about 1½ hours until the orange is completely tender and the liquid is reduced by half. Add the peeled and grated root ginger and chopped stem or crystallised ginger, if used. Stir in the warmed sugar and heat gently, stirring, until the sugar has completely dissolved. Boil fast for about 5–10 minutes or until setting point is reached; test on a saucer (*see page 168*). Leave for about 10 minutes to thicken so that the orange slices will stay evenly distributed in the jar, stir and pot into prepared warmed jars. Cover, seal, wipe and label.

17th Lancers Orange Brandy (c.1860)

This lovely recipe from my great-great-grandmother's cooking book was made while the regiment was stationed in India. I use an inexpensive three star brandy, and keep it for at least one year before drinking, preferably for two or three. It's elegant and a little bitter, and I find it more sophisticated than sweeter liqueurs like Grand Marnier.

Ingredients

1¾ pts (1l) brandy
¾ lb (350g) Seville oranges

½ lb (225g) lemons (thin skinned variety for preference)
¾ lb (350g) granulated sugar

Wash and dry the oranges and lemons and cut into very thin slices (there is no need to remove the pips). Put them in a china or glass bowl with the sugar. Pour over the brandy and keep closely covered for four days, stirring daily. Then strain through muslin into clean bottles and stopper tightly. Filter through double muslin or a coffee filter after about 6 months. Keep for 1–3 years before using. The resulting brandy-impregnated orange and lemon slices can be used to make a very tasty marmalade (*see below*).

Orange Brandy Marmalade

I make this from the orange and lemon slices, having made the 17th Lancers Orange Brandy. If you are using a wide jam pan for this small quantity, cover for part of the cooking time so that the liquid does not evaporate too much. Or use a large saucepan.

Ingredients

weigh your orange and lemon slices

3 pts (1.7l) water
3 lbs (1.35k) sugar } for each 1½ lb (675g) of fruit slices

Remove all the pips and tie up in a piece of muslin. Place in a pan with the slices, add the water and simmer gently for about 2–3 hours until absolutely tender. Remove the bag of pips and squeeze well. Then add the warmed sugar and dissolve completely before boiling fast for 10–20 minutes until a set is achieved (*see page 168*). Pot and label in the usual way.

SWEET SPRING

Spring, the sweet Spring, is the pleasant year's King
—Thomas Nashe

SWEET SPRING

Although the weather is still wild and wet, there is an imperceptible stirring in the earth, and after a few days of pallid sunshine we can see the first signs that nature has remembered us and a new growing year is beginning. It may still be the depths of winter when the aconites and snowdrops bravely put on their show, but now we have a stronger feeling of spring with the early crocuses carpeting the lawn, the iris standing erect in a sheltered corner and, later, primroses and violets, and if you're lucky a few cowslips brightening up the hedgerows. Flowers and the swelling leaf-buds on the trees are what we notice first in the spring, and they warn us to go and look in the kitchen garden or the shops to see what we can find.

Now is the time for the first forced rhubarb, its early pink tones lending so much to dishes like Rhubarb Ice Cream. Then the first salad, probably only a handful of different leaves, but fresh from the garden none the less; Italian chicory, lambs' lettuce, sorrel —which is always up early—and also, perhaps, stonecrop, that invaluable watercress-flavoured weed which more people would use if they knew what it looked like.

Shrove Tuesday pancakes were said to be the traditional way of finishing up the eggs before Lent. Most of us now don't deny ourselves food in the way our ancestors used to, perhaps giving up alcohol, tobacco or chocolates, but in those days Lent was a time of great austerity. Their winter food, monotonous enough at the best of times, was now getting stale and past its best, and by the time the rigours of Lent were over everyone was really ready for a bit of a feast and some good fresh food to cleanse the blood and give them vigour for the spring work. Simnel cake was made during Lent in time for Mothering Sunday, but had to be kept until Easter; what a temptation that must have been, because there is nothing like a bit of abstinence to heighten appreciation.

Although Easter weather can often be horrid, it's the first time many of us really feel like getting out into the garden, and Good Friday is the traditional day to plant potatoes and sow many seeds. By now the garden will usually provide the handfuls of herbs and greenery to make a brilliant fresh green Easter Stuffing for your capon or chicken, and even herbs like salad burnet and bistort, which will be bitter later, are young and tender at this stage. There should be chervil, chives and parsley, and I cover them with a jam jar or cloche to be certain of them as early as possible.

The first asparagus can push through from mid-April onwards, just a few tips springing from the bare earth to start with, but with the strength to push up clods of earth and roll back stones, sometimes growing up to an almost unbelievable nine inches in a night. Enjoy it early, stem by stem, because, although there will be plenty later, it's those first few priceless stalks that we taste most carefully and enjoy the best. Asparagus is such a treat, and so useful at this time of year, that you should find room for it in your garden if you can. Mind you, calabrese or the hardy purple sprouting broccoli are almost as much of a treat; they come even earlier and are delicious with melted butter, Sauce Maltaise or the more conventional Sauce Hollandaise*; if you made a later summer planting of spinach beet, its flat white stalks can be used in the same way.

70   * *Good Food from Farthinghoe*

As well as these early delicacies it is spinach (most useful for salads), spring greens, spring cabbage and cauliflower, all of which are hardy enough to have over-wintered successfully, that see us through this difficult time when everything is growing like mad but isn't yet ready. A bed of over-wintered spring cabbage (I plant 'April', which has a tight, pointed head) can be a godsend for crisp salads, with a good depth of nutty flavour, or cooked as Spring Cabbage with Beurre Noisette. The rhubarb is now in great red sealing-wax sticks, protected by some old dustbins with the bases removed and the rhubarb packed round with loose straw, just right for dishes like Rhubarb and Angelica Pie and rhubarb suet pudding.

Although the garden catches our immediate attention, one can hardly fail to notice the fields are rich with grass. Really good early lamb is expensive, and although I may have it occasionally I am very happy to buy hogget (last year's late lamb, now nearly one year old) from a good butcher; when it's well hung it has real taste and is a very good buy; it can also be used for boiling. Lamb from the hills of Wales or Scotland is darker, leaner and smaller, with the gamey flavour that they get from natural hill grazing. We may not know our mutton as well as the Forsytes did—do you remember Galsworthy writing that old Jolyon swore by Dartmoor mutton, James by Welsh and Swithin by Southdown, while Nicholas maintained that, although people might sneer, there was nothing like New Zealand? —but there's no reason why we shouldn't try lamb from the different areas. Many good southern butchers also stock the late, hill-born lambs that have fed naturally on the hillside (they are probably now one of our few absolutely natural meats) and, as they will be ready in August or September, you can eat young lamb all through the summer. I can see why saddle of mutton was always the crowning point for a Forsyte feast, for 'there is something in its succulent solidity which makes it suitable to people "of a certain position". It is nourishing and—tasty; the sort of thing a man remembers eating.' The fact that it has rather fallen from favour, which is such a pity, may be due not so much to the cost as to the relative difficulty of its carving.

The season for game is now past, but spring is a very good time for fish. Herring (if you can get them—and how I long for those fat herrings we used to get straight from the Ayrshire sea for a few pennies each), whitebait, mackerel and turbot are all at their best; crab is always good value and, although scallops are nearing the end of their best season, salmon, sea trout and brown or rainbow trout are fresh and plump. We live in the midlands, and I have a constant battle to get really fresh fish; our Friday market in the Dordogne, where we have a cottage, has taught me the meaning of fish with firm flesh, silvery skin, a bright eye and fresh pink gills. In this country a large number of people seem neither to notice nor to care; apparently much of the best fish goes abroad to wholesalers who will happily match the full retail price which customers here are so loath to pay.

April and May are traditional months for cheese-making, the months when you will particularly notice the cream looking deep and golden and at the top of the bottle. Our yoghurt tastes best then, for the cows have left the yard and are on the fresh lush grass. Spare or left-over yoghurt makes excellent cream cheese if you drain off the whey and season it in an interesting way.

The need for winter soups and solid, warming dishes diminishes, and it's the best time

71

of year for sneaking in a few inexpensive but refreshing and fragrant sorbets that have the added amusement of being difficult for your guests to identify. Ingredients such as blackcurrant leaves, peppermint, rose geranium or hedgerow elderflower may seem mundane to those who have them or bucolic to the city dweller, but I find them lovely for entertaining.

Make the most of watercress before it shoots in summer; make salads of it, use it in sauces and soups, and don't forget you can freeze some blanched watercress as a purée if you think you might want it in summer for flavouring or colouring a sauce.

Some of the early strawberries can already be full of flavour. I like to catch them with the last of the kiwi fruit and serve them layered in a dish with a little sugar syrup, because the colours and flavours are so good together.

Whitsun comes around the end of May, traditionally a time to eat the young spring veal and a gooseberry pie from the first scarce, hard green fruit, sharp and full of flavour. I use a fairly rich shortcrust pastry and make a double crust plate pie, because the flavour of gooseberry is so strong and I'm usually short of fruit. By this time, summer is really just around the corner. The last three months have seen that glorious change from the dark evenings and cold bleak earth of a silent nature to fully clad trees and shrubs in the full fig of their fresh spring colours, flowers everywhere, and bright long evenings full of birdsong, all proclaiming the joys of spring.

Spring

First Courses and Supper Dishes

Tartelettes aux Fruits de Mer
Broccoli Sauce Maltaise
Asparagus
Asparagus Omelette
Asparagus and Ham Quiche
Petits Flans d'Asperge
Asparagus au Gratin
Oeufs aux Herbes

Soups

Spring Vegetable Soup
Potato and Watercress Soup
Potage Dubarry

Fish

Baked Fish Mornay with Capers
Grilled Mackerel
Dressed Crab

Main Courses

Ham in Parsley Sauce
Poulet au Printemps
Baby Lamb Sauce Paloise
Kidneys in Gin and Juniper Sauce
• Pork Italian
Lincolnshire Stuffed Chine
Easter Stuffing for Capon, Chicken or
    Turkey

Vegetables

Creamed Sprout or Turnip Tops
Caledonian Cauliflower

Spring Cabbage with Beurre Noisette
Spinach Salad with Anchovy and
    Croûtons
Artichoke Salad
Watercress Salad
Spring or Autumn Salad
Broad Bean Leaf Salad
Baby Pod Broad Beans

Puddings

• Tarte au Citron
Rhubarb and Angelica Pie
Rhubarb and Sweet Cicily Pudding in
    Demerara Crust
Rhubarb Ice Cream
Gooseberry Double Crust Pie
Russian Sorbet

Miscellaneous

Yoghurt
Yoghurt Whip
Yoghurt Cheese
Scones
Easter Cakes
Simnel Cake
Muesli
Hot Cross Buns
Chive and Mint Cream Dressing
Mint Sauce
Gooseberry or Gooseberry and Sorrel
    Sauce

• Also quantities for 25 persons

First Courses and Supper Dishes

F ***   **Tartelettes aux Fruits de Mer**

I put this superb dinner-party dish into the early spring section, for fish is good and scallops in particular are at their best in March. One taste of these crisp flaky pastry tartelettes, with their rich seafood filling, usually convinces people that they really must have a go at them. Up to that moment, whilst I have been demonstrating making them, I have usually seen a few balloons floating over people's heads saying things like, 'Huh, those *really* are far too much trouble to do'. But of course the prawn butter, prawn fumet and flaky pastry can all have been made at some other time and frozen until you want them. The prawn butter in particular is worth having in the freezer, for it gets every scrap of flavour from expensive prawns. This is a good dish for entertaining, as the seafood, the sauce and the pastry shells can be kept warm individually, ready to combine and dish up at the last moment.

Ingredients
4–6 people

Flaky Pastry
5 oz (125g) plain 'strong' flour
squeeze lemon juice
3½ oz (85g) butter
iced water
pinch salt

Prawn Butter
3 oz (75g) butter
shells from prawns used for the filling

Prawn Fumet
the shells from the prawns (having made
   prawn butter)
2 lb (900g) white fish skins and bones
   (sole or turbot are best)
1 small sliced onion
6–8 parsley stalks
1 slice lemon with rind
1 bay leaf
6–8 peppercorns
¼ pt (150ml) dry white wine
about 2 pts (1.2l) cold water to cover
¼ teasp salt

Filling
12 oz (350g) prawns in their shells
1 lb (450g) skinned, filleted turbot or sole
prawn fumet to poach fish
2–3 fresh scallops (optional)
1 lb (450g) fresh mussels in their shells
   (optional)
4–6 tbs fried breadcrumbs
salt and pepper

Sauce
1½ oz (35g) prawn butter
1½ oz (35g) flour
½ pt (300ml) prawn fumet
¼ pt (150ml) double cream
squeeze lemon
4–6 oz (100–175g) extra prawn butter or
   butter (optional)
salt and pepper

Set aside a few prawns from the quantity given for the *Filling*, to use as garnish. Shell the remainder and set both shells and prawns aside until ready to use.

Flaky Pastry. Sieve the flour and salt into a bowl and add a squeeze of lemon juice. Divide the firm but malleable butter into quarters. Rub in one quarter until the mixture is like breadcrumbs, then add enough iced water to form a medium firm dough. Knead briefly until smooth and roll into an oblong ¼″ (¾cm) thick. Take a second quarter of butter and, with the point of a knife, place dabs of butter on the top two-thirds of pastry, leaving an inch margin all round. Sprinkle with flour and fold the bottom third up, top third down, press edges to seal and turn pastry one turn to your right. Repeat process with the remaining portions of butter. Refrigerate if the pastry becomes too soft and rest for half-an-hour before using (it can be frozen at this stage). Roll pastry thinly and cut to fit 4–6 individual 4½″ (12cm) tartelette tins. Prick well, line with tinfoil and baking beans and cook in a hot oven (425°F/220°C/Gas 7) for about 10 minutes. Press down any bubbles and remove the tinfoil when set. Continue to cook in a moderately hot oven (375°F/190°C/Gas 5) until a golden brown and crisp right through. Keep warm or re-heat when wanted.

Prawn Butter. Melt the butter in a frying pan, add the prawn shells and toss over high heat until hot through. Turn into a food processor or liquidiser and process until finely chopped. Turn the mixture into muslin and squeeze to separate the prawn butter from the shells.

Prawn Fumet. Having made the *Prawn Butter,* place the chopped prawn shells and washed fish bones, with the gills removed, in a pan with all the other ingredients. Bring to the boil, skim well and simmer for 30–40 minutes (no longer, or you will get a bitter flavour from the fish bones). Strain through muslin and reduce further to strengthen the flavour if necessary.

Filling. Cut the turbot or sole fillets into neat pieces and poach in prawn fumet to cover for 5–10 minutes, depending on thickness, until firm. Drain the fish and set it aside with the peeled prawns. Use the fumet to cook the scallops. Remove the black thread from the scallops, wash, cut the white into 3–4 pieces and the tongue into 2 pieces, and poach for about 2 minutes and 1 minute respectively in the fumet. Steam open the scrubbed and bearded mussels and remove from their shells. Strain their liquid very carefully through muslin to remove sand and add to the prawn fumet in which you have cooked the fish and scallops. Strain it again through double muslin if it looks cloudy.

Sauce. Melt 1½ oz (35g) prawn butter in a saucepan, add the flour and cook gently for 3–4 minutes. Remove the pan from the heat, wait for the sizzling to cease and add ½ pt (300ml) prawn fumet; bring to the boil, whisking hard, and simmer for 1–2 minutes. Add the cream and a little more fumet if the sauce seems too thick, season, and finish with extra prawn butter beaten in. I like to keep the sauce hot for ½–2 hours in a *bain marie* at this stage for the flavour to develop.

To assemble. Fold the fish, scallops, peeled prawns and mussels into the sauce. Heat and keep warm in a *bain marie.* Just before serving spoon into warm pastry shells. Sprinkle with fried breadcrumbs and garnish with reserved prawns. Heat in the oven a few minutes and serve.

✱✱   Broccoli Sauce Maltaise

Hardy purple sprouting broccoli is a treasure in the lean spring days. The more tender calabrese, commonly sold as broccoli, is also quite delicious cooked and served like asparagus (well deserving its name of poor man's asparagus) using any of our asparagus recipes or with this orange-flavoured sauce Hollandaise called Sauce Maltaise. I find steaming, rather than boiling, helps to keep the heads from breaking up.

Ingredients
4–6 people

1–1½ lb (450–675g) purple sprouting
    broccoli or calabrese

Sauce Maltaise
3 egg yolks
3–5 tbs orange juice
grated rind of 1 orange
1 tbs lemon juice
1 oz (25 g) cold hard butter
4–6 oz (100–175g) melted butter
salt and pepper

Wash the broccoli and break into even-sized florets. Steam them over boiling salt water for 10–15 minutes until just tender. Remove and lay on a dish all facing the same way. Serve at once with Sauce Maltaise.

Sauce Maltaise. Beat the yolks in a bowl for 1 minute until thick and pale; beat in 1 tbs of the orange juice, the orange rind, lemon juice and seasoning. Add half the cold butter and place the bowl over a saucepan of hot water. Stir until the yolks thicken, then quickly remove the bowl from the water and add the remaining cold butter to check the cooking. Stir until melted, then beat in the melted butter gradually, whisking all the time.

    Finish by beating in enough of the remaining orange juice to make a thick pouring sauce. It can be kept warm for up to 4 hours over a saucepan of lukewarm water standing in a warm (not hot) place.

Asparagus

Asparagus is the seasonal treat *par excellence*. Its season is short, it really should be fresh, not frozen, and therefore we look forward to it, and buy and enjoy it when we see it, knowing it will soon be gone again. The nicest way to eat it is plain boiled with melted butter, with Hollandaise or Maltaise Sauce, or you might try the old fashioned Melted Butter Sauce*. After you have tried all those, it's nice to serve cold with a vinaigrette, or if there is not enough to go round you might try any of the following ways of using it.

    Aparagus from your own garden is the treat of treats, with the water set to boil as you go out to cut it. One has to be patient, allowing at least 2–3 years for it to establish. To my mind it is much better to buy 1-year-old crowns and wait than try to jump the gun by buying older crowns from which you hope to gather asparagus sooner; they invariably take longer to settle down, and can die more easily in the meantime. If you grow your own, you don't always get enough asparagus for everyone at any one time, so this is why I have evolved these recipes which don't need pounds and pounds of asparagus. To stretch it in this way is also better if you have to buy it, for it is never cheap.

*   Asparagus Omelette

Make this either with the very first few tender spears or when there is only a little bit of asparagus, especially those thin shoots sold as 'sprue'. It can be served hot or cold, and is wonderful cold on a hot spring or summer's day, perhaps using the last asparagus of the season.

Ingredients
2–3 people as a main course
4–6 people as a starter

6–8 oz (175–225g) thinnish asparagus or
   3–4 oz (75–100g) cooked asparagus
   tips
6–8 eggs
1½ oz (35g) butter
½–1 teasp flour
4–6 tbs whipping cream or top of the
   milk
salt and pepper

Cook the asparagus in lightly salted boiling water, drain and refresh under the cold tap to set the colour. Cut the tender tops into 2–3 pieces and set aside. Discard tough stalks or keep for soup.

Heat 1 oz (25g) of the butter in a small pan, toss the cut asparagus in the hot butter, then sprinkle over a little flour. Cook for a moment or two before adding the cream or top of milk, off the stove. Boil up, stirring gently, and season.

Make your omelettes (*see page 123*), using 2–4 eggs at a time, depending on the size of your pan; when nearly cooked, spoon some filling across the middle of each. Fold over and turn out. Serve at once or leave to cool and serve cold with a salad.

F **   Asparagus and Ham Quiche

Sometimes you don't have enough asparagus to go round, or you have un-graded sticks, some fat, some thin and some extra long. All these oddities are perfect for making into a quiche.

Ingredients
4–6 people

12 oz (350g) fresh asparagus	*All-Purpose Pastry*
4 eggs (or 3 yolks + 2 eggs)	1 egg yolk and about 2 tbs cold water *or*
2 fl oz (50ml) whipping cream	3–4 tbs cold water
3 oz (75g) diced ham	6 oz (175g) plain flour
¼–½ oz (6–12g) butter	3 oz (75g) firm butter
salt and pepper	a good pinch of salt

All-Purpose Pastry

By hand. If you are using a yolk, mix it with the 2 tbs cold water. Sift the flour and salt into a wide mixing bowl and add the firm butter cut into hazelnut-sized pieces. Rub in the butter, sprinkling over the yolk and water mixed, or just water, as you work, and pinching the whole lot into a dough. When formed into a rough dough turn out on to a board, and with the heel of your hand smear the pastry down the board in egg-sized lumps finally to amalgamate it. Knead briefly into a flat disc. Rest in a plastic bag in the fridge for 1–2 hours or overnight.

In the Food Processor. Sift the flour and salt into the bowl of the food processor with the metal blade in place, add the firm butter cut into hazelnut-sized pieces and have your yolk and cold water, or just cold water, ready. Switch on, and add the yolk and water at once; process until the mixture just draws together into a lump. Turn out on to a board and smear down the board in egg-sized lumps (though I hardly feel it needs this *fraisage* when made in the food processor). Knead briefly into a flat disc. Rest in a plastic bag in the fridge for 1–2 hours or overnight.

Roll the pastry and line a 9″ (24cm) removable base flan tin. Prick the base, line with tinfoil and baking beans and bake in a hot over (400°F/200°C/Gas 6) for 8–10 minutes; then remove the tinfoil and continue to bake in a moderately hot oven (375°F/190°C/Gas 5) for about 15 minutes until lightly golden and almost cooked, covering lightly with tin foil if the rim seems to be getting too brown.

Cook the asparagus in the minimum of lightly salted water, tying thicker stalks into a separate bundle from the thinner spears and cooking for longer. Drain, reserve the water, and set 8–12 tips aside for garnish. Roughly chop the remainder, discarding tough stalks and purée, adding a little of the reserved water. When very smooth, put through a fine sieve and make up to 10 fl oz (300ml) with some of the reserved asparagus water.

Whisk the eggs and add the asparagus purée, cream and seasoning. Scatter the diced ham over the pastry shell, pour over the asparagus mixture, decorate with reserved asparagus tips and dot with butter. Bake in a moderately hot oven (375°F/190°C/Gas 5) until just set right through. Serve hot, warm or cold.

**   Petits Flans d'Asperge

This is a superb recipe, delicate and fine. I based it on a dish we ate at M. Lameloise's restaurant at Chagny in Burgundy, one of the best in France. It's difficult in this country to get good uncooked prawns, so I generally use scampi, one of the few frozen seafoods sold uncooked.

Ingredients
4–6 people

¾ lb (350g) fresh asparagus
2 eggs
3 egg yolks
2 fl oz (50ml) whipping or double cream
salt and pepper

Sauce
8–12 fresh uncooked prawns or frozen
   unbreaded scampi
5–8 fl oz (150ml–225ml) whipping or
   double cream
squeeze lemon juice
fresh chives
fresh or dried tarragon
salt and pepper

Cook the asparagus in the minimum of lightly salted boiling water; drain and reserve the water. Set 8–12 tips aside for garnish and keep warm. Roughly chop the remainder, discarding any tough stalks. Purée the asparagus, adding a little of the reserved water. When very smooth, put through a fine sieve and make up to 10 fl oz (300ml) with the reserved asparagus water.

Beat the eggs and yolks together, then add the asparagus purée, cream and seasoning. Turn into 4–6 well-buttered cocotte dishes and stand these in a tin with boiling water to come halfway up the cocottes. Bake in a very moderate oven (325°F/170°C/Gas 3) for 20–25 minutes until just set. Leave for a few minutes so that they will turn out easily. Run a knife round the edge of each cocotte and turn out on to individual serving plates. Pour round a little sauce, dividing the scampi fairly. Decorate with the reserved asparagus tips and serve at once.

Sauce. Boil the cream for a few minutes in a small pan until reduced and thickened a little. Add some finely scissored chives and tarragon, seasoning, and a squeeze of lemon juice. Keep warm, covered. When ready to serve, add the peeled prawns or the thawed, drained scampi and boil up once. Heat only until the prawns or scampi begin to firm up, then serve.

*   Asparagus au Gratin

I like to use smoked ham for this, cut in a thick slice so that it can be diced into cubes; if you have not got any you can use diced bacon, also smoked for choice. It makes a more substantial and economical dish than asparagus on its own, and can easily be made with frozen asparagus at any time of year.

Ingredients
4–6 people

1 lb (450g) (or more!) fresh or frozen
   asparagus
2 oz (50g) grated Gruyère cheese
a few breadcrumbs
½ oz (12g) butter

Sauce
1 oz (25g) butter
1 oz (25g) flour
¼ pt (150ml) asparagus water
¼ pt (150ml) milk
2 oz (50g) diced smoked cooked ham
3–4 tbs cream
salt, pepper and nutmeg

Trim the asparagus, tie into small bunches (two strings to each bunch) and boil gently in lightly salted water for about 15–20 minutes until just tender (much less for frozen; follow directions on the packet). Drain well, reserving the cooking liquid. Lay in a buttered gratin dish, cover with sauce, top with breadcrumbs, grated cheese and flakes of butter and brown under the grill or in a hot oven (425°F/220°C/Gas 7) for 10–15 minutes.

Sauce. Melt the butter in a saucepan, add the flour and cook, stirring, for 2–3 minutes over moderate heat; draw the pan off the stove and wait for the sizzling to cease. Add asparagus water and milk and bring to the boil, whisking hard; season with salt, pepper and nutmeg and add the diced ham. Thin with spoonfuls of cream to a coating sauce and pour over the asparagus.

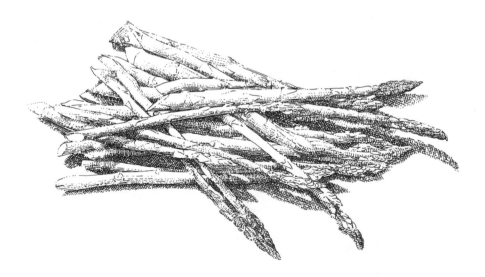

✳✳✳ Oeufs aux Herbes

This spring dish of hot oeufs mollets, coated in a thick but light green herb sauce, is good as a starter or for a light lunch or supper dish. By serving it on fried bread croûtes or in a pastry shell—perhaps using the Cheesy Flaky Pastry (*see page 201*)—it not only becomes more substantial but there is a nice contrast of textures as well. You can make it with watercress and celery leaves if you have not got a great variety of herbs available, and it is still delicious. It's the sort of simple dish which needs careful cooking to be just right, so that the eggs are just runny inside, the sauce is thick enough not to fall off, and the bread or pastry crisp and light. A good test of a cook!

Ingredients
4–6 people

4–6 oeufs mollets (5½-minute boiled
    eggs)
¼ pt (150ml) milk
1 finely chopped onion
a little sprig rosemary
1 oz (25g) butter
1 oz (25g) flour
¼ pt (150ml) single or whipping cream
a good handful fresh mixed herbs
    (parsley, chervil, tarragon, lemon
    thyme, lovage, fennel etc, or any nice
    mix of spring herbs)
4–6 croûtes of fried bread or little pastry
    boats
salt and pepper

As some of the herbs are strongly flavoured, use only one part tarragon, one part lemon thyme and half a part lovage to three parts parsley, chervil and fennel. Pick the herbs from their tough stalks, blanch in boiling salted water for 2–3 minutes, then drain and refresh under the cold tap to set the colour. Squeeze out excess water and set aside.

Heat the milk with the onion and rosemary and simmer gently, covered, until the onion is cooked and the milk well flavoured. Remove the rosemary and discard. Melt the butter in a saucepan, add the flour and cook over moderate heat, stirring, for 2–3 minutes. Draw off the stove, wait for the sizzling to cease, then add the onions and milk and the cream. Season, bring to the boil, whisking hard, and simmer for 1–2 minutes. Place the blanched herbs and the sauce in a food processor or liquidiser and process until smooth and a good green colour. Use at once; you can keep the sauce hot in a bowl over hot water, but it is best used as soon as possible, for the colour spoils quite quickly.

Boil the eggs for 5½ minutes, then run under the cold tap for a moment. Shell and keep in warm water if not using at once. Set the drained and dried eggs in a dish or on croûtes, pastry shells or, in summer, cooked artichoke hearts, and spoon over some sauce. This should be just thick enough to coat them well. Serve at once.

Soups

F ✳✳   **Spring Vegetable Soup**

This is a really useful soup in which you can use whatever you have available, especially when there is not enough of any one vegetable to make a soup on its own. It's also suitable for using up your early thinnings, and I frequently add very young kohl-rabi, broad bean, beetroot or salsify leaves or young borage or marigold plants as well as sprigs of rocket, hyssop or salad burnet. Just balance your flavours so that you do not get one powerful flavour predominating. It will imperceptibly become a summer soup as broad beans, peas and other summer vegetables are included.

    Even without a garden this is still a useful soup, using up many bits and pieces from the vegetable basket and the outside leaves of your bought lettuces, so long as you don't think that yellowing watercress stalks, shrivelled celery sticks and a few tired lettuce leaves are going to give you a soup of any freshness or distinction!

Ingredients
4–6 people

2 oz (50g) butter
8 oz (225g) mixed spring onions, garden leeks or onions (or use just one of these)
handfuls of spinach, sorrel, water or landcress, lettuce, parsley, chervil, chives and sprigs of mint or tarragon to make 8 oz (225g) in all
½ pt (300ml) milk
¼ pt (150ml) double or whipping cream (optional)
1–4 oz (25–100g) butter
finely chopped chervil or chives
some croûtons (optional)
salt and pepper

Velouté Soup Base
1½ oz (35g) butter
1½ oz (35g) plain flour
1¾ pt (1l) light chicken stock
salt and pepper

Melt the butter in a heavy pan, stainless steel, enamel or earthenware for choice. Add the finely chopped onions and leeks and cook gently, covered, without browning for 5 minutes or so before adding the washed and shredded greenery of your choice. Toss in the butter, season lightly with salt and pepper, then cover and cook gently, without browning, for 20–30 minutes until all is tender.

Velouté Soup Base. Meanwhile melt the butter for the velouté soup base, add the flour and cook, stirring, over moderate heat for 2–3 minutes. Draw off the stove, wait for the sizzling to cease, then add the chicken stock. Season, bring to the boil, whisking hard, and simmer for 1–2 minutes.

Once the vegetables are tender, process to a purée in the food processor or liquidiser, adding in the velouté base, and strain through a sieve back into the saucepan (or you can leave it unsieved if you like, provided that there are no stringy bits). Add the milk and reheat.

The soup can be served just like that for a simple supper, but to make a little more of it, add the cream and reheat; then, off the stove, whisk in some butter to enrich and flavour the soup.

Serve sprinkled with finely chopped chervil, parsley or chives, and hand hot croûtons if you like.

$\mathcal{F}$ ** Potato and Watercress Soup

This potato and watercress soup, made with good chicken stock and served with or without the cream and egg yolk liaison, is simple but excellent.

Ingredients
4–6 people

1½ lb (675g) peeled potatoes
1 good bunch watercress
1½ pts (900ml) chicken stock
good squeeze lemon juice
3 fl oz (75ml) cream (optional)
1 egg yolk (optional)
fresh chopped chervil (optional)
fried croûtons (optional)
salt and pepper

Cut the potatoes into even-sized pieces and boil, just covered in lightly salted water, until tender. While they cook, chop up and simmer the watercress stalks in the chicken stock for about 20 minutes; then strain, pressing the stalks well. Drain the potatoes, retaining some of the water, and sieve or pass through a potato masher back into the saucepan. Dilute with the strained, watercress-flavoured chicken stock. When nearly ready to serve, chop the watercress leaves and stir in with a good squeeze of lemon juice and season.

For a richer, smoother soup, whisk the egg yolk with the cream and gradually whisk in some of the hot soup. Return to the pan. Heat the soup gently but *do not boil* or the egg may curdle.

If you wish, serve sprinkled with a little finely chopped chervil and hand tiny hot croûtons of bread, fried in butter and olive oil. I love the delicacy of this soup, but you can, if you like, make it more positive with two bunches of watercress.

**   Potage Dubarry

Vegetables which have overwintered in the open develop much more flavour from growing slowly and being tempered by the elements. So although you can make this classic, rich cauliflower soup at any time of year, I think you will find it has more flavour during the spring. It is care and attention, as well as the fairly large quantity of butter which is beaten in, that gives such a velvety result to this delicate soup, which I often feel has almost a taste of cheese about it.

Ingredients
4–6 people

1 medium sized cauliflower
½ stick celery
¼ small onion
2 pts (1.2l) good stock
4 oz (100g) butter
1 oz (25g) flour
½ pt (300ml) milk
3 egg yolks
2 fl oz (50ml) cream
finely chopped chervil or parsley
salt, pepper and nutmeg

Wash the cauliflower, break into florets, and set a few aside for garnish. Blanch the remaining cauliflower, celery and onion in boiling salted water for 2 minutes. Drain, then simmer in the stock until tender; purée and sieve.

Melt 1 oz (25g) of the butter in a saucepan, add the flour and cook over moderate heat for 2–3 minutes. Draw off the stove, wait for the sizzling to cease, add the milk and bring to the boil, whisking hard. Simmer for 1–2 minutes. Gradually whisk in the cauliflower purée and season with salt, pepper and nutmeg. Simmer gently for 5 minutes.

Whisk the egg yolks with the cream, then gradually add about ½ pt (300ml) of the hot soup, whisking well. Return this mixture to the pan off the stove and heat *very gently* until the yolks thicken, but *do not boil*. On serving, whisk in the remaining butter in little bits and correct the seasoning. Serve with tiny dice of the raw reserved cauliflower and finely chopped chervil or parsley.

Fish

*   Baked Fish Mornay with Capers

I like to bake raw fillets of skinned fish in the oven under a sauce. It is quick and easy, and all the goodness is in the dish. Keep the sauce thick, as juices ooze from the fish during cooking.

Ingredients
4–6 people

Sauce

1–1½ lb (450–675g) fresh haddock or cod fillets
2–3 teasp capers
3 oz (75g) grated Gruyère or strong Cheddar cheese
salt and pepper

1 oz (25g) butter
1 oz (25g) plain flour
½ pt (300ml) milk
3 oz (75g) grated Gruyère or strong Cheddar cheese
salt and pepper

Skin the fish fillets and cut into portions. Tuck the thin tail-ends under to make the fillets of even thickness, and lay them in one layer in a well-buttered, shallow baking dish. Season with salt and pepper and scatter over the capers. Pour over the prepared sauce and top with the cheese. Bake, uncovered, in a moderate oven (350°F/180°C/Gas 4) for about 15–20 minutes or until the fish is just cooked; then pop under a hot grill for a moment to brown.

Sauce. Melt the butter, add the flour and cook for 2–3 minutes over moderate heat, stirring. Draw off the stove and wait for the sizzling to cease before adding the milk. Bring to the boil, whisking with a wire whisk, and simmer for 1–2 minutes. Season lightly with salt because of the cheese but with plenty of pepper, and whisk in the grated cheese. Warm gently, whisking only until the cheese melts, then pour over the fish.

*   Grilled Mackerel

Serve grilled so that the skin is crispy, the slashes filled with mustard if not making the Gooseberry Sauce. (*See page 114*).

Ingredients
4–6 people

4–6 fine fresh gutted mackerel (with head and tail off if very large)
2–3 tbs Dijon mustard (optional)

Wipe the fish and slash diagonally three times down each side, season with salt and pepper and place on a grid under the hot grill. Grill for 5–6 minutes on each side until the skin is crisp and brown and the flesh is cooked. Serve at once with Gooseberry Sauce.

***   Dressed Crab

Crab is available all the year, but is at its best from about May to August. It makes a lovely summer treat for those who are prepared to dress it. Of course, you can serve it whole in the continental way and let everyone, armed with nutcrackers and skewers, get on with cracking and picking the meat themselves, but the English way is to pick all the meat out beforehand and serve it dressed with mayonnaise. You do then get some really good mouthfuls rather than endless little nibbles, but until you have sat down and dressed a crab you won't know how much work is involved. Choose good heavy crab for their size, assessing them by weighing them in your hand, or trust your fishmonger to give you good ones. The females are frequently the fatter, and therefore preferable, with a broader tail than the male, and may be carrying eggs, packed in under their tail. Dressed crab is frequently served in the shell, one per person, but this means that you need 4–6 smallish crabs; these can be the sweetest but are undoubtedly more fiddly to pick. In Britain, crabs are usually sold cooked, but if you get them alive cook them quickly.

Ingredients
4–6 people

4–6 smallish crabs or 2–3 larger ones (the
   dressed weight of the white and
   brown meat will be about ⅓ the
   original weight)
1 lemon
parsley
½ pt (300ml) best handmade mayonnaise
lettuce leaves for garnish

To Cook Crab. A crab must be very much alive when you cook it. To kill them humanely before cooking, plunge a sharp awl or fine screwdriver into the underside of the crab just below the mouth; do this several times at different angles and you will hit the brain and kill it instantly. Plunge it immediately into boiling salt water (which anyway will kill it almost at once); simmer for 10–20 minutes according to weight, but do not overcook as this makes shellfish tough. Remove from the water, run under the cold tap and leave to cool before dressing.

To Dress Crab. Arm yourself with a skewer, nutcrackers and a hammer or heavy knife. Pull the body carefully apart from the shell, starting at the tail end. Carefully remove and discard the mouth and stomach bag which is found in the shell. Press down on the horny mouth with your thumbs until it breaks off, then lift it out with its attached little sack and throw away. Now discard the 'dead man's fingers', which are the soft, greyish, fungus-like gills attached to the body of the crab, and that's all you have to get rid of.

    Scrape the brown creamy meat into one bowl, using the back of a teaspoon to get it all out of the shell. Then set to work on the white meat; twist off each leg and, depending on how thin the legs are and how thorough you're prepared to be, break the legs into sections, carefully bending them backwards at the joints, which will draw out the stiff white tendons. Crack the legs with the nutcrackers and remove the flesh to a separate bowl. A few of the little legs can be used to garnish the dish.

Now turn to the body, where the white flesh lies between layers of thin white shell, rather like a honeycomb. Pick out the meat with a skewer, then break off a bit more shell and pick again, until you have gathered all the meat and have discarded all the body. Take care not to get splinters of shell amongst the meat.

The large claws need careful cracking with a hammer, or they can be tapped sharply round the thickest part with the back of a heavy knife until they break in two. Remove the flesh, discarding the crisp white tendons.

Return to the empty shell, and on the underside you will find a faint marking or 'false line' near the outside of the shell. Tap or press the inside part firmly with your thumbs and the shell will break to this line, giving you a more open shell to serve the crab meat in. Scrub the shell well and oil lightly.

To finish. The white meat can be served as it is, which I prefer, or you can mix it with salt and pepper, a little mustard, oil and vinegar. Cream the brown meat, to which you can add a few breadcrumbs, seasoning and lemon juice if you wish. Place a spoonful of brown meat at each end of the shell and the flaked white meat in the middle, garnished with a little parsley. Lay the prepared shells on a large flat plate, on a bed of lettuce leaves, and garnish with reserved small claws. Serve mayonnaise and lemon quarters separately, handing a plate of thinly cut brown bread and butter.

Main Courses

𝓕 *   Ham in Parsley Sauce

The sight of ruffled rows of green parsley in the garden or a nice fresh bunch in the shops always makes me long for parsley sauce. I love that wonderful smell chopped parsley has when it's really fresh, the smell and taste that go after a day or two on the windowsill. The creamy, bright green sauce is beautiful with a hot whole ham, or can be used when finishing off a stalwart ham or piece of boiled bacon.

Ingredients
4–6 people

**1–1½ lb (450–675g) generously diced
   cooked ham**

Parsley Sauce
**1 pt (600ml) milk
good bunch fresh parsley
1½ oz (35g) butter
1½ oz (35g) flour
3–4 tbs cream (optional)
salt and pepper**

Add the diced ham to the sauce and heat through until it is hot and has been through the boil. If the ham is very lean, I sometimes heat it by tossing the cubes in hot butter in a frying pan, which gives a wonderful flavour and enriches the sauce.

Parsley Sauce. Pull the heads off the parsley and put the stalks in a saucepan with the milk. Heat, covered, till simmering, then leave aside to infuse for 5–10 minutes until needed.

Melt the butter in another saucepan, add the flour and cook over moderate heat, stirring, for 2–3 minutes. Draw the pan off the stove, wait for the sizzling to cease, then strain in all the infused milk. Bring the sauce to the boil, whisking hard, and simmer for 1–2 minutes. Chop the parsley finely, keeping one or two nice sprigs back for garnish, and add 6–8 tbs to the sauce, until it is green with parsley. Add the cream, if used, and season lightly, especially if the ham was salty.

**   Poulet au Printemps

I had trouble with this dish. I wanted to cook a chicken with the fresh herbs of spring, but when I added chopped herbs to the sauce it all seemed rather gritty and bitty. So eventually we cooked the chicken with the herbs, strained the cooking liquid, then thickened this herb-flavoured liquid with egg yolks for a velvety finish. We garnished the dish with crisp glazed cucumber and a little chopped tarragon, which has an amazing affinity for cucumbers. It's surprisingly easy to use for entertaining.

Ingredients
4–6 people

3½ lb (1.6kg) chicken
1 tbs oil
1½ oz (35g) butter
½ oz (12g) flour
6 fl oz (150ml) good chicken stock
4 fl oz (100ml) dry white wine
2 slices lemon
a handful of parsley
1 sprig rosemary
2–3 sprigs marjoram (less of the annual
   sweet marjoram, for it is very strong)
1 tbs scissored chives (approx)
1 sprig fresh or good pinch dried
   tarragon
½ bunch watercress or landcress
½–1 cucumber
2 egg yolks
4 fl oz (100ml) double cream
squeeze of lemon juice
little finely chopped parsley and
   tarragon or use your own choice of
   fresh mixed herbs
salt and pepper

} or use your own choice of fresh mixed herbs

Joint the chicken into four or eight. Heat 1 oz (25g) butter and the oil in a sauté or frying pan and gently cook the chicken pieces on both sides until golden. Sprinkle over the flour and add the stock and wine, shaking the pan as you do so to mix in the flour thoroughly. Add the lemon slices (use only the zest and flesh if it has a thick white pith), the herbs and seasoning. Cover, or turn into a casserole and cook gently on the stove or in a moderately hot oven (375°F/190°/Gas 5) for 20–40 minutes until just cooked. Meanwhile prepare the cucumber. Peel and cut into four lengthways, then cut across into 1" (2–3cm) bits. Blanch in boiling salt water for 2–3 minutes until tender but still crisp, then drain and refresh under the cold tap to set the colour.

Remove the chicken. De-grease the cooking liquid and turn, still with the herbs, into a small pan. Return the chicken to the casserole or sauté pan and keep warm, covered.

Boil up the cooking liquid and reduce until well flavoured, then strain, pressing the débris in the sieve well to get all the flavour from the herbs. Whisk the egg-yolks and cream in a bowl, then gradually whisk in some of the hot liquid. Return to the saucepan and gently bring the sauce to the boil, whisking hard. Simmer for 1–2 minutes (there is enough flour in the sauce to allow the egg yolks to boil without curdling), then add some of the chopped parsley and tarragon and correct the seasoning, adding a squeeze of lemon juice if necessary. You can use this sauce at once, keep it warm in a *bain marie*, or re-heat.

To Serve. Toss the cucumber in the remaining butter in a wide frying or sauté pan until glazed and hot. Place the chicken on a serving dish, and add to your sauce some the liquid they have thrown but don't over-thin it. Scatter the cucumber over the chicken and pour the sauce over, sprinkle with the fresh chopped parsley and tarragon and serve quickly.

**   Baby Lamb Sauce Paloise

Delicate young lamb needs no strong accompaniment, but a delicate type of béarnaise sauce, flavoured with mint and shallot, is almost certain to please.

Ingredients
4–6 people

3 lb (1.35kg) young leg of lamb
1 oz (25g) butter
salt and pepper

Sauce Paloise
3 tbs dry white wine
3 tbs white wine vinegar
2 tbs chopped shallot
2 teasp chopped mint
1 teasp chopped parsley
4–6 oz(100–175g) butter
2 egg yolks
1 teasp cold water
1 teasp finely chopped mint, parsley or chervil
salt and pepper

Bring the lamb to room temperature, pat dry with kitchen paper, season and spread with butter. You can set a meat roasting thermometer into the thickest part of the meat, making sure it does not touch a bone, and remove the meat when it reaches your preferred reading; this will be about 155°F/68°C for medium, 165°F/73°C for a little more done and 180°F/80°C for well done. Roast in a hot oven (400°F/200°C/Gas 6) for 30 minutes, then turn down to moderate 350°F/180°C/Gas 4) and continue to cook, basting from time to time, for another 30–50 minutes, depending if you like your lamb pink or a little more done. Once cooked, leave the meat to rest where it will keep warm but cannot go on cooking, so that the meat fibres relax and the juices re-enter the tissues. The meat can rest for ½–1 hour and will be easier to carve and more succulent and delicious.

Sauce Paloise. Simmer the finely chopped shallot, mint and parsley in the wine and vinegar until reduced to about 1 tablespoonful. Gently melt all but 1 oz (25g) of butter in a saucepan. Beat the egg yolks in a basin for about one minute until thick and sticky. Add 1 teasp cold water to the vinegar and herb mixture and beat into the yolks gradually, drop by drop. Place the bowl over a saucepan of hot water (very gradual heating is the secret), add ½ oz (12g) of cold butter and stir until the yolks thicken. Immediately, before the eggs curdle, remove the bowl from the pan and beat in the remaining ½ oz (12g) of cold butter to stop the cooking, then beat in the melted just warm butter, drop by drop as for mayonnaise. Leave the salty milky residue in the pan. Season and beat in the finely chopped mint, parsley or chervil. Cover and keep warm for up to 5 hours over a saucepan of lukewarm water set in a warm place. Turn into a gently warmed sauceboat and serve with the lamb.

Any left-over sauce can be kept in the fridge or freezer and beaten into soups and sauces when they have finished cooking.

F **   Kidneys in Gin and Juniper Sauce

Lambs' kidneys need last minute cooking to be good because they toughen if over-cooked. This is not easy when you are entertaining, so I have evolved this way of getting round it. Make the sauce in advance; then sauté the kidneys briefly and make up the dish. It will keep warm successfully if you don't let the kidneys go on cooking.

Ingredients
4–6 people

1–1½ lb (450–675g) lambs' kidneys
1 tbs olive oil
1½ oz (35g) butter
1–2 tbs gin
salt and pepper

Sauce
1 tbs castor sugar
1 oz (25g) dripping, fat or lard
1 finely sliced onion
1 diced carrot
1 diced stick celery
¾ oz (20g) flour
¾ pt (450ml) chicken stock (or stock cube
   and water)
½ teasp juniper berries, slightly crushed
½ clove garlic, slightly crushed
1 teasp tomato purée
½ bay leaf
a sprig thyme
2–3 parsley stalks
1–2 tbs red currant jelly
½ teasp wine or sherry vinegar
salt and pepper

Sauce. Sprinkle the sugar on to the base of a wide saucepan and heat gently until it melts and then goes a golden brown caramel colour. At once (before it burns), add the fat and prepared onion, carrot and celery. Cover the pan and shake over high heat for several moments until the caramel has dissolved, then remove the lid and fry to a good brown. Add the flour and cook gently for 3–4 minutes to a light brown. Draw the pan off the heat and wait for the sizzling to cease before adding the stock. Bring to the boil, whisking hard, and add the slightly crushed juniper berries and garlic, the tomato purée and bay leaf, thyme and parsley stalks. Season lightly and simmer (skimming if necessary) for 20–40 minutes until reduced, shiny and syrupy. Add the red currant jelly and dissolve, correct the seasoning and add a few drops of vinegar. Strain through a fine sieve, pressing the debris well; you should have about 10 fl oz (300ml) sauce. Keep warm, covered, until required, or the sauce can be made ahead and re-heated.

Skin the kidneys (if they are not already skinned), cut in half, carefully removing the white core, and cut each half into 2–3 pieces. Heat the oil and butter in a wide frying pan until very hot and the froth is subsiding. Add the kidneys, which must lie in one layer in the pan (cook in two lots if necessary) and sauté over high heat for 1–2 minutes until just firm and lightly browned. If they exude a lot of liquid and start to boil, remove from the pan and boil the liquid away, for they will toughen if they boil for long.

    Season the kidneys, add the gin to the hot pan and flame, shaking the pan until the flames go out. Add the kidneys and pan juices to the sauce, or vice versa, correct seasoning and simmer for a moment or two before serving.

F ** **Pork Italian**

Osso Buco is so good, but as it is not always possible to get veal shank I have evolved this dish, which uses tender shoulder of pork with the characteristic blend of tomato, garlic, anchovy and lemon that is the signature of *osso buco*. I serve it with either saffron rice or Risotto Doré.

Ingredients
4–6 people

25 people

2–2½ lb (900g–1.15kg) shoulder of pork	10 lb (4.5kg) boned skinned shoulder of pork
1 oz (25g) seasoned flour	4 oz (100g) seasoned flour
2 tbs olive oil	4 tbs olive oil
2 oz (50g) butter	3 oz (75g) butter
2 finely chopped onions	8 finely chopped onions
2–3 tbs tomato purée	6–8 tbs tomato purée
14 oz (400g) tin tomatoes, drained	4 × 14 oz (400g) tins tomatoes, drained
¼ pt (150ml) dry white wine	½ pt (300ml) dry white wine
2 cloves garlic	4–6 cloves garlic
¼ pt (150ml) stock	½ pt (300ml) stock approx.
2–4 anchovy fillets	8–10 anchovy fillets
salt and pepper	salt and pepper

To Serve
3 tbs parsley ⎱
grated rind ½ lemon ⎰ finely chopped together to make
1 clove garlic ⎰ a *gremolata*

To Serve
6–8 tbs parsley ⎱
grated rind 1 lemon ⎰ chopped finely together to make
2 cloves garlic ⎰ a *gremolata*

Heat the oil and butter together in a frying pan. Cut the meat into 1½″ (4cm) cubes, toss in the seasoned flour and brown in the heated oil and butter. Remove the meat to a casserole and add the onion to the pan. Fry until lightly browned, then add the tomato purée and fry for 1–2 minutes. Add the roughly chopped tomatoes and the wine and boil hard for 3–4 minutes. Pour this sauce over the meat, season, and add the flattened garlic and the stock. Cover and cook very gently in a slow oven (300°F/150°C/Gas 2) for 2–3 hours or until very tender. Half-an-hour before serving, add the chopped anchovy fillets.

To Serve. Remove the meat and boil down the sauce if it's not already thick and rich. Serve on a bed of saffron rice or Risotto Doré (*see page 204*) and sprinkle heavily with the *gremolata* of finely chopped parsley, lemon rind and garlic.

$\mathcal{P}$ ** ## Lincolnshire Stuffed Chine

This stuffed collar of bacon was a traditional dish for Trinity Sunday. It makes use of fresh herbs, including young blackcurrant leaves, which give a delicious fragrance to the stuffing, and young raspberry leaves, which add a certain dry astringency. It is very easy to prepare and simple to cook, eats extremely well cold and is a perfect example of a dish which makes the most of what's around at a certain time of year but which nowadays could easily be lost. Make it any time from when the first young leaves appear in April till they get a bit tough in mid June.

Ingredients
8–12 people or more

**4 lb (1.8kg) piece of smoked collar of
    bacon (the whole piece would weigh
    up to 8 lb (3.6kg) if you want to do it
    for a party)**
3–4 spring onions
5–6 tender lettuce leaves
good handful parsley
2–3 sprigs thyme
**2–3 sprigs marjoram (or less of the
    annual one)**
5–6 young blackcurrant leaves
2–3 young raspberry leaves

Soak the bacon for 2–3 hours or overnight as recommended by your butcher.

Chop together the spring onions, lettuce leaves, herbs and blackcurrant and raspberry leaves. Undo the strings on the bacon and open it up. Cut a few slits or pockets on the inside and spread with the herb mixture. Re-tie with string in several places (the larger piece you do, the easier it is to tie). Place the bacon on a double sheet of tinfoil on a roasting tin, cover it with another double sheet and fold the edges together to make a parcel (it used to be done in a flour and water pastry, but I find tinfoil is the modern answer). Bake for 25 minutes for each pound (450g) and 30 minutes over in a hot oven (400°F/200°C/Gas 6).

Leave until cold in the tinfoil parcel, then remove strings and skin before serving thinly sliced.

*   Easter Stuffing for Capon, Chicken or Turkey

It always gives me great pleasure to prepare this fresh herb stuffing for the Easter bird. I enjoy the early walk round the spring garden, gathering all the young leaves and herbs I can find. I always include a small sprig of rue, the bitter herb of the Cross, and I add hard-boiled eggs to the stuffing as another symbol of the rebirth at Easter. The stuffing has a lovely fresh, clean flavour that epitomises spring, though it can of course be used at any time as a stuffing for roast chicken. If you have not got a garden, you can make the stuffing with parsley, watercress and celery leaves, with a pinch or two of dried herbs to get a good mixture of flavours, and it will still be wonderfully fresh and green.

Ingredients
Enough for the cavity of a 10–12 lb (4.5–5.4 kg) turkey or capon

4 eggs
3 oz (75g) chopped herbs (plenty of parsley, watercress, chives and spring or Welsh onion, some sorrel, bistort, salad burnet, chervil and marjoram and a little thyme, lemon thyme, lovage, winter savory and rosemary, with a tiny sprig of rue)
8 oz (225g) white or brown breadcrumbs (we usually use the crumbs from stale home-made granary bread)
1 lemon
1 tin of anchovies (optional)
5–6 oz (125–175g) soft butter
salt, pepper and nutmeg

Hard boil two of the eggs. Chop all the herbs and combine with the breadcrumbs, chopped hard-boiled eggs, the grated rind of lemon and chopped anchovies (if used). Cream the softened butter and stir in the mixture. Add plenty of salt, pepper and freshly grated nutmeg. Then add the lemon juice, bind with the remaining eggs and stuff the bird.

Vegetables

Creamed Sprout or Turnip Tops

Young sprout tops in spring or tender turnip leaves in spring or autumn make a delicious and useful vegetable purée.

Ingredients
4–6 people

1–1½ lb (450–675g) sprout tops or turnip
  leaves
2–3 oz (50–75g) butter
4–6 tbs cream
salt, pepper and nutmeg

Wash the sprout tops or turnip leaves well and throw them into plenty of boiling salted water. Boil, uncovered, until just tender, drain well, and process in a food processor until well chopped.

Heat the butter in a pan until browned and smelling nutty and add the purée. Heat gently, stirring, season, and add cream to make a soft mixture. Serve at once or keep warm in a *bain marie*.

* **Caledonian Cauliflower**

Crispy fried oat flakes (the jumbo ones from a health food shop are nice) and chopped hard-boiled egg make a nice topping for a tasty spring cauliflower

Ingredients
4–6 people

1 fine cauliflower
1½ oz (35g) butter
2–3 tbs oat or wheat flakes
1 hard-boiled egg
2 tbs fresh chopped parsley or ¼ teasp
  Italian seasoning
salt and pepper

Steam the cauliflower or cook in salted boiling water until just cooked. Drain thoroughly and keep warm in a serving dish.

Heat the butter in a frying pan and fry the oat or wheat flakes until crisp and golden. Add the finely chopped egg, parsley or Italian seasoning and salt and pepper. When ready to serve, sprinkle over the cauliflower and serve at once.

*   Spring Cabbage with Beurre Noisette

The fresh green leaves and hearts of spring and summer cabbages need little cooking, so I like them in *beurre noisette* (browned butter with a distinctive flavour) in this very quick and simple way.

Ingredients
4–6 people

1 firm young cabbage
1½ oz (35g) butter
squeeze lemon juice
1 tbs water
½ teasp cornflour (optional)
salt and pepper

Slice the cabbage finely; if it is not absolutely crisp and firm, soak it in cold water with a small handful of salt added for about 10 minutes, and drain and dry it in a kitchen cloth before cooking.

Chop the butter up and heat it in a saucepan large enough to hold the cabbage (I use a wok). Swirl the pan from time to time and cook the butter until it is nut brown with a delicious nutty smell.

Add the cabbage, seasoning and a good squeeze of lemon juice, and toss the cabbage over high heat until it is coated in butter and wilted but not browning. Add 1 tbs water, cover, and continue to cook, shaking the pan from time to time, for between 3–7 minutes, depending how you like your cabbage, how thick you have cut it and how much you have in the pan.

When cooked but with the stalks still crunchy, remove from the pan and serve. If there is quite a lot of liquid left, either boil fast for a moment or two to evaporate it or add the cornflour, slaked in a little cold water, and boil until the juices thicken and adhere to the cabbage. Or just simply drain the cabbage from the liquid, because it will still have its distinctive buttery flavour.

✳✳　Spinach Salad with Anchovy and Croûtons

Spring is just the time for a spinach salad. The leaves will be delicious, tender and full of vitamins. I find Greenmarket a good variety to grow; it hasn't too powerful a flavour for eating raw but is excellent cooked. So many varieties are available now and some, like perpetual spinach, are rather coarse for salads, except when caught very young, but they are useful all-year standbys.

Spinach needs quite a strong dressing to complement its full flavour, and I love it either with anchovies and croûtons or as Spinach and Bacon Salad*. In both I feel a really good, full-flavoured olive oil makes all the difference.

Ingredients
4–6 people

½–¾ lb (225–350g) young spinach

Dressing
8–10 anchovy fillets
1 teasp Dijon mustard
4 teasp wine vinegar
3–4 tbs fruity olive oil
1 tbs oil from the anchovies
plenty of pepper and very little salt

Croûtons
3 slices stale bread
½ oz (12g) butter
2 tbs fruity olive oil

Remove tough stalks and midribs from the spinach, wash and shake dry. Crisp in a sealed bag in the fridge if necessary.

When ready to serve, turn the salad into the dressing, add the croûtons, toss well and serve at once.

Croûtons. Heat the butter and oil in a frying pan, de-crust and dice the bread, add it to the hot fat and sauté until crisp and brown; keep warm.

Dressing. Chop the anchovy fillets into pieces and place in a salad bowl with salt, pepper and mustard. Add the vinegar, stir well to dissolve the salt and gradually whisk in the oils.

* *Good Food from Farthinghoe*

**   Artichoke Salad

The rich garlicky Aioli Dressing with anchovy fillets and black olives make this a salad to serve on its own, either as a first course or with cold meat or hard boiled eggs.

Aioli is always supposed to be made in mortar because the flavour is rather pungent if it is made in a food processor, though of course it is much quicker to make by machine.

Ingredients
4–6 people

1½ lb (675g) Jerusalem artichokes
6–8 anchovy fillets
a little milk
3 oz (75g) black olives
some finely chopped parsley

Aioli Dressing
2–3 cloves of garlic
1 egg yolk
¼ pt (150ml) olive oil
½ lemon
salt and pepper

Either peel the artichokes and boil them in salted water for about 10–12 minutes until just tender or scrub them, boil them and then peel them; leave to cool. Soak the anchovies in a little milk to plump them up.

Mix the chopped up artichokes with the Aioli Dressing and pile on a serving dish. Garnish with the anchovies and olives and sprinkle with parsley. Serve well chilled.

Aioli Dressing. Peel the cloves of garlic and crush them in a mortar with a little salt and pepper; then work in the egg yolk with the pestle and gradually drip in the oil, stirring with the pestle all the time. Add a little lemon juice to taste and correct the seasoning.

**   Watercress Salad

Watercress makes a lovely healthy spring salad. The hard-boiled egg adds a smooth texture, while the croûtons add crunch and the bacon and oil soften the flavour.

Ingredients
4–6 people

2 bunches fresh watercress
2 oz (50g) diced streaky bacon
1 tbs walnut or hazelnut oil
2–3 tbs sunflower or light oil
1 tbs wine or shallot vinegar

½ teasp Dijon mustard
2 hard-boiled eggs
a handful of croûtons, preferably fried in
    bacon fat or walnut oil
salt and a little pepper

Wash and dry the watercress, discarding the tough stalks and any yellowed leaves, and crispen in a sealed bag in the fridge if necessary. Fry the diced bacon but do not let it get too crisp. Mix the salt, pepper, mustard, vinegar and oils into a dressing. Peel and slice the eggs. Arrange the watercress in a bowl, scatter over the croûtons, pour over the dressing and the bacon and toss well. Add the egg slices and serve at once.

**   Spring or Autumn Salad

These vegetables are at their best in spring, though also available in autumn. The individual character of this dish comes from the use of hard-boiled egg to thicken the dressing and the use of fruit juice in place of vinegar (though you may need a drop or two of vinegar as well if the fruit is very sweet and lacks acidity).

Ingredients
4–6 people

	Dressing
½ **small cauliflower**	**salt**
4 oz (100g) button mushrooms	**pepper**
1 bunch watercress	**1 teasp French mustard**
1 bunch radishes	**juice of ½ grapefruit or 1 orange**
2–3 small carrots (optional)	**4 tbs olive oil**
2 hard-boiled eggs	

Break the cauliflower into small florets, blanch in boiling salted water for 2–3 minutes, refresh under the cold tap and drain. Wash and trim the watercress. Slice the mushrooms, radishes and carrots. Keep one egg yolk for the dressing and roughly chop the remaining egg and white. Arrange all attractively in a salad bowl. When ready to serve, dress and toss.

Dressing. Crush the egg yolk in a bowl with salt, pepper and mustard until smooth. Beat in 2–3 tbs fruit juice and then the oil.

*   Broad Bean Leaf Salad

The new leaves of broad beans, picked while they are still curled like baby witches' claws, are tender and deliciously flavoured; so, by the way are sweet pea or young green pea shoots. These broad bean shoots make an appetising addition, as long as they free from blackfly, to what can be a rather meagre salad at this time of year. You can also stir-fry them in the Chinese way for an unusual vegetable, or make them into a salad on their own.

Ingredients
4–6 people

a double handful of curled young broad bean leaves	**1 tbs shallot-flavoured vinegar, wine vinegar or lemon juice**
4 tbs full-flavoured best olive oil	**salt and pepper**

Wash and shake the broad bean leaves. If they need crispening, place them in a sealed, damp plastic bag in the fridge for a while before turning into a salad bowl. I like to dress this sort of salad by sprinkling the leaves with fine sea salt and freshly ground black pepper, then trickling over the vinegar or lemon juice and a generous amount of olive oil just before we toss and eat it.

*   # Baby Pod Broad Beans

When the little pods have formed and are 3"–5" (7–12cm) long but the beans have hardly started to swell, you can cook them whole to give yourself a culinary preview of the special spring flavour of baby broad beans. They come in May or early June, especially if autumn-sown, and are very welcome as it is a sparse time in the garden, before most summer crops get going.

Ingredients
4–6 people

1½ lb (675g) baby pod broad beans
1–1½ oz (25–35g) butter
finely chopped summer savory, sage or
**   parsley (optional)**
salt and pepper (optional)

Break the beans into 2–3 pieces and toss into boiling salted water. Cook for 8–12 minutes or until just tender, then drain and refresh under the cold tap to set the colour. When ready to serve, heat the butter in a frying pan or saucepan until browning. Throw the beans in and toss until heated through, season with salt and pepper if you wish (though the first time try them plain) and scatter with a little finely chopped herb.

Puddings

𝓕 ✳✳   Tarte au Citron

This sharp lemon curd flavoured tart in its crisp pastry is a great favourite all the year, but perhaps most useful in early spring when fruit or other fillings can be expensive. This is excellent from the freezer, either cold or slightly re-warmed, and is nice for large parties.

Ingredients
4–6 people

Pastry
6 oz (175g) plain flour
3 tbs icing sugar
4 oz (100g) firm butter
1 egg yolk
1–2 tbs iced water
pinch salt

Filling
grated rind and juice 1 lemon
2½ oz (60g) butter
2 eggs
3 oz (75g) castor sugar

Pastry 25 people
Make 4 × 9″ (24cm) tarts using 3 batches
of pastry and using trimmings for the
fourth tart

Filling
grated rind and juice 4 lemons
10 oz (275g) butter
8 eggs
12 oz (350g) castor sugar

Pastry. Sift the flour, salt and icing sugar into a bowl or the food processor. Add the firm butter, cut up into hazelnut-sized pieces, and rub in or process to the breadcrumb stage. Bind with the yolk and a very little cold water. Form into a flat disc and rest for ½–2 hours in the fridge in a plastic bag.

Roll the pastry to fit a 9″ (24cm) removable base flan-tin. Prick the pastry, line with tinfoil and baking beans and bake in a hot oven (400°F/200°C/Gas 6) for 8–10 minutes until the pastry is set. Remove the tinfoil and return to a moderately hot oven (375°F/190°C/Gas 5) until golden brown and almost cooked.

Filling. Gently melt the butter. Lightly whisk the eggs. Whisk in the sugar and then the melted butter and grated lemon rind and juice. Pour into the pastry case and continue to bake in a slow oven (300°F/150°C/Gas 2) for 20–25 minutes until the filling has set. Serve hot, warm or cold.

**   Rhubarb and Angelica Pie

Angelica comes up in great white umbrellas of flower in spring and early summer. Its sweet flavour goes well with rhubarb, counteracting some of the rhubarb's acidity. Of course, even without angelica this classic fruit pie, using a rich short pastry, is delicious. It's the perfect English Sunday lunch pudding for this time of year, preferably served with thick cream or Crème Fraîche.

Ingredients
4–6 people

Pastry
6 oz (175g) plain flour
⅜ teasp baking powder
2 oz (50g) butter
1 oz (25g) lard
1 oz (25g) castor sugar
2–3 tbs cream or milk
pinch salt

Filling
1¾ lb (800g) rhubarb cut into 1" (2cm)
lengths
6 oz (175g) sugar or to taste
1–2 teasp cornflour
6–8 stems of tender young angelica in
2"–3" (5–8cm) pieces or some
crystallised angelica

Pastry. Sift the flour, baking powder and salt into a bowl or the food processor, add the butter and lard, cut into small cubes, and rub in or process to the breadcrumb stage. Add the sugar and bind with the cream or milk. Form into a flat disc and chill for ½ hour in a plastic bag in the fridge, though you can use this pastry immediately.

Filling. Mix the sugar and cornflour and layer with the rhubarb and angelica in a pie dish, mounding the rhubarb up well. Use more cornflour if there has been a lot of rain and the rhubarb is very juicy.

Roll the pastry to an oval a little larger than the top of the dish and cut a ¾" (2cm) wide strip from the outside to fit round the rim of the pie dish. Wet the pie dish rim with water and set the border in place. Moisten the strip and lay the pastry over the pie, trim the edges, press into place and decorate the pie with cut trimmings. Bake the pie in a hot oven (425°F/220°C/Gas 7) for about 20–30 minutes until the pastry has browned and set. You want the pastry to set firm before the rhubarb cooks and sinks beneath it. Lower the oven temperature to 375°F/190°C/Gas 5 and continue to cook for another 20–30 minutes, covering lightly if the pastry gets brown enough.

Try to serve this pie straight from the oven, for the steam from the rhubarb will soften the pastry if it sits keeping warm. It is, however, at least as good cold.

**   Rhubarb and Sweet Cicily Pudding in Demerara Crust

Sweet cicily not only has an attractive flavour but also has a sweetening effect on acid fruit like rhubarb. You can use the leaf or tender stem of the green cicily fruit. Or try some fresh or crystallised angelica instead, as it has much the same effect, and the flavour is quite entrancing. The Demerara crust makes this steamed suet pudding a great favourite.

Ingredients
4–6 people

1 oz (25g) butter
1½ oz (35g) Demerara sugar
½ teasp mixed spice (optional)

Suet Crust
10 oz (275g) self-raising flour
5 oz (125g) suet
8–10 fl oz (225–300ml) milk (approx)
½ teasp salt

Filling
2 lb (900g) rhubarb
2 teasp cornflour
3–4 oz (75–100g) Demerara sugar
4–5 sweet cicily leaves or angelica stems or ½–1 oz (12–25g) crystallised angelica

Prepare a 3 pt (1.7l) pudding bowl by spreading generously with butter and sprinkling with the Demerara sugar and mixed spice (if used).

Suet Crust. Sift the flour and salt into a bowl, add the chopped suet and, using a fork, mix with enough milk to make a soft, scone-like dough. Knead lightly together on a floured board (a delicate touch is needed for good suet crust) and then break a bit off for a lid and set aside. On a well-floured board, roll the large piece to a round of about 10" (25cm) in diameter, keeping it thicker in the middle than round the edges. Sprinkle well with flour and fold in half with the fold away from you. Draw the edges gently towards you and carefully roll out the centre to form the pastry into a bag which will fit the pudding basin. Slip your hand in to check that the middle is not sticking together and keep well floured. Turn the pastry over halfway through rolling or the top layer will roll thinner than the bottom; then with your hand inside it, lift the bag and fit it into the prepared basin, leaving the excess hanging over the rim. Put in the rhubarb filling. Roll the dough for the top and fix in place with cold water. Cover with a butter paper and pleated tinfoil, greaseproof paper or a floured cloth securely tied. Leave a loop of string so that you can remove the bowl from the steamer.

Fill a steamer or saucepan with boiling water to come halfway up the bowl. Set the bowl on a trivet, heat diffuser or a couple of skewers so that it does not rest directly on the bottom of the pan. Cover tightly and steam or boil for 2½–3 hours. Replenish the pan with boiling water, if necessary, and keep boiling all the time. Turn out into a deepish dish, for there may be quite a lot of juice.

Filling. Cut the rhubarb in 1" (2–3cm) pieces and mix with the cornflour, sugar and sweet cicily or angelica (dice the crystallised angelica and distribute evenly).

F ✳✳   Rhubarb Ice Cream

A delicately flavoured ice cream that I first came across in June in a rather nice restaurant in Alsace. I was confused by its soft pistachio green colour, but this is how it turns out late in the season, made with unforced sticks of rhubarb.

Ingredients
4–6 people

1½ lb (675g) rhubarb (pink rather than
    greenish for choice)
8 oz (225g) sugar or to taste
1–2 tbs water
½ pt (300ml) milk
3 egg yolks
8 fl oz (225ml) whipping cream

Cut up the rhubarb and stew with the sugar and 1–2 tbs water until tender. Drain and purée (you should have approximately 12 fl oz (350ml) of rhubarb purée). Cool.

Heat the milk. Whisk the egg yolks and gradually pour the hot milk on to them, stirring. Return to a double saucepan (not aluminium, which discolours egg yolks) or heavy pan and heat gently, stirring all the time, until the egg yolks thicken and the custard coats the back of a spoon. Do not let it boil. Cool.

Combine the cooled custard with the cold rhubarb purée and the cream. Pour into shallow metal or tinfoil containers and freeze, stirring in the edges once or twice as they freeze. When firm, process in the food processor or beat well until smooth. Re-freeze. Or make in an ice-cream machine. Mellow in the fridge before serving.

F ✳✳   Gooseberry Double Crust Pie

By Whitsun the gooseberry bushes should be well hung with small green fruit. Cull them carefully to thin the crop; they will still be very hard and green, but will make a good filling for this double crust pie which uses a short, crisp pastry. The filling may be a little runny when hot but should be just right when cold, which I'm told is the traditional way to serve a Whitsun gooseberry pie, with lashings of thick cream, of course!

Ingredients
4–6 people

Filling
1 lb (450g) green gooseberries
4 oz (100g) Demerara sugar or to taste
1 teasp cornflour
1 tbs cold water

Pastry
8 oz (225g) plain flour
½ teasp baking powder
2½ oz (65g) butter
1½ oz (35g) lard
1½ oz (35g) castor sugar
3–4 tbs cream or milk
good pinch salt

Filling. Top and tail the gooseberries. Mix the sugar and cornflour and put with the water and gooseberries, in a saucepan. Cover and simmer gently until soft and pulped. If it seems very runny, as it can be in a rainy year, add a little more cornflour mixed with a teaspoon of water. Leave to cool before using in the pie. You can add a few chopped leaves of sweet cicily, angelica or scented rose geranium, or later in the year cook a head of elderflower with the gooseberries, but for this first pie of the year I prefer pure gooseberry.

Pastry. Sift the flour, baking powder and salt into a bowl or the food processor. Rub or process in the butter and lard, add the sugar and bind with the cream or milk. Form into two flat discs of equal size and chill for ½ hour or longer in a plastic bag in the fridge, though you can use this pastry immediately.

Grease a 9″–10″ (24–28cm) pie plate and roll one disc to fit. Fill with the cold filling (if the filling still seems rather runny, rub ½–1 teasp of cornflour into the pastry base; it thickens the filling and keeps the pastry from going soggy). Top with the second round, pinch the edges together, cut off excess pastry round the edge and decorate the pie, cutting a slit in the top to allow steam to escape. Cook in a hot oven (400°F/200°C/Gas 6) for about 10–15 minutes until brown, then lower the temperature to moderately hot (375°F/190°C/Gas 5) and continue to cook for a further 20–30 minutes until the pastry is crisp and brown right through. Serve hot, warm or cold.

One is at an advantage with either an Aga or convection oven; in the Aga you can put the pie on the base of the oven for a little while to get direct heat, and so cook the bottom layer of pastry; in the convection oven there is all-round, even heat to cook the pastry evenly top and bottom. The conventional gas or electric oven is hotter at the top than the bottom, so pies usually need covering lightly with a double layer of tinfoil to keep the top from burning whilst the pastry underneath cooks.

ℱ *   ## Russian Sorbet

Why this is called Russian sorbet I don't know, but I found it called this in a delightful old book. The title gives nothing away, so you can have everyone trying to guess the flavour, elusive but somehow familiar. It's the colour, of course, that muddles people, who expect a blackcurrant flavour to be dark!

Ingredents	a good handful of young blackcurrant
4–6 people	leaves
	rind and juice 2–3 lemons
1 pt (600ml) water	
8 oz (225g) granulated sugar	

Combine the sugar and water in a very clean pan. Heat gently, stirring, until the sugar dissolves completely, then boil hard for 5–6 minutes. Throw in the blackcurrant leaves and the pared lemon rinds and leave to infuse for 2–3 hours. Strain the liquid and add lemon juice to taste. Turn into a shallow (preferably metal or tinfoil) dish and freeze, turning the edges into the middle as they freeze. When the whole lot is fairly firmly set, place in the food processor or liquidise until soft, smooth and light. Pack into a container or bowl and refreeze.

These sorbets usually need softening for 30 minutes in the fridge before serving, and if kept for any length of time may get rock hard and need softening, re-processing and re-firming. Serve with little biscuits or slices of sponge cake.

Miscellaneous

ℱ *   ## Yoghurt

Yoghurt, a fermented milk which keeps for longer than fresh milk, has been used for centuries from the Adriatic to India, where the bacillus *lactobacillus bulgaricus* can survive naturally in the air.

More recently, it has become very popular in the West, but the bacillus has to be raised in laboratory conditions and will then survive in our atmosphere for only about one month. So when you buy a natural live yoghurt or ferment starter to make your own yoghurt, you will need to replace it every month or so. The benefits of making a live yoghurt which, as well as containing streptococci to thicken or curdle the milk, also contains the *lactobacillus bulgaricus*, are fairly well known. Briefly, this particular bacillus can survive in the human digestive system for some time, combatting harmful bacilli, cleaning the skin and aiding slimming. Of course, yoghurt can be made without this bacillus included; it will taste good and be as easy to make, but will not have such health-giving properties. To make your own yoghurt, which I have done for ten years or more, you need only a genuine 'live' Balkan yoghurt or a packet of dry ferment starter.

Ingredients

1–2 pts (600ml–1.2l) fresh cows' or goats'
    milk (pasteurised is fine)
1 tbs 'live' yoghurt starter (or powder
    ferment, in which case follow
    instructions on packet)

Place the milk in a pan and bring to the simmer, preferably with a simmer saver so that it cannot boil over. Simmer for several minutes to drive off some moisture and condense the milk a little, for cows' milk, in particular, is rather watery. Then turn the milk into a container; I prefer earthenware, glass or pottery to plastic, but I don't know that it really makes much difference. Allow the milk to cool to 120°–130°F (50°–55°C) on a thermometer or, as it has been tested for thousands of years, by dipping your middle finger into the milk and counting slowly to ten (10 seconds); it should feel quite stingy hot by 9 or 10 but all right to keep your finger in (lukewarm milk usually makes thin, insipid yoghurt). While the milk cools, prepare a warm spot for it 'to make'. I use an insulated picnic box with two bottles of hot water placed in it to keep the temperature at about 110°F(34°C)—half boiling and half cold water or hot tap water is fine—but you can use a warm airing cupboard or anywhere with a constant temperature and no draught.

Now add 1–2 tablespoons of the hot milk to the live yoghurt starter in a small bowl and stir. Should the mixture curdle, your milk was too hot, so wait a moment and try again with a little more starter yoghurt (as little as ½ teaspoonful of starter yoghurt will make 2–3 pints of yoghurt). Some yoghurts prefer to culture at different temperatures, but I have always found the best results came from quite a warm culture. Now pour the mixed milk and yoghurt back into the container of milk and cover lightly (loose tinfoil is good). Quickly place the container, before the milk temperature drops, into your prepared warm spot and leave it to culture. A first batch will usually take about 8 hours (longer for a powdered ferment) and subsequent batches about 5 hours. Too long in the warm will give a layer of watery liquid on top of the yoghurt and rather a sharp taste. Too short a time and the yoghurt will be bland and not thick enough.

Once made, carefully remove to a cool place without shaking or jolting. Cover closely and leave until cold and set. After making several batches, the yoghurt should get thicker and creamier, but after 3 weeks or so you will find it becoming watery and it is time to get another starter.

The plain yoghurt can be used for cooking savoury dishes, or of course fruit, honey, sugar or any other flavour can be added. Any rather stale yoghurt or a batch that over-heats and curdles can always be turned into muslin to drain, then made into cream cheese. Or after being drained, it can be mixed with milk or cream and eaten with sugar and fruits as *fromage blanc*.

𝒫 ∗   Yoghurt Whip

Natural yoghurt, folded into whipped cream and left to set, makes a fresh-tasting accompaniment to fruit. Topped with dark brown sugar, which melts to a dark and tasty sauce, it can also be served on its own.

Ingredients
4–6 people

8–10 fl oz (225–300ml) double cream
8–10 fl oz (225–300ml) natural yoghurt
soft dark brown sugar (optional)

Whisk the cream until thick, carefully fold in the yoghurt and turn into a serving dish. Sprinkle the top heavily with the sugar, if desired. Leave for 6–24 hours to set. Serve alone or to accompany fruit, especially the Brandied Pears (*see page 216*) or Winter Fruit Salad (*see page 58*).

𝒫 ∗   Yoghurt Cheese

If your home-made yoghurt does not get eaten and becomes sharp and strong, don't waste it. It's lovely for making scones, or it can be drained to make a simple, good cream cheese. I usually vary the seasoning, sometimes adding paprika or cayenne and whatever herbs I feel like trying or have available.

Ingredients
approx 8 oz (225g) cheese

1 pt (600ml) yoghurt (approx)
1–2 tbs cream
2 tbs chopped herbs such as parsley and
    chive
pepper or cayenne pepper
¼ teasp salt

Drain the yoghurt in a muslin-lined sieve, stirring the thick part to the middle from time to time, until you are left with about 8 oz (225g) thick cheesey mixture. Mix it in a bowl with the cream, seasoning and flavouring and pack it into a pot, where it will last for days.

𝓕 ∗   Scones

The best liquid for making scones is buttermilk or naturally soured dairy milk, but neither of these is readily available these days; sour milkman's milk will not do. But I find yoghurt does the job well, especially if it is rather sharp and sour, and for this reason homemade yoghurt is better than some processed bought ones. The acidity makes the scones feather-light, but you do also need a 'light touch' to make good scones.

Ingredients
6 large or 12 small scones

8 oz (225g) plain flour
1 teasp cream of tartar   } *or* 1½ teasp baking powder
½ teasp bicarbonate of soda }
1 oz (25g) butter
1 oz (25g) castor sugar (optional)
3 fl oz (75ml) yoghurt   } *or* use all yoghurt, buttermilk or sour milk
3 fl oz (75ml) milk   }
½ teasp salt

Sift the flour, salt, cream of tartar and bicarbonate of soda (or baking powder) into a wide mixing bowl. Chop up the butter and add and rub in to the breadcrumb stage. Mix in the sugar (if used), then the yoghurt and milk, stirring lightly with a fork and adding enough liquid to make a soft spongy dough. Lightly draw together with your fingers and press out ¾" (2cm) thick on a floured board. Cut into rounds with a 2–2½" (5–6cm) cutter (or you can pat into one round and cut into 8 segments). Place the scones on a baking sheet and cook in a very hot oven (450°F/230°C/Gas 8) for 8–10 minutes until risen and light brown. Cool on a rack, covered with a cloth if you want soft scones, and preferably serve while still warm.

*   Easter Cakes

Not as crisp as a biscuit or as crumbly as a cake, these brandy flavoured, scone-like cakes (the brandy makes all the difference) were made in Somerset at Easter. They are ideal for packed lunches or picnics, or for slipping into your pocket for an anytime munch.

Ingredients
approx 20 cakes

8 oz (225g) plain flour
4 oz (100g) butter
4 oz (100g) currants
4 oz (100g) castor sugar
½ teasp cinnamon
½ teasp mixed spice
1 egg
2 tbs brandy

Rub the butter into the flour until it resembles fine breadcrumbs and add the currants, sugar, cinnamon and mixed spice. Whisk the egg and brandy together and add to bind the mixture. Draw the dough together, knead very lightly and roll out to ½" (1cm) thickness. Cut into 2" (5cm) rounds with a fluted cutter and bake in a moderate oven (350°F/180°C/Gas 4) for 20–25 minutes until light golden and cooked through. Cool on a rack and store in a tin.

** **Simnel Cake**

This cake was originally made by young girls in service and taken home to their mothers on Mothering Sunday. It was kept for three weeks and eaten at Easter. The name comes through old French from the Latin word *simila* meaning fine flour. The almond paste balls used for decoration are early pagan fertility symbols of spring and also represent the eleven apostles, other than Judas, an example of Christianity superimposed on earlier pagan rites.

Ingredients

4 eggs
8 oz (225g) flour
½ teasp freshly grated nutmeg ⎫
½ teasp ground cinnamon ⎬ *or* 1½ teasp mixed spice
½ teasp ground allspice ⎭
8 oz (225g) currants
8 oz (225g) raisins
8 oz (225g) sultanas
4 ox (100g) cut mixed peel (or your own
    Crystallised Grapefruit, *see page 276*)
4 oz (100g) glacé cherries   *Almond Paste*
8 oz (225g) soft butter   12 oz (350g) ground almonds
4 oz (100g) soft brown sugar   6 oz (175g) castor sugar
4 oz (100g) castor sugar   6 oz (175g) icing sugar
2 oz (50g) ground almonds   1½ teasp almond essence
2 oz (50g) flaked almonds   1 egg and 1 yolk
6 tbs (approx) milk
¾ teasp salt   1–2 tbs sieved apricot jam

Prepare the tin. Line a 9″ (24cm) diameter round cake tin with two thicknesses of greaseproof or Bakewell paper, bringing the paper well above the rim of the tin (this protects the top of the cake from direct heat so that it will not brown too soon). Paint the inside of the greaseproof-lined tin with melted butter, but Bakewell paper does not need buttering. Tie a double layer of brown paper round the outside of the tin, also coming well above the top.

Almond Paste. Sift the sugars into a bowl, add the ground almonds, the essence and the egg and yolk and work up to a stiff dough. Knead lightly. Set aside roughly one third to make 11 balls to decorate the top of the cake. Divide the remainder into two equal halves. Form one into a flat disc and keep in a plastic bag until ready to use on the top of the cake. Roll the other into a 9″ (24cm) circle in diameter, using icing sugar and cornflour instead of flour on your pastry board and pin, to use in the middle of the cake.

Lay the eggs in a bowl and cover with hand-hot water so that they warm while you assemble everything. Sift the flour, salt and spices together. Quarter and wash the cherries in hot water, dry well and roll into a little of the flour so that they remain evenly dispersed through the cake. Mix together the dried fruit, the ground and flaked almonds and peel, and toss with a little flour.

Cream the butter until pale and creamy, then beat in the sugars; cream really well. Remove the eggs from the warm water, break into a bowl, whisk until frothy, then gradually beat into the creamed butter and sugar. If the butter and sugar have been really well creamed, they should hold all the eggs without curdling, but add a tablespoonful of flour if the mixture looks like curdling. When all the egg is added, stir in the cherries, fruit and nut mixture and the sifted flour mixture. Stir well and add enough milk for the mixture just to drop off the spoon. Turn half the mixture into the prepared tin, level off, and place the prepared circle of almond paste on the mixture. Spread the remaining cake mixture on top, making a bit of a dip in the middle so that the cake rises evenly. Bake in a slow oven (300°F/150°C/Gas 2) for 1½ hours, then lower the temperature to 250°F/130°C/Gas 1 for a further 2¾–3¼ hours till cooked (when a skewer comes out clean). Cool in the tin and turn out on to a rack. When absolutely cold, spread the top with apricot jam and cover with the remaining rolled out almond paste. Decorate with eleven balls of almond paste set around the edge. Put the cake into a hot oven or under a moderate grill until the almond paste is browned and blistered. Keep the cake as long as you can before eating it (but it won't be bad even after only a few days!).

** Muesli

For years now we have mixed up our own muesli. It has no added sugar, but the sultanas and toasted nuts make it quite sweet enough. A small bowl for breakfast with home-made yoghurt and stewed fruit is almost *de rigueur*. Do make sure the barley, oat and wheat flakes and especially the wheat germ have not gone off and acquired that bitter, rancid flavour which they will get if stored for too long in the shop or cupboard.

Ingredients
2 large jars

½ lb (225g) whole hazelnuts	1 lb (450g) porridge oats (such as Quaker)
½ lb (225g) sunflower seeds	¾ lb (350g) sultanas and raisins
¼ lb (100g) sesame seeds	¼ lb (100g) bran
1 lb (450g) wheat flakes	¼ lb (100g) wheat germ
1 lb (450g) large oat flakes	¼ lb (100g) flaked millet (optional)
1 lb (450g) barley flakes	1 oz (25g) dried apple flakes (optional)

Roast the hazelnuts and sunflower seeds until golden brown and the sesame seeds until nutty flavoured and just colouring; this will be about 15 minutes in a moderately hot oven (375°F/190°C/Gas 5) for the hazelnuts, 6 minutes for the sunflower seeds and 3 minutes for the sesame seeds, which could otherwise be toasted by tossing in a heavy dry frying pan. Stir and turn the nuts from time to time for even browning. Roughly crush or chop the hazelnuts, using a food processor or heavy plastic bag and rolling pin; some should be quite fine and some in nice big bits.

Combine all the ingredients in a large bowl and mix well together. Keep in tightly sealed containers.

$\mathcal{F}$ ✳✳   **Hot Cross Buns**

Home-made hot cross buns are such a treat; the spicy baking smells fill the kitchen and house as they're being made with the scent of old fashioned celebration. As we make most of our own bread, we are a bit spoilt and find the flabby bought buns with insipid spicing just won't do. Try to buy a really good mixed spice; they can vary quite a lot but should be fragrant and fresh. The spice, butter, eggs and salt all slow down the yeast's working so allow plenty of time and find a nice warm place to rise the dough (*see below*).

Ingredients
24 buns

1 lb (450g) strong white flour
2–3 teasp mixed spice
1 oz (25g) fresh yeast
2 oz (50g) soft brown sugar
8–9 fl oz (225–250ml) tepid milk
2 oz (50g) butter
2 eggs
6 oz (175g) currants
2 teasp salt

Pastry for Crosses
2 oz (50g) plain flour
1 oz (25g) butter
a little cold water

Sugar Glaze
3 oz (75g) sugar
2 fl oz (50ml) water

Sift the flour, spice and salt into a bowl. Cream the sugar and yeast together and add 5 fl oz (150ml) of the tepid milk. Make a well in the flour and add the yeast mixture, stirring in a little of the flour. Flick flour over the mixture and leave in a warm place for about 10 minutes. When the mixture starts to bubble and ferment and the flour crust cracks, add the softened butter and beaten eggs and mix to a soft dough with the remaining milk. Knead for about 5–10 minutes until the mixture is pliable and elastic, then work in the currants. Turn the dough into a bowl and cover with a large plastic bag; leave to double in bulk, out of draughts and in a nice warm place at about 80°F (28°C). This may take 1–2 hours or longer, for rich doughs can be slow to rise.

Make the pastry for crosses whilst the dough rises.

When well risen, knock down the dough, turn out on to a well-floured board and knead for a few moments. Keep the dough cocooned in flour so that it does not stick, but try not to work in any more flour. Roll into a sausage shape, divide into 24 pieces, form into slightly flattened buns and place well apart on greased baking sheets.

Roll the prepared pastry thinly and cut into narrow strips. Fix a generous pastry cross over the top of each bun with cold water. Place the baking sheets inside large plastic bags (trap air and seal the bags so that they balloon over the buns; buns like a nice steamy atmosphere to rise) and leave in a warm draught-proof place to rise again until they are well risen (most people making buns at home do not let them rise enough). Bake the buns in a hot oven (425°F/220°C/Gas 7) for about 10 minutes until well browned and cooked. Cool on a rack. You can brush them over with sugar glaze for a shiny finish as they cool, but this goes a bit sticky if you are not using them at once. Serve warm for tea or breakfast. Stale buns, even a week old, are lovely split, toasted and buttered.

Pastry for crosses. Rub the diced butter into the flour and bind with water to make a pliable pastry. Left-over shortcrust can also be used.

Sugar Glaze. Dissolve the sugar in the water, and boil fast for a few minutes.

Bread Rising. To provide draught-free warm, humid conditions for yeast to work best, you can put a washing-up bowl inside a large plastic bag or bin liner and pour a little hot water into the bowl. Set a trivet in the water, and on this place the bowl with the dough in it, keeping the bottom just above the water. Then seal the bag and leave in a warm place.

*   Chive and Mint Cream Dressing

In spring and early summer we often use lettuce thinnings for salads. I think they need a rather more generous dressing like this than do really crisp sweet lettuce hearts.

Ingredients
Dressing for a salad for 4–6 people

2–3 tbs scissored chives (or Welsh onion
   in winter)
1 teasp chopped mint
   or mint or tarragon vinegar in winter
1 tbs vinegar
pinch sugar
2 tbs olive oil
2 tbs cream
salt and pepper

Stir the herbs, sugar, seasoning and vinegar together until the salt and sugar have dissolved before gradually stirring in the oil and cream. Leave for ¼–½ an hour, if possible, for the vinegar to thicken the cream, then add to the salad and toss well.

113

* Mint Sauce

Fresh chopped mint, with a touch of sugar and sharpened with wine vinegar, is the traditional British accompaniment for lamb, and this version is minty and mild but tasty. I have to admit to a sneaking personal preference for mint jelly because it does not run all over the plate, and because it is not vinegary is less likely to spoil your wine. You might like to try the Sauce Paloise, a mint flavoured hollandaise, as an alternative with baby lamb.

Ingredients

2 oz (50g) mint leaves from their stalks	4 tbs boiling water
3 tbs castor sugar	4 fl oz (300ml) wine vinegar

Chop the mint with the sugar and, when finely chopped, scrape into a bowl and add the boiling water. Stir well to dissolve the sugar before adding the wine vinegar. It can be made in a food processor. It will keep for some time in a jar in the fridge.

ℱ * Gooseberry or Gooseberry and Sorrel Sauce

This was traditionally served with mackerel, but is also good with roast pork in spring and summer in place of apple sauce. The version with a white sauce base is quite soft and bland and best with the first green gooseberries; that with the sorrel is rather more piquant and is perhaps best when the gooseberries are riper later in the summer.

Ingredients

Gooseberry Sauce	*Gooseberry and Sorrel Sauce*
½ lb (225g) green gooseberries	½ lb (225g) green gooseberries
¼ pt (150ml) thick white sauce (made with ½ oz (12g) butter, ½ oz (12g) flour and ¼ pt (150ml) milk)	1 oz (25g) butter
	2–3 hand-sized tender sorrel leaves
	a little grated fresh root ginger (optional)
a little sugar (optional)	a little sugar (optional)
salt and pepper	salt and pepper

Cover the gooseberries in water, simmer until tender and drain. Then prepare the sauce of your choice.

Gooseberry Sauce. Purée and sieve the gooseberries. Add them to the white sauce base, correct seasoning and add a little sugar if desired. Serve hot.

Gooseberry and Sorrel Sauce. Melt the butter and add some very finely shredded sorrel; soften for several minutes but don't let it become a purée. Add a little grated ginger, if desired, and the crushed gooseberries. Stir well together and season with salt, pepper and several pinches of sugar if you wish. Serve hot.

SPIRIT OF SUMMER

Oh, bring again my heart's content
Thou Spirit of the Summertime!

—William Allingham

SUMMER

Suddenly it's summer. Sometimes this happens positively and we wake up one morning and feel that summer's here. In other years, so I've noticed, the change is imperceptible, and with the weather still changeable it's only the fallen blossom, the fully clad trees and long hours of daylight that announce it. The early mornings in June have always something new and fresh to offer and it's no effort to be up early. The scents, delicate in the cool air, haven't yet blended into the dreamy perfumes of the afternoons. And think of the growing hours! The plants thrust and get bigger in every moment of daylight, and the rows of seeds planted in the spring change day by day from a thin wavery thread to thick bands of green. I love to garden in these long evenings, hoeing between the rows and thinning out the young vegetables; the light strikes from a different angle and the plants throw shadows; the old brick walls and flags of the kitchen garden reflect the heat of the day and the swallows are hawking over the water.

But early summer is a difficult time for vegetables. The broccoli and the purple sprouting are finished, the asparagus season traditionally closes on 20 June, and, though you may still have spinach and spring cabbage, the beans, peas and carrots are probably some way off. You may be short of lettuce, depending on whether you managed an autumn planting or got some early seeds in, so you can be a bit bare for a week or two before the plenty of summer. Autumn-sown broad beans will be ready an important week or two ahead of a spring planting; I grow Aquadulce overwinter, a variety that flourished even through that dreadful 1981–82 winter, and use Exhibition Long Pod as a spring planting. By now they will be growing very fast, and are very easy to miss if you want to start early by eating the whole pod as Baby Pod Broad Beans.

These are our salad days, the quick growth of early summer making the lettuces crisp and juicy, and a base to which we can add an endless choice of leaves such as sorrel, salad burnet or rocket while they are still delicate and tender. Herbs like chives never seem to be used nearly enough, and lovage will have everybody guessing, though it needs to be added with great discretion. All the mints, especially spearmint and the variegated ginger mint *Mentha x gentilis*, add freshness and excitement to salads, as do the vivid flowers of borage, marigold and nasturtium—all edible and bringing flashing colours and bright flavours to a galaxy of salads.

Salads are really a subject in themselves and we eat them all year round. They are healthy and quick to prepare, and we never tire of them because of the unending variety of the green ingredients and all the other things that can be added to them. Think of the range of oils and all the vinegars you can make or buy. There are interesting seasonings to try, dressings to invent or adapt and a miscellany of things like fruit and nuts to add—anything that takes your fancy. A jar or two of Gooseberry and Elderflower Jelly is fun and can be made before the serious strawberry and raspberry season comes along and you hot-foot it to the nearest pick-your-own farm or clamber under your own nets. Little alpine strawberries, the commercial variety rather than the smaller and more sparsely fruiting woodland kind, fruit all summer from before the

116

maincrop strawberries till late October or early November, when they are almost at their best. They are hardly out of flower all year, and the birds don't seem to touch them. Grow a non-runner variety like Alexandria, or they will scramble everywhere. They are a fiddle to pick, only a few ripening on each bush at any one time, and it's no good picking them till they are really fat and a dark purply red because they will not have the true flavour of *fraises de bois*. But they are superb in Little Strawberry Tarts with Almond Pastry, and even better, if that's possible, on their own with Crème Fraîche and castor sugar.

When it's hot I'm disinclined to cook by day, preferring the early morning or the cool of the evening to prepare dishes like Escabèche of Mackerel or Raised Pork Pies that can stay in the larder till we need them. Cut and come again meats last and go well with our summer salads. Cold Loin of Pork with Pistachio and Green Peppercorns or the more economical but equally delicious Spiced Pork* or Lincolnshire Stuffed Chine take only moments to prepare before long slow cooking.

It's surprising how far meat goes when it's served cold and thinly sliced, and even Boned Stuffed Duck*, made from a rather expensive basic ingredient, can turn out very good value if eaten in this way. I think we can also learn a lot from the way the Germans produce a quick bite of *Aufschnitt* from sliced sausage, preserved meats and various ryebreads; or the Scandinavian equivalent, smorgasbord, a dazzling array of tempting variety, and the way the Italians and French are so clever in their use of pickled vegetables and preserves, like the Mixed Pickled Vegetables that I have adapted, which will keep in the fridge or on the shelf and into which we can dig at will. A Pot au Feu* cooked for Sunday lunch will keep you in meat for a week, and how delicious the cold chicken, ham and beef are with such a good flavour from the long slow cooking with vegetables and herbs. You can eat them sliced thin with salads and baked potatoes, dressed with a mayonnaise or vinaigrette, diced and made into Cold Beef and Potato Salad or stir-fried with vegetables in a wok.

Summertime is picnic time, and although the weather may let you down you will still have to plan a picnic for the school sports day, a day on the river, a trip to Glyndebourne or picnics while you're on holiday. How much easier they are to prepare these days. We no longer need large cool cabbage leaves as wrapping or a stream to chill the wine. Cling film and the insulated cool box may be more prosaic but they are highly efficient and easy to use, and allow you to produce a cool salmon mayonnaise, cream for the strawberries and a perfect glass of Mosel on a hot day. Talking of cream, the strawberry and raspberry months are the time for making a few batches of your own Crème Fraîche, the thickened, delicately soured cream of France. I try to bring back a pot (or you can buy it from Harrods or a good delicatessen) and, by culturing it in the same way as you make yoghurt, you can make ordinary and rather tasteless commercial whipping cream into a thick spooning cream with a fine flavour. I make a batch and freeze several small doses to use as future starters. Cold salmon has style for a good picnic (and kudos, if that matters!), but what about cold, hard-boiled quails eggs, now reasonably available, good travellers and easy to shell, giving that dash of do-it-yourself that any picnic needs, however elegant? If you really wanted to have something extra special, and don't mind spending a bit of time in preparation, try my recipe for Boned Stuffed Quails, filled with herbs and cream cheese and nibbled delicately off the legs, which have the bones left in to act as handles. Simpler,

* *Good Food from Farthinghoe*

but also stylish, are Lamb Cutlets in Sweet-Sour Mint Aspic, pink and succulent. Salads need to be easy to eat and, while nothing beats raspberries or strawberries and cream, a well made summer pudding or Blackcurrant Mousse is excellent and easily portable in its bowl.

For the simpler picnic, perhaps on holiday where you have to make do with what you can buy en route, fresh baps or French bread will usually form the basis. Add a deep bowl of pâté, some well chosen cheese and a few not too ripe tomatoes, sliced on the spot and dressed with plenty of salt and pepper and vinaigrette from a well sealed bottle, and you've got all you could want. If you're on an expedition, rather than a journey, and lunch is part of the day's entertainment, then a small barbecue or portable gas cooker will widen the scope and add to the fun. You can cook the local sausages (or buy *crépinettes* in France) or kebabs, marinaded for a moment in oil, lemon and herbs, though these last may have to be from the picnic box unless you find yourself on a tuffet of wild thyme with a bush of rosemary at your elbow. Trout can be fried straight from the loch or mackerel from the sea—and how much better they are only minutes from the water.

Barbecuing is easy at home and is fun in the summer, and husbands and children should be encouraged to become masters of the barbecue. Spiced Tandoori Style Chicken is particularly convenient, because it can be prepared when you choose and can sit marinading for one or two days, or even longer, while you wait for the English clouds to roll away. Or cubes of lamb can be marinated in oil, lemon and oregano to make those little souvlakia or Marinated Lamb Kebabs which sizzle on Greek and Turkish grills, emitting clouds of fragrant smoke which can draw you down several streets, your mouth watering in anticipation. These thoughts of kebabs are so evocative that I can recall the astringent taste of retsina (from the barrel, of course!) and hear the sizzling of tiny batter-covered squid frying in olive oil. Great dishes of stuffed vegetables lurk in the corners of my memory, and my tongue recalls the glorious texture of aubergine. Some might say these are not part of English country cooking, but why not? They probably weren't a few years back, but travel has now brought them to many people and we can grow or buy tomatoes, aubergine and garlic, and our lamb is streets ahead of stringy Macedonian mutton. Excellent squid can also be bought, fresh or frozen.

New potatoes are now available and how good they taste. Nice as the imported earlies are, they never quite replace home-grown ones, ideally picked straight from a garden. There is really no need to peel or scrape them, because much of the flavour lies just under the skin. If picked straight from the garden, however, the skin will almost fall off in shreds when cooking, so their looks are improved if you rub the skin off with the ball of your thumb. Desirée and Vanessa are good as new or maincrop potatoes; if you can find Fir Apple, a long knobbly tuber with a fine flavour and waxy texture, you have one for salads or on its own.

Summer food is glorious food and, to me at least, it means a feeling of plenty, lashings of baby vegetables and mounds of strawberries and raspberries (and plenty more for the children to 'steal' from under the nets). It's not so much a time for cooking and complicated recipes but more for using what is fresh and at its best, in the garden or from the shops, treating it simply and enjoying all its natural summer flavours to the full.

SUMMER

First Courses and Supper Dishes

Courgette and Smoked Ham Quiche
Chicken Livers in Green Peppercorn
    Jelly
• Fruits de Mer en Salade
Cold Prawn Omelette
Salade Composée
Oeufs Mollets aux Epinards
Tomatoes Stuffed with Cream
    Cheese and Herbs

Soups

Etta's Tomato Soup
Broad Bean Soup
Summer Vegetable Soup with Pistou
Crème Louise

Fish

Fillets of Cod in Parsley Sauce
Escabèche of Mackerel
Cold Trout and Cucumber and Dill
    Sauce

Main Courses

Spiced Tandoori-Style Chicken
Chicken Sauté à la Clamart
Lamb Cutlets in Sweet-Sour Mint
    Aspic
Boned Stuffed Quail
Quail Prince William
Escalopes of Liver with Lemon and
    Garlic
Filet d'Agneau avec sa Salade
    d'Epinards
Marinated Lamb Kebabs
Raised Pork Pies
Cold Beef and Potato Salad
Cold Loin of Pork with Pistachio
    Nuts and Green Peppercorns
Stir-Fried Curried Pork and
    Vegetables

Vegetables

Broad Beans in Summer Savory or
    Parsley Sauce
Kohl Rabi with Lemon and Thyme
Stir-Fried Courgettes with Pistou Sauce
Cucumber in Old English Butter Sauce
Stir-Fried Green Beans and
    Mushrooms
French Beans à la Crème
• French Bean Salad
Salt and Sesame Glazed Potatoes
Potato Salad with Walnut Oil and Lovage
Cheesy Potatoes

Puddings

Gooseberry Fool
Gooseberries in Elderflower Syrup
• Blackcurrant Mousse
Pavlova
Soufflé Glacé
Little Strawberry Tartlets with
    Almond Pastry
Rose Petal Ice Cream
Vacherin
Raspberry Sorbet

Miscellaneous

Vinaigrette Dressing and Variations
Whipped Cream Dressing
Thorpe Mandeville Old English
    Boiled Dressing
Potted Cheese with Herbs
Mixed Pickled Vegetables
Jam Making
Gooseberry and Elderflower Jelly
Strawberry Jam
Raspberry and Red Currant Jam
Sieved Raspberry Jam
Crème Fraîche
Little Almond Finger Biscuits
Courgette or Pumpkin Cake
Lemon Squash

• Also quantities for 25 persons

119

First Courses and Supper Dishes

** Courgette and Smoked Ham Quiche

If you have no time to de-gorge the courgettes, wring them out in a tea towel to expel their excess moisture. This combination of flavours is most successful and makes a good hot or cold quiche.

Ingredients
4–6 people

Filling
¾–1 lb (350–460g) small courgettes
4 oz (100g) smoked ham or smoked
  sausage
1 oz (25g) butter
1 tbs olive oil
1 large chopped onion
3 eggs
4 fl oz (100ml) cream *or* mixture of cream
  and milk
1 teasp chopped fresh or good pinch
  dried marjoram
2–3 oz (50–76g) grated Cheddar cheese
salt and pepper

All Purpose Pastry
1 egg yolk and about 2 tbs cold water *or*
  3–4 tbs cold water
6 oz (175g) plain flour
3 oz (75g) firm butter
good pinch salt

Pastry. If you are using a yolk, mix it with the cold water. Sift the flour and salt into a bowl or food processor with metal blade, add the firm butter, cut into hazelnut sized cubes, and rub in or process, adding the yolk and water as you go, until a pastry forms. If not thoroughly combined, turn the pastry on to a board and smear it down the board in egg sized lumps with the heel of your hand (*fraisage*) finally to amalgamate it. Knead briefly into a flat disc and rest, in a plastic bag, in the fridge for ½–2 hours. Roll and line a 9″ (24cm) flan tin with the pastry, prick the base lightly with a fork, line with aluminium foil and baking beans and cook in a hot oven (400°F/200°C/Gas 6) for about 10 minutes. Remove the foil and baking beans, lower the temperature to 375°F/190°C/Gas 5 and continue to cook for 10–15 minutes longer before adding the filling.

Filling. Slice the courgettes and layer in a colander, sprinkling each layer with salt. Press with a plate and weights and leave to de-gorge for 20 minutes or so before draining off all the expelled water and patting dry on kitchen paper.
  Meanwhile heat the butter and oil in a frying pan and fry the onion until soft and golden. Turn up the heat, add the drained courgettes and sauté over fierce heat for several minutes until just beginning to brown. Layer the prepared pastry case with the sliced or diced ham or sausage and the courgette filling. Whisk the eggs with the cream or milk and cream, seasoning and marjoram, and pour over the filling. Scatter with grated cheese and bake in a moderate oven (350°F/180°C/Gas 4) until the filling has set. Serve hot, warm or cold.

P ✳✳   Chicken Livers in Green Peppercorn Jelly

Marinated and lightly cooked chicken livers, set in a pepper and Madeira consommé, make a nice starter or cold summer lunch dish. If you have some home-made consommé, so much the better.

Ingredients
4–6 people

¾–1 lb (350–450g) chicken livers
2 tbs Madeira
1 tbs brandy
1 teasp finely chopped fresh lemon
    thyme
1 teasp green peppercorns
1 teasp salt
2–3 tbs chicken or duck fat or oil

Green Peppercorn Jelly
½ pt (300ml) Campbell's condensed
    consommé
1¼ teasp gelatine
1 tbs cold water
2 teasp tarragon vinegar
1 tbs Madeira
1–2 teasp green peppercorns

Carefully pick over the chicken livers, removing threads and any green-tinged flesh, and divide large ones into 2 or 3 pieces. Sprinkle well with salt and put in a bowl with the crushed green peppercorns, finely chopped lemon thyme, the Madeira and brandy. Leave in the fridge for 12–24 hours, turning from time to time.

Drain the livers and pat dry on kitchen paper. Sauté briskly in hot fat until just done but still pink in the middle. Drain on kitchen paper and cool.

Line the base of 4–6 cocotte dishes with a layer of the peppercorn jelly, and when it has set lay several bits of chicken livers in each dish. Fill up with the remaining pepper corn jelly distributing the peppercorns evenly, and chill to set. Turn out by dipping the cocottes into hot water for a few moments, then dry and invert on to plates with a good shake. Serve with toast or a Brioche Loaf* and butter.

Green Peppercorn Jelly. Sprinkle the gelatine on to the cold water in a small bowl, leave for a few minutes to soak, and then stand the bowl in a pan of hot water until the gelatine has melted. Add to the consommé with the vinegar, Madeira and green peppercorns. Cool, either over crushed ice or in the fridge, until syrupy and almost setting.

* *Good Food from Farthinghoe*

$\mathcal{P}$ **   Fruits de Mer en Salade

I'm very proud of this dish. When made with the freshest of fish and shell fish (half of which is marinated in lime juice while the remainder is poached), fresh herbs and a carefully made dressing, it is quite delicious, and perfectly possible for a 'special occasion' large party. As a bonus, it can be made in advance, for it benefits from a little marinading though as little as 15 minutes in the lime juice and one hour in the sauce is enough —especially in hot countries. Serve it with Piquant Melba Toast.

Ingredients

4–6 people	*25 people*
6 oz (175g) small squid (optional, and could be replaced with more of the others)	1¼ lb (550g) small squid (optional and could be replaced with more of the others)
6 oz (175g) fine scallops	1¼ lb (550g) fine scallops
6 oz (175g) turbot, haddock or cod fillet	1¼ lb (550g) turbot, haddock or cod fillet
4 oz (100g) peeled cooked prawns	14 oz (400g) peeled cooked prawns
1 bay leaf	1 bay leaf
3 limes or 2 lemons (approx)	12–14 limes or 6–8 lemons (approx)
salt and pepper	salt and pepper
salad leaves, preferably of various colours and textures	salad leaves, preferably of various colours and textures

Sauce

2–3 tbs mayonnaise (made from 1 yolk, 4 fl oz (100ml) olive oil, about 1 tbs lemony juice from the fish, salt, pepper and mustard)	10–12 fl oz (300–350ml) mayonnaise
1 tbs natural yoghurt	4 tbs natural yoghurt
1 tbs thick or whipped cream	4 tbs thick or whipped cream
½–1 teasp pernod (optional)	½–1 tbs pernod (optional)
1 tbs fresh chopped or ¼ teasp dried basil	2–3 tbs fresh chopped or ½–1 teasp dried basil
1 teasp fresh chopped or ¼ teasp dried tarragon	1 tbs fresh chopped or ½–1 teasp dried tarragon
1 tbs each fresh chopped chives, parsley and chervil *or* 2–3 tbs any fresh herb mixture	2–3 tbs each fresh chopped chives, parsley and chervil *or* 6–8 tbs any fresh herb mixture

Clean the squid, removing the hard, transparent quill which runs up inside the body and the little beak in the middle of the rosette of legs. Remove the intestine and cut off the head. Simmer the squid for about 1–4 minutes in salt water to cover, with a slice of lemon and a bay leaf. Cut the orange coral 'tongues' off the scallops and add them to poach for 1 minute until firm. Drain (discarding the liquid, but don't throw it away—it's delicious in soups or sauces). Cut the squid into pieces and cool.

Remove any skin and bone from the fish, cut into rectangular strips 1″ × ½″ (2½cm × 1cm) and place in a glass or china bowl. Cut each scallop white into 2–3 discs, then across into strips, combine with the cold squid and the scallop 'tongues' and add to the fish. Just cover with lime or lemon juice, add the bay leaf and season with salt and pepper. Leave to marinate in the fridge for 2–12 hours, or less at room temperature.

While you make the sauce leave the fish mixture to drain very well and press lightly. Fold into the sauce. Leave refrigerated and well covered for another 2–12 hours. Serve on a bed of salad leaves on individual plates, decorated with thin slices of the scallop coral and a few chopped herbs.

Sauce. Make the mayonnaise, whisking hard so that it will take a little of the lemony juice from the fish and still remain stiff (or whisk some fish juice into ready made mayonnaise). Stir in the yoghurt, thick or whipped cream, pernod if used, and herbs.

✳✳ Cold Prawn Omelette

I like to serve this barely lukewarm for a summer lunch, making individual omelettes or two larger ones that can be divided. I have included the method for making prawn butter, but if you have some in the freezer (it freezes well), this dish can be very quickly and easily made with a packet of frozen prawns.

Ingredients
2–3 people (or for 4–6 as a starter)

6 eggs
½ oz (12g) butter
salt and pepper

Prawn filling
6 oz (175g) prawns in their shells
2 oz (50g) butter
½–1 teasp flour
4–6 tbs cream
a pinch mace
salt and pepper

Prawn filling. Shell the prawns and add the shells to the melted butter in a frying pan. Toss over high heat for a few minutes, then turn into a food processor or liquidiser and process until well chopped. Scrape the mixture into a square of muslin and squeeze out all the prawn butter. Melt 1 oz (25g) or so of prawn butter in a pan and add the prawns; toss over moderate heat for 10–15 seconds and season with pepper and mace. Sprinkle on a little flour and cook gently for several moments before adding the cream and simmering to make a thick creamy sauce. Correct the seasoning.

Break 2–3 eggs into a bowl, season and whisk with a fork. Heat an omelette pan and, when very hot, add a scrap of butter; once melted, pour in the egg and make an omelette, spooning on some of the filling when nearly done. Fold and turn out. Make the remaining omelettes. Leave to cool and serve with fresh rolls, butter and a salad.

✱✱   Salade Composée

Delicate *nouvelle cuisine* salads look pretty arranged on the plate, but I cannot recommend them for large numbers when you are entertaining because they must be done absolutely at the last minute. Even with everything ready and prepared in the fridge, the amateur (unlike the professional chef, who assembles dozens of platefuls daily) will find it takes time to make even quite a simple arrangement. But this is a versatile recipe, using either various bought sliced meats or chicken or turkey breast cooked in a simple but delicious way with a variety of salad ingredients. The method of cooking the chicken or turkey breasts is based on Chinese cooking and deserves to be used frequently for all sorts of other dishes.

Ingredients
4–6 people

6–8 oz (175–225g) thinly sliced meats (such as kassler, Westphalian ham, smoked chicken or turkey breasts)
or ¾–lb (350–450g) raw chicken or turkey breast

To Cook the Chicken or Turkey Breast
½ pt (300ml) water
2 teasp green peppercorns
2–3 slices fresh root ginger
2 spring onions
1 tbs sherry
1 teasp salt

Dressing
2 teasp lemon juice
2 teasp tarragon vinegar or other herb vinegar
1 teasp finely chopped chervil, fennel or parsley
4 teasp walnut oil (or best olive oil)
4 teasp sunflower or light vegetable oil
salt and very little pepper

Salad
2–3 large carrots and/or a handful of tiny french beans
1 avocado pear
juice of ½ lemon
1 crisp head lettuce
1 bunch watercress
handfuls of mixed salad leaves if available (rocket, lambs lettuce, radicchio, young salsify leaves, marigold leaves, young spinach or sorrel leaves, etc.)
1–2 teasp green peppercorns

To Cook Raw Chicken or Turkey Breasts (if used). Bring the water to the boil with the salt, peppercorns, ginger, onion and sherry. Add the chicken or turkey breast, bring back to the boil, then set aside covered until cold and cooked. Slice very thinly for the salad.

Dressing. Stir together the lemon juice, vinegar, seasoning and the herb until the salt has dissolved; then drip in the oils, stirring hard.

Salad. Cut the carrots (if you are using them) into wide ribbons with a peeler (or cut into long julienne strips). Blanch in boiling water until just limp. If you are using beans, blanch separately. Drain and refresh under cold water to set the colour. Peel and slice the avocado thinly and brush with lemon juice to prevent discolouration. Toss all the remaining salad ingredients with the dressing and arrange in a large bowl or on individual plates. Arrange the carrots (or beans), the meat and the avocado over it and scatter with the green peppercorns.

** Oeufs Mollets aux Epinards

These oeufs mollets, soft hard-boiled eggs, are set in a spinach and mayonnaise mixture. This appeals to those who like a fresh taste allied to smooth, rich, contrasting textures. Do not prepare too far ahead or the spinach will discolour.

Ingredients
4–6 people

4–6 eggs
1 lb (450g) fresh or 10 oz (275g) cooked
    spinach
1 lemon
¼ pt (150ml) mayonnaise (made with 1
    yolk, salt, pepper, mustard, ¼ pt
    (150ml) mixed olive and vegetable oil
    and about 2 teasp wine vinegar)
salt, pepper and nutmeg

Toss the spinach into plenty of boiling salted water in an enamel or stainless steel saucepan (aluminium reacts with spinach). Cook until just tender, drain and refresh with cold water; press excess water out of the spinach.

Boil the eggs for 5½ minutes (6 if they are very fresh, which means they will be difficult to peel) so that they are '*mollets*' (just soft inside). Peel and keep in cold water.

Purée the spinach in a food processor or liquidiser and add the mayonnaise; season and sharpen with lemon juice, and thin with water to a purée which will just drop off the spoon. Place the eggs in individual cocotte dishes and spoon over the spinach sauce. These are nice served with cheese straws or sesame fingers.

You can if you prefer make the mayonnaise in the food processor or liquidiser and add the spinach to it.

**   Tomatoes Stuffed with Cream Cheese and Herbs

This is a most delicious dish, the flavours blending admirably when carefully made with tasty fresh tomatoes. It's perfect for a summer starter or light summer lunch, served with slices of ham or salami and a few black olives.

Ingredients
4–6 people

4–6 fine ripe tomatoes
6 oz (175g) cream cheese (such as Eden
    Vale Somerset soft cream cheese)
1–2 tbs very finely chopped shallot
2 teasp fresh chopped or ¼–½ teasp
    dried basil
1 tbs finely scissored chives
½ teasp green peppercorns
4 fl oz (100ml) double cream ⎫
2 tbs plain yoghurt   ⎬ *or* use Crème Fraîche
chopped chervil or parsley ⎭
salt
pepper (if necessary)

Cover the tomatoes with boiling water and leave for 30 seconds or so before plunging into cold water and peeling. Cut off the tops and remove the inner pulp carefully, especially around the stalk end. Salt lightly inside and leave upside down to drain for about ¼ hour.

    Combine the cream cheese with the very finely chopped shallots, basil and chives. Stir in the green peppercorns and season with salt. Add 2–3 tbs of the cream to make a soft mixture. Drain and dry the tomatoes, fill with the cheese mixture and replace tops. Place on a serving dish and, just before serving, pour over the remaining cream, mixed until smooth with the yoghurt (or you can slightly acidulate the cream with lemon juice). Scatter with chopped chervil or parsley and serve.

Soups

ℱ *   Etta's Tomato Soup

I first learned to cook at about the age of eight with my grandmother's cook Etta. She made cakes and biscuits with me and I used to watch her at work in the kitchen as I ate my supper. Things learned at that age stay so clearly in the mind, and I still see the perfectly formed, tiny dice of tomato appearing from under her huge steel knife at incredible speed. This soup is really only a white sauce base, thinned with chicken stock and served with diced tomato and chopped parsley. It's simple and good, and useful when you have only a few, fine-flavoured tomatoes.

Ingredients
4–6 people

2 oz (50g) butter
1½ oz (35g) flour
½ pt (300ml) milk
1¾ pts (1l) good white chicken stock

3 firm tasty tomatoes
1–2 tbs finely chopped parsley or chives
salt and pepper

Melt the butter in a saucepan and add the flour. Cook, stirring, over moderate heat for 2–3 minutes, then draw off the stove and wait for the sizzling to cease. Add the milk and return to the heat. Bring to the boil, whisking hard, and simmer for 1–2 minutes before seasoning with salt and pepper. Now gradually thin this white sauce with the chicken stock to cream soup consistency (¼ or ½ a chicken stock cube can be added if the stock is lacking in flavour).

Meanwhile skin the tomatoes. Cut them in half round their middles, squeeze out and discard the pips and cut the tomato flesh into even, small dice. Add to the soup with the fairly finely chopped parsley or chives and correct the seasoning only when ready to serve, for the tomato should keep its freshness and shape. The creamy coloured soup is very pretty with its dice of tomato and green flecks of parsley.

ℱ * Broad Bean Soup

If your broad beans get fat and floury and are wearing their leather jerkins, you can always use them up in this simple summer soup.

Ingredients
4–6 people

1 lb (450g) podded broad beans
4 oz (100g) young peas for colour, fresh
  or frozen (optional)
1½ oz (35g) butter
2 oz (50g) bacon or ham
1–2 fresh young onions
½ oz (12g) flour

1½ pts (900ml) chicken or ham stock or 1
  stock cube and water
½ pt (300ml) milk
3–4 fl oz (75–100ml) cream or 1 oz (25g)
  butter
2–3 sprigs summer savory or parsley
salt and pepper

Melt the butter, chop the bacon and onions small and cook them gently in the butter, with the sprigs of savory, till tender. Add the flour and cook for a minute or two, stirring; then add the stock and seasoning and bring to the simmer, whisking. Throw in the beans and simmer until very tender, adding the peas, if used, for the last 5–10 minutes. Process and sieve the soup, then add the milk and cream. If you are enriching it with butter rather than cream, add it off the stove in tiny pieces at the end. Re-heat, check the seasoning and serve, if you wish, scattered with finely chopped summer savory or parsley or with fried croûtons.

For a finer flavour, you can remove the tough outer skins of the broad beans before cooking, but then you rather lose the point of this quick and simple soup.

F ✳✳   Summer Vegetable Soup with Pistou

Having given a very acceptable winter version of Soupe au Pistou in another book*, I feel I must now tell you how to make a summer soup that is almost a meal in itself. It's made from all that there is fresh in the garden, or readily available in the shops, with the glorious addition of fresh basil, tomatoes, oil and garlic, made into a fragrant and unctuous sauce to add as you dare. I simmer it in a heavy earthenware *marmita* which always seems to enhance the flavour. You can use either stock or water, adding 2 stock cubes if you want—though I don't myself think they are necessary if the vegetables are well flavoured. I sometimes add diced kohl rabi, turnips, leeks if I have them, and even lettuce or a touch of Florence fennel. If there are no fresh haricots, and you haven't time to soak and cook dried ones, you can just add more pasta instead, probably the tiny shells, stars or broken spaghetti.

The Pistou Sauce will keep in the fridge for a week or so and can be used with pasta, handing parmesan separately, or with courgettes (*see page 147*).

Ingredients
6–8 people

3–4 tbs good fruity olive oil
2 onions
2 medium potatoes
2–3 carrots
1–2 leeks (optional)
1–2 sticks celery (optional)
2–4 slim courgettes
6–8 oz (175–225g) or a good handful
   young French beans
4 tomatoes, peeled and roughly chopped
1 tbs tomato purée
3 pts (1.7l) stock *or* water + 2 chicken
   cubes (optional)
1 clove garlic
1 bay leaf
sprig thyme
3–4 chopped leaves fresh basil
3–4 oz (75–100g) pasta, elbow macaroni,
   shells, stars or broken spaghetti
6 oz (175g) fresh or 4 oz (100g) dried
   haricot beans, soaked and cooked,
   their cooking liquid retained
fresh chopped parsley
salt and pepper

Pistou Sauce
3 cloves garlic
a good handful of basil leaves and
   flowers
2 tomatoes, peeled and seeded
1 tbs tomato purée
4–6 tbs good fruity olive oil
salt and pepper

Gently warm the oil in a wide pan. Dice the onions, potatoes and carrots, and slice the leeks and celery if used. Dice the courgettes, but set half of them aside with the French beans, which should be topped, tailed and broken into 1" (2–3cm) lengths. Add to the oil the diced and sliced vegetables, the chopped tomatoes and the tomato purée, with 2 tbs cold water, and cook gently for 10 minutes, until all the liquid has gone and the vegetables have softened but not browned. Add the stock or water, the flattened clove of garlic, bay leaf, thyme, basil and fresh haricot beans, if used. Boil quite briskly, uncovered, for 20–30 minutes, then add the remaining diced courgette (the first lot dissolves into the soup giving it texture and body, the second lot stays fresh and crisp), the French beans, the pasta and the cooked, dried haricot beans, if used. Season generously with salt and pepper and simmer for 15–20 minutes more, adding the bean cooking liquid or water if necessary (though it should be almost a vegetable stew) until the beans and pasta are well cooked but not flabby. Stir in a little fresh chopped parsley.

Serve the soup piping hot and let everyone add a spoon or so of Pistou Sauce to their own bowl, depending on the warmth of their love affair with basil and garlic. You stir it in and catch the mouth-watering aroma as it rises with the steam. You can also add freshly grated parmesan to the pistou or sprinkle it over the soup if you wish.

Pistou Sauce. Pound the basil and garlic in a mortar, or process. Add the tomato purée, then gradually add the chopped tomato and olive oil alternately until you have a fairly smooth emulsified sauce. Season generously with salt and pepper.

ℱ ✳✳ Crème Louise

Iced summer soups are delicious and always popular. To get round the problem of too jellied a stock, resulting in a thick vegetable porridge, I often use a Chinese method of making stock. The chicken carcass, preferably raw, is chopped up into small bits to get the flavour from the marrow in the bones and boiled with flavouring ingredients for 1 hour only, during which time the liquid reduces by half. This will only set very lightly to jelly but will be full of flavour. This soup uses the felicitous combination of summer cucumber and tomato with cream and cream cheese to thicken it, yoghurt to freshen it and prawns to enhance it if you wish. Should you freeze it, it is good re-heated and served hot.

Ingredients
4–6 people

Chinese Style White Chicken Stock

1 large cucumber
1 pt (600ml) approx white chicken stock
1 lb (450g) ripe tomatoes
3 oz (75g) cream cheese (optional)
½ pt (300 ml) plain yoghurt
¼ pt (150ml) whipping cream
2 oz peeled prawns (optional)
finely chopped chives
salt and pepper

1 chicken carcass (preferably raw)
2 slices bacon (no fat or rind)
1 sliced small leek or onion
2–3 slices fresh root ginger
½ clove garlic
8 peppercorns
½ chicken stock cube
3 pts (1.7l) water
¼ teasp salt

Chinese Style White Chicken Stock. Chop the chicken carcass up, breaking the bones, using a chopper or strong kitchen scissors. Place in a saucepan with the remaining ingredients and bring to the boil. Skim well and boil for 1 hour, the pan half covered, so that the liquid reduces to about 1½ pts (900ml), of which you will need about 1 pt (600ml), skimming from time to time. Strain through muslin or a fine sieve and remove any fat after standing a few minutes or when cold.

Peel and slice the cucumber and cook until tender in ½ pt (300ml) of the chicken stock. Process until smooth, then strain into a bowl; I use a liquidiser in preference to a food processor because it produces a more velvety result. Process the roughly chopped tomatoes with the remaining ½ pt (300ml) of stock and sieve into the bowl. Mix the cream cheese, if used, yoghurt and cream until smooth, or process briefly. Strain into the bowl and whisk all together. Check seasoning and chill well. Serve in chilled bowls, scattered with prawns, if used, and chopped chives.

Fish

* Fillets of Cod in Parsley Sauce

When thick fillets of cod have that fresh glisten and their dappled skin looks bright and clear, enjoy them with a simple fresh parsley sauce and our quick way of cooking skinned fish under its sauce.

Ingredients
4–6 people

1–1½ lb (450–675g) fresh cod or haddock
    fillet

Parsley Sauce
½ pt (300ml) milk
a good bunch fresh parsley
1 oz (25g) butter
1 oz (25g) flour
3–4 tbs cream
salt and pepper

Skin the fish fillets with a flexible knife (it's much easier to skin fish when it's raw), starting from the tail end and keeping the knife flat. Remove any bones and cut the fish into portions, doubling the tail under itself to even out the thickness. Lay the fish in a buttered shallow gratin dish in one layer and coat with the sauce. Bake uncovered in a moderate oven (350°F/180°C/Gas 4) for 15–20 minutes or until cooked.

Parsley Sauce. Heat the milk and parsley stalks to boiling point and set aside, covered, to infuse. Chop the parsley heads finely. Melt the butter, add the flour and cook over moderate heat for 2–3 minutes. Draw the pan off the stove, and wait for the sizzling to cease. Strain the infused milk and add. Bring to the boil, whisking with a wire whisk; simmer for 1–2 minutes. Season, and stir in plenty of parsley until the sauce is a bright speckled green. Thin with tablespoonfuls of cream until it is of a thick coating consistency. It must be thick as it is going on raw fish, which will exude some juices during cooking.

P *   Escabèche of Mackerel

Pickling fish to enhance its flavour and help it to keep has always been part of a cook's skill. The word escabèche intrigues me because one finds it with so many variations all round the world. Heavily pickled dishes to keep a great while are found in old books. Hanna Glasse in the eighteenth century has a recipe for pickled mackerel called *caveach*, and Meg Dods, the eminent Scottish cook of the early nineteenth century, has a recipe for *Cabeached Cod* which she says comes from the Spanish word escabèche, and means fish pickle. The escabèche crossed the Atlantic to become the Mexican Zeviche or Ceviche, changing to become uncooked fish, lightly pickled in lime or lemon juice.

Nowadays we don't need to preserve for quite so far ahead, and can get away with a lighter pickle, much more to today's taste. But how useful it is, especially in summer when you may not feel like cooking, to be able to dip into a dish of pickled fish or, perhaps for week-end visitors, to prepare a dish several days before you need it.

Ingredients
4–6 people

4–6 fine mackerel
a little flour
8 fl oz (225ml) oil
1 sliced onion
1 diced carrot
8 fl oz (225ml) white wine vinegar
2 fl oz (50ml) water
several sprigs thyme
3–5 cloves garlic
½ bayleaf
2–3 parsley stalks
3–4 whole allspice
6–8 peppercorns
2 cloves
1 blade mace, or good pinch ground
   mace
salt and pepper

Gut the mackerel and cut off the head and tail. Cut each fish into 3–4 pieces through the backbone. Season, dip in flour, brush off the excess and fry in the hot oil, turning once, until brown and just cooked; remove to a deep dish. Add the onion, carrot, vinegar, water, thyme, garlic (either flattened under the blade of a knife or chopped small), bay leaf, parsley stalks, allspice, peppercorns, cloves, mace and 1 teasp salt to the oil in the pan; boil together for 5–10 minutes, then pour over the mackerel to cover. Cool, cover and keep for at least 24 hours before eating. It will keep for a week or so—longer if you salt the fish before cooking it.

✳✳ Cold Trout and Cucumber and Dill Sauce

Baked trout, skinned and served cold with this light summer sauce, make a good lunch dish or dinner party starter when the weather is warm; mind you, we have eaten them in cold weather and they are still excellent.

Ingredients
4–6 people

4–6 fine (preferably pink) trout
½ oz (12g) butter
1 lemon
2–3 tbs white wine (optional)
2–3 tbs water
salt and pepper
parsley or watercress

Cucumber and Dill Sauce
½ cucumber
1–2 teasp castor sugar
1–2 teasp fresh chopped or ½ teasp dried
  dill (or use fennel or chives)
lemon juice
5 fl oz (150ml) whipping cream
3–4 tbs mayonnaise
salt and pepper

Wipe the trout inside and out and lay, in one layer, in a wide baking dish rubbed generously with the butter. Season the trout, squeeze over the lemon juice and add the wine and water. Cover loosely with a sheet of Bakewell or buttered greaseproof paper and bake in a moderately hot oven (375°F/190°C/Gas 5) for about 20 minutes until the eye goes white and the flesh feels firm. Set aside to cool, and when completely cold remove the skin and arrange the fish on a dish. Keep covered and chilled, then garnish with parsley or watercress when ready to serve.

Cucumber and Dill Sauce. Dice the cucumber into tiny dice, leaving on the skin if it is tender, and lay in a colander. Sprinkle with salt, press with a plate and weight and leave for 20–30 minutes before patting dry with kitchen paper. Add sugar, dill, seasoning and lemon juice to the cream and whisk until it is just holding its shape. Whisk it into the mayonnaise and then stir in the cubes of drained cucumber. Correct the seasoning and turn into a sauceboat.

It takes about an hour for the flavour of dill to come out and flavour the cream.

Main Courses

𝒫 **   Spiced Tandoori-Style Chicken

This is spicy but not hot and peppery, can be prepared a day or so ahead and will be ready to barbecue when the sun comes out. Just drumsticks on their own make very good finger food for barbecues. Ghee can be used instead of clarified butter.

Ingredients
4–6 people

3½ lb (1.6k) chicken or 10–12 drumsticks
2 teasp whole coriander seed
1 teasp whole cumin seed
1″ (2cm) piece fresh root ginger
2 finely chopped onions
2 cloves garlic
5 fl oz (150ml) plain yoghurt
juice 1 lemon
2 tbs wine vinegar
¼ teasp chilli powder *or* cayenne pepper
2 teasp salt
1 teasp paprika
2 teasp garam masala or curry powder

1 oz (25g) clarified butter or ghee

Pound the coriander and cumin to a powder in a pestle and mortar and grate or pound the ginger. Place all the ingredients except the chicken and clarified butter in a good processor or liquidiser and process well or beat together by hand.

Skin the chicken, divide it into portions and prick all over with the point of a knife. Pour over and rub in the mixture and leave for 24 hours. Tandoori chicken should be cooked in a clay tandoori oven! Failing this use a charcoal grill, grill, rôtisserie or very hot oven (450°F/230°C/Gas 8). Place the chicken pieces on a rack in a roasting tin, bake for 20–25 minutes and brush with the ghee or clarified butter. Or cook the chicken under a hot grill, turning frequently until it is a good red-brown and nice and crusty. Serve with Pitta or Indian bread or French bread and salads.

To Clarify Butter. Chop up some butter and heat gently in a heavy pan. Once the frothing diminishes, skim off the top froth and carefully pour off the golden oil, leaving the salty, milky residue behind. This can be used in mashed potatoes but watch out, it's very salty. Clarified butter will keep almost indefinitely.

**   Chicken Sauté à la Clamart

A delicate and simple way of cooking chicken and petits pois together. I think it is best to buy the petits pois seeds in France, though I have to admit that I have not grown them for the last year or so. Best quality frozen petits pois, although not really the same, still make a lovely dish.

Ingredients
4 people

3½ lb (1.6kg) chicken
2 oz (50g) thick cut smoked bacon
2½ oz (65g) butter
12 spring onions
a little fresh chopped tarragon or
    summer savory (optional)
1 head lettuce
1 lb (450g) shelled petits pois, fresh or
    thawed from frozen
2–3 teasp sugar
a few tbs chicken stock if necessary
1 teasp potato flour, slaked with water or
    cream
salt and pepper

Joint the chicken into four or eight portions and dice the bacon small. Melt the butter in an ovenproof casserole (not iron or aluminium), place in the chicken joints in one layer and fry them very gently until sealed but not brown. Turn and seal the other sides. Add spring onions and bacon and fry for a little, season with salt and pepper (a little tarragon or summer savory is good too), cover with the chicken carcass if there is room and close tightly. Place in a slow oven (300°F/150°/Gas 2) for ½ hour.

Shred the lettuce and drain the peas if they were frozen. Remove the carcass from the casserole, add the peas, shredded lettuce, sugar and, should it be necessary, a little chicken stock, though the chicken will probably have produced enough juice. Stir well together, cover closely and continue to cook at 300°F/150°C/Gas 2 for another ½ hour. Then turn up to moderate (350°F/180°C/Gas 4) for 30–60 minutes more until the chicken is done and the peas soft and tender. Remove the chicken joints to a serving dish and keep warm.

Thicken the peas with a little potato flour, mixed with water or cream, boiling down if there is too much; you could use egg yolks and cream for a richer dish if you wish. Pour the peas over the chicken and shake the dish to settle them. Heart-shaped croûtes of fried bread are nice around this dish and Salt and Sesame Glazed Potatoes (*see page 150*) or Lemon New Potatoes* also go well with it.

✳✳   Lamb Cutlets in Sweet-Sour Mint Aspic

It can be difficult to think of cold dishes for smart picnics or special summer lunches, but I have evolved two which I find particularly useful. These lamb cutlets in mint jelly are one and the following Boned Stuffed Quail is the other, perhaps a little fiddly but really quite something.

Carefully cooked, so that they are still pink, cutlets set into a delicate sweet-sour minty aspic are easily transportable and can be nibbled off the bone.

Ingredients
4–6 people

8–12 lamb cutlets
2 tbs oil
salt and pepper

Sweet–Sour Mint Aspic
1 pt (600ml) pkt aspic (the Swiss make
    Haco is good)
5 fl oz (150ml) cold water with extra to
    make up the volume
3 fl oz (75ml) white wine vinegar (or basil
    vinegar if you have it)
6 tbs finely chopped mint
2 tbs Demerara sugar
salt and pepper

Sweet-Sour Mint Aspic. Sprinkle the aspic on to 5 fl oz (150ml) cold water in a saucepan and heat gently until the crystals all melt. Place the aspic in a measuring jug and add the wine vinegar, mint and sugar. Stir to dissolve the sugar, then make up to 1 pt (600ml) with cold water. Season lightly and leave until cold and syrupy, stirring from time to time.

Bring the cutlets to room temperature before cooking, if possible, for if cold from the fridge they will cool the pan and cannot seal and brown quickly. Trim away excess fat and cut off the meat to expose the bone ends, to a length of 1"–2" (2.5cm–5cm). Bat gently with the heel of your hand, pat dry with kitchen paper and season with salt and pepper just before cooking.

Heat the oil in a frying pan until just smoking hot and add the cutlets in one layer. Cook them for about 30 seconds until sealed and browned on one side, then turn and cook the other side. Lower the temperature and continue cooking until just done but still pink inside. Press them with your finger and you will soon learn when they are no longer squishy and raw but have not yet become firm and resilient as when too well cooked. Remove them individually as they are cooked because some will be thicker and take a little longer. Drain on kitchen paper and cool.

If you wish to turn them out of their dish to serve, spoon some of the syrupy mint aspic into a shallow dish and leave to set; then arrange the cold cutlets on this jelly, keeping them arranged quite close together. Spoon over the remaining setting aspic, which should now be heavy enough for the mint not to float to the top, and leave to set. It will keep in the fridge, covered, for 24 hours or more. Turn out on to a serving dish if you wish and decorate, or take on your picnic in the dish.

*** Boned Stuffed Quail

If you want something a bit special you might feel like tackling these boned quail, stuffed with cream cheese and herbs and wrapped in bacon. They are delicious served hot but are also designed for the elegant picnic where they can be picked up and nibbled. They are not really difficult to bone; my new students tackle them with no pre-conceived inhibitions and manage quite easily, though they are small and a bit fiddly. A little cooked rice can be incorporated with the cream cheese to give the stuffing rather more body.

Ingredients
4–6 people

4–6 quail
4–6 oz (100–175g) cream cheese
1–1½ tbs chopped fresh herbs (parsley
    and sage, marjoram, chives or
    tarragon)
½–1 egg yolk
3 rashers of thin-cut streaky bacon per
    quail
salt and pepper

Take a nice balance of fresh herbs with parsley predominating (or all parsley). Chop them finely and mix with the cream cheese, egg yolk and seasoning. De-rind the bacon and stretch as thin as possible with your thumb on a wooden board.

Bone the quail, starting by cutting through the skin right down the back with a sharp boning knife. Work the skin and flesh away from the carcass, detaching the wings and legs from their sockets. Work carefully round one side to the breast bone, then round the other. Next detach the carcass along the breast bone very carefully so that the skin does not tear. Cut the end two joints off the wings and remove the third wing bone by cutting round the little joint to detach the ligaments; then pull out the bone which will pull the flesh through to the inside. Leave the leg bones in, but push the flesh well up the drumstick bones so that the bones are clean and well exposed.

Spread out the quail, skin side down, on the table and place a spoonful of cream cheese mixture on each. Fold the skin over to enclose the cream cheese with the two legs pulled out straight together at the back end. Wrap the quails in the stretched bacon in a torpedo shape, using 2–3 rashers for each bird, and secure with two tooth picks, passed right through each bird.

Lay the prepared quails on a rack in a roasting tin and roast in a very hot oven (450°F/230°C/Gas 8) for 15–20 minutes. Don't worry if a little cream cheese oozes out as it is rather inclined to do. Serve hot, possibly garnished with watercress, or leave until cold and serve cold with salads.

*** Quail Prince William

I created this dish in 1982 to honour the birth of Prince William. A quail, with a filling of apricots, pine nuts and smoked ham, is set on a heart-shaped croûte of fried bread, spread with a purée of leeks and garnished with blue borage flowers for a boy. The sauce is made with a careful balance of fresh, symbolic herbs; rosemary, a protection from evil, is for fidelity and remembrance; marjoram is added for happiness; lemon thyme for vigour and strength; and basil because it is the royal herb. Bay is a symbol of glory and bringer of good luck, and borage is for courage and to drive away sadness. The only difficulty is finding fresh leeks in summer, usually possible on the continent (and perhaps in Wales) but less easy for the rest of us.

Ingredients
4–6 people

4–6 quail or 2 per head
2–3 oz (50–75g) smoked ham (fat and lean)
4–6 dried apricots
2–3 tbs pine nuts
2–3 oz (50–75g) butter
1 bay leaf
sprig rosemary, lemon thyme or thyme and marjoram
borage flowers for decoration (optional)
salt and pepper

Leek Croûtes
12 oz (350g) finely sliced leek (white only)
1½ oz (35g) butter
2–3 tbs cream
4–6 heart-shaped croûtes of fried bread
salt and pepper

Sauce
1 sprig dill
1–2 basil leaves
2–3 mint leaves
1 small to medium borage leaf
4–6 lemon thyme or thyme leaves
} *or* any nice mix of fresh herbs
8 fl oz (225ml) double cream
1 oz (25g) butter (optional)
a few drops lemon juice
salt and pepper

Finely chop the ham and dice the apricots. Mix with the pine nuts and a little pepper and use to stuff the quail. Truss them (a cocktail stick does the job well), season and set to roast on the bayleaf and herbs, in a covered roasting tin or casserole in the melted butter. Roast in a hot oven (425°F/220°C/Gas 7) for 20–25 minutes, basting once. Remove from the roasting tin or casserole and keep warm.

Leek Croûtes. Meanwhile, gently cook the shredded leek in the butter with salt and pepper until absolutely tender. Purée in the food processor or liquidiser, adding enough cream to make a purée that will just hold its shape.

Sauce. Chop the herbs very finely, ending up with 1–1½ teasp. Discard the sprigs of herbs from the pan in which the quail were cooked, pressing out all butter and juice, add the cream, and boil up to amalgamate with the butter and reduce. Add the herbs, correct the seasoning and add a few drops of lemon juice. Reduce to a coating sauce. Stir in flakes of butter, if desired, to thicken and enrich the sauce.

To Serve. Mound a little leek purée on each hot croûte, set a quail on the leek and coat with the sauce. Scatter with borage flowers and serve at once.

F ✱✱   Escalopes of Liver with Lemon and Garlic

The Italians cook liver beautifully and frequently use calves' liver, which is difficult to get in this country—and pricy. They usually cut it into thin, thin escalopes that are briefly cooked, often with sage, and served with the buttery cooking juices. You need a nice thick centre piece of lambs' liver (the thin outer lobes are too thin and fiddly when sliced); cut it into thin escalopes to make a delicious alternative to British liver, bacon and onions. Cook it with fresh sage, or try this recipe with green peppercorns, lemon and garlic. Just be certain that you barely show the liver to the pan so that it has no time to overcook and get dry and crumbly.

Ingredients
4 people

1 lb (450g) calves' or lambs' liver cut in
   ⅛" (4mm) thick slices
2 tbs olive oil
1½–2 oz (35–50g) butter
½–1 teasp green peppercorns
1 clove garlic
½ lemon
salt and pepper

Season the escalopes lightly on both sides.

Heat the oil in a large frying pan until just smoking, then lay in the escalopes in one layer. Almost at once turn them over, then remove them from the pan while they are still faintly squishy to the touch. Remove to a serving dish and keep warm while you cook the remainder, if they have not all fitted into the pan.

Add the diced butter, finely chopped garlic and green peppercorns to the pan and heat until the garlic softens and the butter bubbles. Add a good squeeze of lemon juice and pour over the escalopes. Serve at once, possibly with Salt and Sesame Glazed Potatoes (*see page 150*) and a crisp salad, dressed with the Chive and Mint Cream Dressing (*see page 113*). It makes a lovely summer lunch.

** Filet d'Agneau avec sa Salade d'Epinards

This elegant and easy way of serving a summer loin of lamb for entertaining combines a boned joint with a little rich sauce, thickened only with a sweet onion purée, and a little fresh salad. It is served carved in thin slices on individual plates with the sauce over it and salad arranged around it. The idea came from something I saw being served at another table in a French restaurant, hence its French title!

Ingredients
4–6 people

3 lb (1.35kg) loin of lamb, boned, but
   keep the bones
1 finely chopped shallot
3 tbs olive oil
½ lemon
a little wine, stock or water
salt and pepper

Sauce
bones from the lamb
1–2 large onions
3 tbs olive oil
1 slice bacon
1 carrot
1 stick celery
½ clove garlic
bouquet garni of parsley, thyme and
   bayleaf
½ pt (300ml) red wine
½ chicken stock cube
3 fl oz (75ml) good stock
salt and pepper

Salade d'Epinards
½–¾ lb (225–350g) fresh little spinach
   leaves or use curly endive or
   watercress
2 teasp lemon juice
2 tbs olive oil
salt, pepper and mustard

Bone the lamb (retaining the bones) and marinade with the shallot, oil, lemon juice and seasoning for 4–24 hours. Then roll and tie with string in 3–4 places. Pat dry and set in a roasting pan. Cook in a hot oven (425°F/220°C/Gas 7) for 25–34 minutes. Watch that the pan juices do not burn by adding a dash of wine, stock or water when they are a good brown. Rest the lamb, in a warm place but where it cannot continue to cook, for 15–45 minutes before carving into thin slices.

Sauce. Having boned the lamb, break up the bones and set them to roast in a hot oven (425°F/220°C/Gas 7) for about 15 minutes until browned. Drain off any accumulated fat.

   Cut the onions into thick slices and gently cook in the olive oil, in a frying pan, until soft and golden. Drain, purée and set aside. To the oil in the pan add the diced bacon, carrot and celery. Cook until golden brown, then add to the pan the browned bones, garlic, bouquet, wine, stock cube, a very light seasoning and stock. Cover and cook gently for 10–15 minutes, then remove the lid and boil fast to reduce down to 3–4 fl oz (75–100ml). Strain, pressing the bones and vegetables well, and set this rich sauce aside.

On Serving. Carefully drain the fat from the roasting tin, add a little wine, stock or water, boil up and de-glaze the pan, stirring in all the brown tasty bits. Add the reserved sauce to the pan, boil up and add 1–2 tbs of onion purée to thicken and flavour the sauce. Correct the seasoning and serve over the sliced lamb, or serve in a sauce boat.

Salade d'Epinards. Toss the washed and dried spinach leaves, curly endive or watercress in a dressing made by stirring the salt, pepper and mustard with the lemon juice, then gradually whisking in the oil to make a dressing. Serve a little salad around each plate with the carved lamb; its crunchy freshness contrasts well with the rich meat and sauce. Alternatively, a hot purée of cooked spinach or turnip leaves, with generous quantities of butter and cream, goes well with the lamb.

$\mathcal{P}$ *   Marinated Lamb Kebabs

The smell of barbecuing meat, with its hint of herbs and suggestion of the Near East, is one of the most evocative and tantalising smells I know. A really sharp fire, or a very hot grill, is needed to get the necessary crisp brown outer crust while still keeping the interior succulent. None of those dreadful bits of totally unauthentic onion, pepper, tomato or mushroom should be interspersed with the meat; if you absolutely must, use a bay leaf, a scrap of lamb fat or a tiny sliver of onion. But do not neglect the generously chopped parsley (flat leafed for choice) on serving. I use dried oregano for the marinade, preferably the wild sort with flowers included, bought from a Cypriot grocer.

Ingredients
4–6 people

2 lb (900g) lean leg of lamb
1 finely chopped onion
2 tbs good olive oil
juice ½ lemon
1 tbs chopped fresh parsley
1 teasp chopped fresh or pinch dried
    thyme (use one of the mountain or
    creeping thymes if you have them)
¼–½ teasp dried oregano
salt and pepper

To accompany
pitta breads
bowls of chopped parsley, chopped
    spring onion or leek, yoghurt,
    quartered tomatoes and cucumber
    sticks
half-lemons

Cut the meat into 1" (2–3cm) cubes and place in a bowl with all the other ingredients. Mix well and leave to marinate for 2–4 hours; it's amazing how much more succulent this makes the meat. Thread the lamb on to long flat skewers, keeping it well up to the point and closely packed together.

When the barbecue or grill is really hot, grill the kebabs very fast and close to the heat, turning until browned on all sides; they should stay succulent inside if cooked fast.

Serve with warmed pitta bread, the accompaniments, half-lemons to squeeze over the meat and—need I say it?—a glass of wine.

✳✳✳ Raised Pork Pies

The written recipe for pies always looks rather daunting, but when you tackle it you find it is really quite easy and quick. My students can usually produce a pretty good pie first time, though of course seeing it done, rather than reading about it, is always easier. These are so tasty and good that I do recommend you to try them some time. You can, if you wish, construct one large pie and just continue the second part of the cooking time, or make the pie in a removable base cake tin, though the crust is not so crisp and brown.

Ingredients
4 × 1 lb (450g) pork pies

Jelly Stock
1–2 pigs' trotters
scraps of pork, bones and skin (from the filling)
1 onion
1 carrot
bouquet garni or parsley stalks, thyme, bay leaf and 1 clove
½ teasp vinegar or lemon juice
gelatine (if necessary)
2–3 egg whites to clarify stock (optional)
salt and pepper

Hot Water Crust
1 lb (450g) 'strong' flour
6 oz (175g) lard
5 tbs water
5 tbs milk
1 oz (25g) butter
egg wash
1 teasp salt

Filling
1¼ lb (550g) lean shoulder pork
¾ lb (350g) pork fat (back fat is best)
¼ lb (100g) streaky bacon or good pinch of saltpetre to keep the filling pink
1 teasp anchovy essence (optional)
½ teasp ground black pepper
a good ¼ teasp mace
1½ teasp salt

Jelly Stock. Place the trotters, scraps, bones and skin in a pan, cover with cold water, bring to the boil and drain. Rinse the trotters and replace in the pan with the vegetables, vinegar, bouquet and a little salt and pepper. Simmer for 3–4 hours until the trotters are completely tender, strain the stock through muslin, then de-fat and reduce to about 1 pt (600ml). Check the seasoning, which should be spicy. To clarify the stock if you wish, use 2 or 3 slightly whisked egg whites and their crushed shells. Add them to the stock and simmer for 10 minutes. Leave to stand for 10 minutes, then strain through 3–4 layers of muslin. Check that this sets to jelly or, if necessary, add gelatine.

Hot Water Crust. Chop up the lard, melt it in the milk and water and bring to the boil. Sift the flour and salt into a bowl, rub in the butter, then add hot lard. Beat really well with a wooden spoon or in a food processor, processing for ½–1 minute. Cover the bowl with a cloth and leave the pastry to cool for 20–40 minutes. As it's so rich, it must be cool enough to handle but not cold, or it will not mould. Make up the filling.

Divide the pastry into four and keep three parts warm. Take one part and keep aside a quarter of it for its lid. Place the dough in a ball on a greased baking sheet. Gently shape into a pot, gradually pressing out the base to 5"–6" diameter and drawing up the sides to 3" high. Carefully fill with your prepared meat, pressing it in tightly or the meat will toughen; mound well up on top. Press the remaining quarter of crust into a circle to fit the top, moisten the edges with water and seal on well. Make a hole in the centre and stick in it a little tinfoil funnel. Having made all four pies, use the scraps to make decorative leaves etc; decorate pies and brush with egg wash. Bake in a hot oven (425°F/220°C/Gas 7) for 10–20 minutes until a good brown and the pastry has set; then turn down to 325°F/170°C/ Gas 3 and continue to bake for 1–1½ hours until crisp, brown and tender; a skewer plunged through the hole will tell if the meat is tender. Leave to cool, but when still warm fill through the funnel with the just warm jelly stock. Top up several times as the warm meat will absorb the warm stock.

Make the pies several days before serving for the flavour to mature. They will keep for up to one week.

Filling. Cut the meat and fat into little finger-nail size pieces (minced meat is not so succulent). Finely chop the bacon. Add the anchovy essence, if used, sprinkle with seasoning and mix well together.

✳ Cold Beef and Potato Salad

Cold boiled or roasted meat, mixed with sliced cooked potatoes and dressed with a herby spicy vinaigrette dressing, is one of the best ways of using up the remains of the joint in summer.

Ingredients
4–6 people

10 oz (275g) or more cooked sliced beef
1 lb (450g) potatoes
1–2 tbs wine vinegar
watercress or lettuce leaves
2 oz (50g) black olives (optional)
salt and pepper

Dressing
1 shallot or small onion
1 tbs Dijon mustard
3 tbs fresh chopped parsley or mixed
    herbs (parsley, marjoram, chives,
    thyme, etc) or 1 teasp dried Italian
    seasoning soaked in 1 tbs boiling
    water for 5 minutes
2–3 tbs wine vinegar
6–8 tbs olive or groundnut oil
salt and pepper

Boil the potatoes in their skins, then peel, slice, season, sprinkle with vinegar and leave to cool (or use left-over boiled potatoes).

Cut the beef into strips, combine with the potatoes and dressing and toss all together well. Line a bowl with watercress or lettuce leaves, arrange the beef and potato salad on them and, if used, scatter with black olives.

Dressing. Finely chop the shallot or onion and combine with the mustard, plenty of salt and pepper, the chopped fresh herbs or soaked dried ones and their water. Stir in the vinegar, then gradually stir in the oil to make a thick dressing (or shake it all up in a tightly closed jar).

𝒫 **   Cold Loin of Pork with Pistachio Nuts and Green Peppercorns

This cold spiced loin of pork, spiked with pistachio nuts, is a lovely and useful dish which can be prepared several days ahead. You can dispense with the pigs' trotters and jelly if you wish, and increase the amount of pistachio nuts or forget about them and use a herb stuffing instead. The Spiced Pork* is a less elegant and cheaper but very useful variation on this theme.

Ingredients
6–8 people

3½ lb (1.6kg) loin of pork or larger piece
   if you wish, boned, but keep the bones
2 pigs' trotters
½ clove garlic
½ teasp green peppercorns
4 sage leaves
2 sprigs lemon thyme or thyme
1 teasp brandy
2 teasp salt

1 oz (25g) pistachio nuts
2–3 slices lemon
1 clove garlic
bouquet garni of parsley, sage, thyme
   and bay leaf
1 onion stuck with 2 cloves
1 stick celery
1 carrot
¼–½ pt (150–300ml) dry white wine
water to cover

Remove the skin and any excess fat from the loin of pork and bone out.

Pound the salt, garlic, green peppercorns, sage and lemon thyme in a mortar and moisten with the brandy. Rub this flavouring paste well into all sides of the meat and leave in a cool place for 12–24 hours.

Place the pigs' trotters in plenty of cold water, bring to the boil to blanch, simmer for 15–30 minutes and discard the water.

With the point of a knife, make little pockets on the inside of the meat and tuck pistachio nuts in these pockets and also down the length of the meat in the middle; if you are feeling generous spike them into the fat side too. Roll and tie the joint 3–4 times.

Place the meat, with its skin underneath it, snugly into a casserole, tuck the blanched pigs' trotters around it and add the lemon, garlic, bouquet, onion, celery and carrot. Pour in the white wine and add enough water to cover. Put on a tight fitting lid and cook in a slow oven (250°F/130°C/Gas 1) for about 4–5 hours until very tender. Leave to cool in the stock for about an hour, then strain off the stock through muslin. The stock should be clear, but if it's not you could clarify it with egg whites. Check the seasoning and test the set; boil down or add a little gelatine if it does not set to a jelly.

Carve the cold meat into thin slices and serve surrounded by the chopped jelly. Or you can coat the sliced meat with the jelly, if you wish, or encase the whole loin in jelly by repeatedly spooning over layers of almost setting jelly.

** Stir-Fried Curried Pork and Vegetables

Quick-cooked dishes are always at a premium and this stir-fried dish, not very authentic but nevertheless delicious, has proved very popular. A block of creamed coconut will keep almost indefinitely on the shelf, even opened, and can add richness and savour to many dishes. The Chinese curry powder, not as hot as an Indian one, adds an oriental fragrance. As with all Chinese dishes, get everything prepared before you start, because when you cook, you work quickly.

Ingredients
4–6 people

¾–1 lb (350–450g) lean pork (shoulder or
    tenderloin)
1 large aubergine
1 red pepper
1 large onion
2 cloves garlic
2 tbs dry sherry
4 tbs stock
2 tbs soy sauce
1 tbs cornflour
3 tbs creamed coconut
4 tbs oil
1–2 tbs Sharwood's Chinese Curry
    Powder
2 teasp grated fresh root ginger
a squeeze lemon or lime juice
salt and pepper

Cut the aubergine into ⅜" (1cm) slices, then into chip-like strips, or use a food processor chip disc. Sprinkle with salt in a colander and leave under a plate and weight for about 30 minutes. Cut the meat into 1" (2–3 cm) narrow strips across the grain. Remove stalk and seeds and slice the pepper. Cut the onion in half lengthways, then in slices lengthways. Finely chop the garlic.

Mix the sherry, stock and soy sauce with the cornflour, and add to it the chopped up creamed coconut (it won't mix in).

Pat the aubergine dry on kitchen paper. Heat 2 tbs oil in a wok or large frying pan and, when smoking, toss in the aubergine and stir-fry for about 2 minutes. Remove and set aside. Add the onions and peppers and stir fry for 1 minute; set aside. Now add the remaining oil to the pan and, when smoking, toss in the meat and stir-fry for about 2 minutes until just browning. Sprinkle with the curry powder, garlic and grated ginger and cook for a further minute, taking care the curry powder does not burn (do it in two batches if your wok won't get hot enough to do quickly in one). Now stir the prepared coconut sauce and add to the pan with the aubergine, onion and pepper. Simmer gently until the sauce thickens, season, and squeeze over some lemon or lime juice. Serve at once with rice.

Vegetables

Broad Beans in Summer Savory or Parsley Sauce

Broad beans should be eaten at thumb nail size when their outer skins are still tender. A light sauce is made from their cooking water, thickened, enriched and flavoured with summer savory which is known as the bean herb because of its affinity to beans. This dish is good when you have had enough of just tossing them in butter but don't yet want to coat them in a true white sauce (much quicker too!).

Ingredients
4–6 people

1–1½ lb (450–675g) podded broad beans (3–4 lb (1.35–1.8kg) unpodded beans)
12 fl oz (350ml) cooking water from the beans
2–3 teasp potato flour, arrowroot or cornflour

2 fl oz (50ml) cream or milk
1–2 tbs finely chopped summer savory or parsley
1½ oz (35g) butter
salt and pepper

Throw the beans into just enough lightly salted boiling water to cover them and cook until just tender. Drain the beans into a colander, reserving the cooking liquid. Return 12 fl oz (350ml) of cooking liquid to the pan. Mix the potato flour with the cream or milk and stir it into the cooking liquid in the saucepan. Add the summer savory or parsley, the butter and light seasoning (remember the cooking liquid was salted) and simmer until thickened. Return the beans and stir to coat them all in the light sauce. Turn into a dish and serve at once or keep warm.

*   Kohl Rabi with Lemon and Thyme

This unusual looking vegetable has a delicate flavour and is used extensively in Germany but not so much here. It can be bought from good greengrocers or will grow quite easily in the garden, where it needs rich damp ground for quick growth, so that it is tender and not fibrous.

Ingredients
4–6 people

4–6 kohl rabi (approx 1½ lb (675g))
1 oz (25g) butter
chopped fresh lemon thyme or thyme
½ lemon
salt and pepper

Peel the kohl rabi, making sure you remove the outer fibrous layer of skin, before cutting into slices and then across into batons. Cook these in boiling salt water until just tender but still quite crisp, and then drain. Heat the butter in a saucepan or a wok or frying pan, and when hot throw in the kohl rabi and toss over high heat. Season and add chopped lemon thyme or thyme (or chives, parsley, summer savory or whatever herb you may feel like) and a good squeeze of lemon juice. Toss for a moment more before serving.

** Stir-Fried Courgettes with Pistou Sauce

Courgettes are a wonderfully versatile vegetable and Quick Jade Courgettes* are perhaps our favourite way of having them. Grated courgettes wrung out in a cloth, then sautéd in butter and finished with thick cream and tarragon, run it a close second, as does this recipe for Stir Fried Courgettes. It can be simply finished with onions and herbs or tossed with Pistou Sauce to make it robustly delicious.

We use the Chinese roll-cut to make courgette pieces with a wide surface area, which is desirable for stir-frying because they don't stick to the bottom of the pan as ordinary slices are rather inclined to do.

Ingredients
4–6 people

1–1½ lb (460–675g) fresh slim courgettes
2 tbs olive oil
3–4 tbs Pistou Sauce (*see page 129*)
1 finely chopped onion ⎫
1 finely chopped clove garlic ⎬ optional in place of Pistou Sauce
finely chopped fresh parsley, marjoram ⎪
   or basil and chives ⎭
salt and pepper

Wash or wipe the courgettes. Then, holding your knife at an angle, cut a ½" (1cm) slanting slice. Turn the courgettes through a quarter turn and, with your knife at the same angle, cut another slice, and so on. The pieces will come out as triangular wedges, quite large but with plenty of surface area to cook quickly.

Heat the oil in a wok or wide frying pan, and when very hot add the courgettes and stir-fry until browning. Add the onions and garlic, if used, and cook for a minute more before seasoning heavily and, off the stove, stirring in either the fresh chopped herbs or the Pistou Sauce. Serve at once while still crisp.

Sometimes I add ½ teasp potato flour or cornflour, mixed with 3–4 tbs of cream, and boil to thicken; then stir in the Pistou Sauce for a wonderfully creamy, rich flavoured version.

* *Good Food from Farthinghoe*

**   Cucumber in Old English Butter Sauce

Melted butter sauce was used in the past and much care was taken in its making. It is delicious with many vegetables such as broccoli, cabbage, carrots and cauliflower, but I give it here with cucumber, which is often overlooked as a cooked vegetable. Ridge cucumbers from the garden are prolific and have great sweetness and flavour. Tarragon has a close affinity with cucumber.

Ingredients
4–6 people

1–2 large or more smaller cucumbers
squeeze lemon juice
a little finely chopped tarragon, chives or
   chervil (optional)

Butter Sauce
2 oz (50g) butter
1 teasp plain flour
4 tbs milk
1 tbs cream (optional)
a squeeze of lemon juice (optional)
salt and pepper

Peel or half-peel the cucumbers if you wish, cut into quarters lengthways and remove any seeds if necessary; then cut across into 1″ (2–3 cm) segments. Toss into plenty of salted boiling water with a good squeeze of lemon juice added. Cook until just tender but still crisp, drain well and toss with the sauce, adding a little chopped herbs if you wish. Serve at once.

Butter Sauce. Place about ¾ oz (20g) butter, chopped up, in a saucepan and mix in the flour. Add the milk and bring to the simmer, shaking all the time; boil for a moment only to achieve a creamy sauce. Off the stove, add in the remaining butter in little bits, shake in, season and finish with a little thick cream if you like. A squeeze of lemon could also be added.

*   Stir-Fried Green Beans and Mushrooms

Cook fresh green beans alone or add in the mushrooms for a nice combination of flavours. Sometimes, to add extra colour and flavour, I toss in a handful of prawns just at the end of the cooking so that they don't get tough and hard. I like this dish, with its delicate soy and sherry flavour, cold as well as hot, and have successfully made it with mange-tout peas in place of the beans. You can, of course, just cook beans this way with oil, water and seasoning.

Ingredients
4–6 people

1 lb (450g) young French beans
2 cloves garlic
2 tbs oil
4 oz (100g) fresh sliced mushrooms
4 teasp light soy sauce
1 teasp sugar
1 tbs pale dry sherry
4 oz (100g) prawns (optional)

Flatten the garlic and remove its skin. Wash and dry the beans and snap them into finger lengths if they are too long. Heat the oil in a wok or large frying pan and fry the garlic until golden; discard. Add the beans to the pan and stir-fry for 1–2 minutes before adding the mushrooms and tossing and frying for a further 1–2 minutes. Now add soy and sugar and cook 2 minutes longer. Add the sherry, reduce the heat and cook until the beans are crisply tender, stirring from time to time (adding prawns at this stage if desired). Serve at once or leave until cold.

* French Beans à la Crème

One of my favourite ways of serving French beans, though they must be served the moment they are ready. It's not a dish you can do for too many because the cream stews rather than reducing. Baby beans are best without garlic, but the garlic gives a wonderful flavour to slightly more mature beans. If you are careful and drain them well, you can even use frozen beans.

Ingredients
4–6 people

1–1½ lbs (450–675g) French beans
2 oz (50g) butter
1 clove garlic (optional)
2–3 tbs double cream
½ lemon (optional)
salt and pepper

Cook the beans in plenty of boiling salted water until just tender. Drain and refresh under the cold tap to set the colour. Drain well. Heat the chopped-up butter in a wide pan until sizzling and add the finely chopped garlic (if used) and well drained beans. Toss over high heat until the beans are heated through and buttery and the moisture has all gone. Add the cream and seasoning and continue to toss over high heat until the cream reduces, leaving the beans coated in a creamy sauce. Squeeze over a little lemon juice (optional) and serve at once.

✻ French Bean Salad

Pick finger-length French beans whilst tender and slim, cook until *croquant*, and dress with this dressing while they are still warm. Serve plain or add diced ham, flaked tuna, cooked cubed potato and hard-boiled egg for a lovely summer lunch.

Ingredients

4–6 people	*25 people*
1–1½ lb (450–675g) crisp and tender French beans	6–7 lb (2.7–3.2kg) crisp and tender French beans
salt	salt

Dressing	*Dressing*
1 tbs finely chopped shallot	4 tbs finely chopped shallot
1 teasp Dijon mustard	1 tbs Dijon mustard
1 tbs wine, basil, shallot or herb vinegar	3 tbs wine, basil, shallot or herb vinegar
1 teasp lemon juice	1 tbs lemon juice
2 tbs fruity olive oil	6–8 tbs fruity olive oil
3 tbs cream	5 fl oz (150ml) cream
a little finely chopped summer savory, parsley or coriander	2–3 tbs finely chopped summer savory, parsley or coriander
salt and pepper.	salt and pepper

Top and tail the beans and snap in two if necessary.

Bring a large saucepan of water to the boil and salt heavily (about 1 tablespoon for each 2 pints (1.2l) of water). Toss in the beans and cook, uncovered, until just tender but still with some snap. Drain and refresh under the cold tap for about 10 seconds to arrest the cooking, and wash off the excess salt which will have kept them green and speeded the cooking. Drain thoroughly and dress while still warm.

Dressing. Stir the shallot, mustard, salt and pepper, vinegar and lemon juice together (in the salad bowl). Then trickle in the oil and cream whilst stirring hard to make a thick dressing. Stir in the chopped herbs and beans and toss well.

Variation for 25 people. You will probably need to cook the beans in several batches.

Salt and Sesame Glazed Potatoes

Unpeeled baby potatoes are boiled and finished in a salt glaze. They are lovely served just like that, but if you want you can toss them in oil or butter and sesame seeds for an unusual crunchy finish. Serve them on their own with cream cheese and chives for a good but very simple supper dish.

Ingredients
4–6 people

1½–2 lb (675–900g) baby new potatoes
1–2 tbs oil or 1 oz (25g) butter
1–1½ tbs sesame seeds
¼ teasp black peppercorns
sea-salt

Place the scrubbed but unpeeled potatoes in a wide pan and cover with boiling water. Cook until nearly tender, then drain away all but a little water. Add 1 teasp additional salt and continue to boil fast, shaking the pan, until all the water has evaporated and the potatoes are covered in a whitish bloom of salt.

Crush the peppercorns roughly in a mortar. Remove the potatoes, wipe out the pan and add the oil or butter. When it is hot, return the potatoes, sprinkle with the sesame seeds and crushed black pepper and toss over high heat until the sesame seeds have toasted a little and the potatoes are coated in them. Serve at once or keep warm, uncovered, until ready to serve.

* Potato Salad with Walnut Oil and Lovage

Walnut oil has a powerful flavour and lovage, if used with a heavy hand, can overwhelm a dish. Here they are both used with discretion on a warm potato salad with shallot and bacon dice, and they make a robust, earthy dish which is good with a plate of cold meat in summer. With more bacon and some lightly hard-boiled eggs it also makes an excellent simple lunch or supper dish.

Ingredients
4–6 people

2 lb (900g) new (or middle aged!)
   potatoes
2–3 oz (50–75g) diced bacon, preferably
   smoked and cut thick
6–8 tbs walnut oil
1–2 finely chopped shallots or a mild
   onion
3–5 tbs wine vinegar

1 teasp castor sugar
1 teasp finely chopped fresh or a pinch
   dried lovage (or use rather more
   chopped celery leaf)
plenty of finely chopped chives
3–4 tbs yoghurt or cream
salt and pepper

Boil the potatoes in their skins until just done. Slice or dice generously into a bowl and season fairly lavishly. Fry the bacon in the walnut oil until just brown before adding the shallot for a moment or two to soften a little. Now add the vinegar to the frying pan with the sugar and stir well. Pour this dressing over the potatoes and add the lovage, chives and yoghurt or cream. Fold and stir all together and serve while still a little warm.

*   Cheesy Potatoes

I turn to this when I want a nice simple lunch and there is not much around from which to make it. With good potatoes and fresh herbs it makes a tasty dish.

Ingredients
4–6 people

2 lb (900g) even-sized potatoes
fresh lemon thyme, thyme or dried
   Italian seasoning
plenty of scissored chives

Sauce
1 oz (25g) butter
1 tbs oil
1 large onion
14 oz (400g) tin tomatoes (4–8 fresh
   tomatoes)
2 fl oz (50ml) cream
4–6 oz (100–175g) grated strong cheese
salt and pepper

Boil the unpeeled potatoes in salted water until they are just cooked, then peel them and cut into quarters or thick slices. Lay them in a buttered gratin dish, scatter with chopped lemon thyme, thyme, or Italian seasoning, pour over the sauce, sprinkle heavily with scissored chives and serve.

Sauce. Heat the butter and oil and cook the chopped onion until golden and tender. Add the drained and roughly chopped tinned tomatoes (or peeled fresh tomatoes) and fry for about 5 minutes until tender and sauce-like. Stir in the cream, cheese and plenty of seasoning, heat gently, stirring, until the cheese has just melted, and pour over the potatoes.

Puddings

F **   Gooseberry Fool

Sharp gooseberries make one of the best of fools. Careful cooking of the fruit produces the finest flavour, so cook it gently in a jar in water or a double boiler (not aluminium) if you have time. I prefer not to purée some of the gooseberries, which provides a more interesting texture, and sometimes I add a head or two of elderflower or 1–2 rose geranium leaves to the gooseberries while they cook for a more complex flavour.

Ingredients
4–6 people

1½ lb (675g) green gooseberries
1–2 heads elderflower or 1–2 rose
   geranium leaves (optional)
4–6 oz (100–175g) sugar or to taste
½ pt (300ml) double cream

Place the topped and tailed gooseberries and the elderflowers or rose geranium leaves (if used) in a jar with 2 tbs cold water and about 3 oz (75g) of the sugar. Stand the jar in a deep pan of boiling water to come within 1 inch (3cm) or so of the top of the jar and simmer the water until the fruit is tender. Strain into a sieve (you probably won't need the juice), then set one third of the gooseberries aside, roughly crushed, to fold in later. Purée the remainder, sieve, then sweeten further to taste. Cool.

Whip the cream until fairly stiff and fold in the cold fruit purée and the remaining roughly crushed gooseberries. Turn into a serving dish and chill for 12–24 hours. Serve with sponge fingers or Little Almond Finger Biscuits. (*see page 170.*)

P ✳✳   Gooseberries in Elderflower Syrup

Gooseberries, blanched and carefully cooked so that they keep their colour and shape, are delicious in an elderflower-flavoured syrup. Once elderflowers are over you could flavour the syrup with rose geranium leaves.

Ingredients
4–6 people

1 lb (450g) green gooseberries
6–8 oz (175–225g) sugar
8 fl oz (225ml) water
1–2 heads elderflower

Top and tail the gooseberries and throw them into a pan of boiling water, or pour a kettle of boiling water over them. Drain and refresh under the cold tap to set the colour.

Prepare a syrup by dissolving the sugar in the water, and when completely dissolved boil for 1–2 minutes. Add the gooseberries to the syrup and cook exceeding slowly and carefully until just tender but still whole. Remove the gooseberries to a serving dish, add the elderflower head to the syrup and boil for a few minutes until you have a well flavoured thick syrup. Strain this through a fine sieve over the gooseberries and leave until cold or, better still, till the next day for the flavours to blend.

F ** Blackcurrant Mousse

A fresh fruity mousse is always popular. This one can be made with fresh blackcurrants, in which case include a few of their leaves for flavour while they cook, or from frozen fruit at any time of year, in which case a stick of cinnamon can be cooked with them. The finished mousse freezes well.

Ingredients

4–6 people	*25 people*
12 oz (350g) blackcurrants	3 lb (1.35kg) blackcurrants
6 oz (175g) sugar	1¼ lb (550g) sugar
a few blackcurrant leaves (optional) or 1 stick cinnamon	6–8 blackcurrant leaves or 2 sticks cinnamon (optional)
2 tbs *liqueur de cassis* (optional)	6–8 tbs *liqueur de cassis* (optional)
2½ teasp gelatine	3 tbs and 1 teasp gelatine
2 tbs cold water	8 tbs cold water
8 fl oz (225ml) whipping cream	1¾ pts (1l) whipping cream
3 egg whites	12 egg whites
whipped cream and frosted blackcurrants to decorate (optional)	

Place the blackcurrants, sugar, leaves or cinnamon stick in a saucepan with a little water. Cook until tender, then remove leaves or cinnamon and purée and sieve the blackcurrants. Stir in *cassis* if used. Sprinkle the gelatine on to the cold water in a small bowl and soak for several minutes; then stand the bowl in a pan of hot water until the gelatine has completely melted. Add to the blackcurrants and chill until completely cold but not yet setting. Whip the cream until it just holds its shape and fold in, followed by the egg whites whipped until they just hold a peak. Turn into a 1½ pt (900ml) soufflé dish and chill or freeze. Decorate with whipped cream and frosted blackcurrants, if you wish.

Frosted Blackcurrants. Lightly whip a white of egg until mousse-like and dip small bunches into it, coating evenly. Then dip into castor sugar till coated all over, shake off excess and leave to dry on a rack.

Variation for 25 people. You will need 3 × 2 pt (1.2l) bowls to hold the mousse.

F ** Pavlova

Anyone who enjoys fresh summer fruits will find the soft marshmallow meringue of a pavlova the perfect foil for their sharp-sweet flavour, the cornflour and vinegar changing the texture of the meringue from the classic crisp dry finish. Once cooked, the pavlova is best served crisp side down, so that it does not stick to the serving dish, with the fruit piled all over the soft upper surface. Don't worry if it cracks. Pineapple, passion fruit, kiwi fruit, mango, peaches, apricots or banana and ginger can all be used to fill a pavlova, but to me nothing beats the tart freshness of summer soft fruit.

Ingredients
4–6 people

3 egg whites (at room temperature)
6 oz (175g) castor sugar
1 teasp cornflour
½–1 teasp vanilla essence
¾ teasp vinegar

Filling
¾–1 lb (350–450g) raspberries or
   strawberries
½ pt (300ml) double cream
a little vanilla sugar
1 or 2 drops vanilla essence

Mark an 8" (20cm) circle on Bakewell paper or tinfoil, grease lightly and sprinkle with flour; shake off the excess. Whisk the egg whites in a deep bowl until just holding a peak. Gradually whisk in one-third of the sugar, then keep whisking until the mixture is very stiff and shiny. Fold in the remaining sugar and finally the vanilla essence, sifted cornflour and vinegar. Spoon on to the prepared paper on a baking sheet, forming the edges higher than the middle. Bake in a slow oven (275–300°F/150°C/Gas 2) for about 1 hour, until the top is a pale golden brown but the middle is soft and marshmallowy. Turn upside down on to a serving dish and peel off the paper. Leave until cold.

Filling. Whip the cream and sweeten lightly with vanilla sugar, or castor sugar, and a drop or two of vanilla essence. Fold most of the fruit, halved or quartered if large, into the cream, keeping back some to decorate. Pile the filling on to the pavlova and decorate. reserved fruit.

**   Soufflé Glacé

The recipe for this simply made frozen soufflé can be adapted to practically any liqueur.

Ingredients
4–6 people

3 egg yolks
2 eggs
4 oz (100g) castor sugar
2–3 tbs Grand Marnier, rum or almost
   any other liqueur

8 fl oz (225ml) whipping cream
a little cocoa and icing sugar or drinking
   chocolate

Tie a band of doubled greaseproof or Bakewell paper round a 1 pt (600ml) soufflé dish to come 2" (5cm) above the rim.

Put the eggs, yolks and sugar in a bowl, placed over a pan of hot water; the water should not touch the bowl and the water should not boil. Whisk the mixture over heat until thick, pale and forming 'the ribbon' when dropping off the whisk. Remove from the heat and continue whisking (less vigorously) until cold, standing the bowl in iced water to speed this up. Whip the cream until stiff, whisking in the Grand Marnier, then fold the two mixtures together gently. Turn into prepared soufflé dish and freeze for a minimum of about 8 hours.

To Serve. Serve frozen. It may need mellowing in the fridge for a while before serving. Remove the greaseproof paper carefully and sprinkle the top with a little cocoa and icing sugar mixed, or drinking chocolate, to make it look like a hot browned soufflé.

155

*** Little Strawberry Tartlets with Almond Pastry

Crisp almond pastry shells and a cream cheese filling, topped with strawberries, raspberries or *fraises de bois*, make an elegant and delightful summer dessert. Of course, you can always make a large tart if you find little ones too fiddly.

Ingredients
12 tartlets

Almond Pastry
5 oz (150g) plain flour
2 oz (50g) ground almonds
2 oz (50g) icing sugar
4 oz (100g) soft butter
2 egg yolks
pinch salt

**about 2 lb (900g) strawberries,
  raspberries, *fraises de bois* or other
  fruit**
redcurrant glaze

Cream Cheese Filling
1 oz (25g) butter
**8 oz (225g) unsalted cream cheese (such
  as Eden Vale Somerset soft cream
  cheese)**
1 oz (25g) vanilla sugar
a few drops vanilla essence
4–6 fl oz (100–175ml) double cream

Almond Pastry. Sift the flour on to a large board or table top and sprinkle over the ground almonds. Make a well in the middle and place the soft butter, yolks, sugar and salt in the well. Pinch and mix these together, without the flour, with your finger tips, and when amalgamated draw in the flour to make a paste. Knead a little and form into a flat disc. Alternatively, place the well-softened butter, sifted icing sugar and yolks in the food processor and process together briefly until amalgamated; then add the sifted flour, salt and ground almonds and process briefly. Scrape round the bowl, process again until all is incorporated, turn out on to a floured board and knead briefly into a flat disc. Rest the floured pastry, whichever way it's made, in a plastic bag in the fridge for 1–2 hours.

Let the pastry soften a little in the kitchen so that it will roll easily, then roll and line 12 little tartlet tins (or a 9″ (24cm) tart tin if you prefer). Prick the base and line with tinfoil and baking beans. Bake in a hot oven (400°F/200°C/Gas 7) for 5–8 minutes. Once set, remove the tinfoil and beans and continue to cook in a moderately hot oven (375°F/190°C/Gas 5) for 10 minutes or so until an even golden colour all over and glistening with butter bubbles. Remove from the tins and cool on a wire rack.

Cream Cheese Filling. Cream or process the butter until soft, add the cream cheese, vanilla sugar, vanilla essence and, when smooth, add enough double cream to make a soft mixture.

To Assemble. Hull the strawberries, dividing any large ones. Place a spoonful of cream cheese filling in each pastry shell and arrange the strawberries on top. You can glaze the strawberries with a little red currant glaze, if you wish (*see page 211*).

✳✳   Rose Petal Ice Cream

I love ice creams and sorbets and, having already included a rose petal sorbet in my previous book, was intrigued by the idea of a rose petal ice cream. I experimented using the fragrant red rose 'Mr Lincoln', and I find this velvety smooth ice cream quite delicious with its wonderful fragrance of roses.

Ingredients
4–6 people
approx 1¼ pts (700ml)

12 fl oz (300ml) milk or single cream
1 strip lemon rind
1 egg
2 egg yolks
6–7 oz (175–200g) castor sugar
good handful rose petals (3–4 roses fully
    open but *not* past their best)
8 fl oz (225ml) whipping cream

Heat the milk with a strip of lemon rind and leave to infuse, covered, for a few minutes. Whisk the egg and yolks with the sugar until thick and pale, then gradually whisk in the strained milk. Return to the stove in a heavy pan and cook gently, stirring, until the custard thickens a little and coats the back of a wooden spoon. Do not let the mixture boil or the eggs will curdle. You can, if you like, cook the mixture in a double boiler, but not in aluminium, which discolours egg yolk mixture, nor in pyrex in which custards never seem to thicken. Pour the custard over the picked-over and clean but unwashed rose petals, cover, and leave until cold or overnight.

Strain the custard, pressing the rose petals well before discarding. Add the lightly whipped cream and freeze the mixture. This takes about 25 minutes in an ice cream maker that freezes and churns simultaneously. Alternatively, you can turn the mixture into a shallow container (tinfoil is good as it conducts cold well) and freeze, stirring the sides to the middle once or twice as it freezes. Then process the near-frozen mixture in the food processor or whisk hard until absolutely smooth.

Freeze until required, and mellow in the fridge for about 20–30 minutes before serving with little biscuits.

$\mathcal{P}$ ✳✳✳   Vacherin

Although the usual definition of a vacherin is a meringue (or almond paste) basket or container filled with cream, ice cream or fruit, you will find that in some French restaurants they serve a vacherin of layered ice cream and meringue rounds. For a special occasion, or when you want a pudding prepared and ready in the freezer, this looks and tastes spectacular. If you use an electric ice-cream maker, or if you keep containers of Honey Ice Cream and Raspberry Sorbet (both excellent on their own) in the freezer, the vacherin's construction becomes much simpler.

Ingredients
6–8 people

Meringue Rounds
3 egg-whites
6 oz (175g) castor sugar
½ teasp lemon juice
pinch salt

Honey Ice Cream
5 oz (125g) honey
½ pt (300ml) milk
3 egg yolks
¼ pt (150ml) double cream

Raspberry Sorbet
8 oz (225g) raspberries
6 oz (175g) sugar
½ pt (300ml) water
1 lemon

or use the Raspberry Sorbet recipe (*see page 000*)

To Finish
⅓ pt (200ml) whipping cream

Meringue Rounds. Place the egg whites and salt in a deep bowl and whisk until the whites just hold a peak. Beat in the lemon juice and the sugar, a tablespoonful at a time, until you have added about 4 oz (100g) and the mixture is very stiff and glossy. Fold in the remaining sugar and spread the meringue as evenly and smoothly as possible on two 9″ (24cm) circles on Bakewell paper (flan rings can be used to keep the meringue in shape). Bake the meringue in a very slow oven (250°F/130°C/Gas 1) for 1–2 hours, then, if crisp, remove flan rings if used, invert on to racks and peel off paper. Return to the oven to crispen the base for a few minutes if necessary. Cool and store in an airtight tin if not using at once.

Honey Ice Cream. Heat the honey and milk together, but do not let them get too hot or the acidity in the honey will curdle the milk. Whisk the yolks until thick and pale, then whisk in the cream. Gradually, whisking all the time, pour on the hot honey and milk. Place over a saucepan of hot, not boiling, water (or in a very heavy pan) and cook the custard gently, stirring, until the yolks thicken and coat the back of a spoon, but *do not boil*. Cool, and freeze the mixture in a shallow dish or tinfoil trays. Stir in the edges from time to time, and when stiff beat well or process in the food processor until smooth. Re-freeze until spreadable but firm before assembling. Or freeze in an ice cream maker.

Raspberry Sorbet. Place the sugar and water in a saucepan and heat gently, stirring, until the sugar has completely dissolved; then turn up the heat and boil fast without stirring for 5 minutes. Cool. Purée or process the raspberries, add the syrup and sieve. Add lemon juice to taste and freeze the mixture, stirring in the edges from time to time. When firm, beat well or process until smooth. Re-freeze until spreadable but firm before assembling. Or freeze in an ice cream maker.

To Assemble and Finish. Place one meringue round on a serving dish inside a 9" (24cm) baseless removable-base cake tin. Spread the Honey Ice Cream in an even layer. Freeze until firm, then spread with the Raspberry Sorbet. Cover with the remaining meringue round and freeze until firm. Remove the cake ring carefully. Whip the cream and place in a piping bag with a rose nozzle. Pipe stars of cream all round the side of the Vacherin. Keep the Vacherin in the freezer, but mellow in the fridge for ½–¾ hour before serving, cut like a cake.

*   Raspberry Sorbet

Fresh fruit sorbets are nearly always my choice at the end of a meal in a French restaurant. I love the way Madame reels off the *parfums* in a sing-song chant: 'vanille-chocolat-fraise-framboise' before adding the inevitable crème caramel! But I have only just discovered how easy the very best of these rich fruity sorbets are to prepare. I used to make the raspberry sorbet I have used in the Vacherin. It makes an excellent sorbet, and of course yields rather more than the recipe below, but to make a superlative simple sorbet try this one.

Ingredients
1 pt (600ml) sorbet

1 lb (450g) raspberries
5 oz (125g) castor sugar
½–1 lemon

Purée and sieve the raspberries; this is most quickly done in a food processor, followed by a soup mouli with a fine plate, or by using a large sieve. Add the sugar (it's usually about ⅓ of the weight of fruit purée), whisk and stir until the sugar has dissolved, and add just enough lemon juice to make the flavour sharp and clear. Freeze and beat in the normal way. I usually turn the mixture into shallow tinfoil containers to freeze, stirring in the sides once as they freeze, until the mixture is fairly firmly frozen; then process in the food processor until light, smooth and without any crystals. Pack into a bowl or container and refreeze until ready to use.

It is most important to mellow sorbets for about ½–1 hour in the fridge before serving.

The electric ice-cream makers which beat and freeze the mixture, although expensive, do produce superb ice-creams and sorbets. With this recipe you could be eating a fresh sorbet just over ½ hour after picking the fruit.

Miscellaneous

* Vinaigrette Dressing and Variations

Vinaigrettes are used throughout the year, but this seems as good a moment as any to expound the basic recipe and expand on a few variations. I wholeheartedly believe that we should eat a salad, or raw vegetables of some sort, every day for their vitamins and living vitality; we should also use as much unrefined, expeller or cold pressed oil as we can afford, to provide the lecithin (this helps to remove polyunsaturate fats), vitamins and minerals which our bodies need. One of my real hates is 'de-odorised edible oil' coming from unspecified sources and subjected to unimaginable processes.

Many oils make good dressings. Olive oil is richly flavoured and often gives just that authentic taste to a dish, especially if it's from the Mediterranean. Walnut, hazelnut and almond are all lovely but very strongly flavoured, and need diluting with a lighter oil like safflower or sunflower, which is especially healthy, full of polyunsaturates and on the increase, if those nodding golden fields of France are anything to go by. Peanut or groundnut oil, *arachide* in France, is a steady standby. I can pass corn oil and soya oil by, but a dash of sesame or an oil flavoured with something like basil adds variety and flavour to a dish.

Then there is a wide choice of vinegars. Avoid malt vinegar and anything powerful or coarse, and use red or white wine vinegar or those delicious ones flavoured with tarragon, basil, mint or even rose petal. If you search you will find cider or sherry vinegar (I have my own brew of this, the basis formed by a very old vinegar I was given in Jerez), but I doubt whether you can buy (though you could make) gooseberry, rhubarb or primrose vinegar, though a peck or even half a peck of primroses might be a bit hard to come by!

Mustards also add variety to your dressing, and there are plenty of interesting ones on the market from the classic, powerful English mustard to sharp Dijon or those mild sweet German and Scandinavian varieties. They can be smooth or grainy, herbed or made with ale or wine or with peppercorns added, and all of them have something interesting to offer to give character to your dressings.

For salt read sea-salt in all my recipes (*see page 14*).

In all my cooking I use a variety of freshly ground peppers. The black peppercorn or the rather stronger white one (the same peppercorn but with the outer skin rubbed off) are the standards, but I also used dried green peppercorns. Soft green peppercorns from brine are rather different, being added whole or chopped to add texture and flavour to dishes.

Next consider all the other ingredients which can be included like herbs, sugar, cream, cheese, capers, anchovy—the list is endless, and you will realise that there is no reason ever to have a boring salad dressing. It is also fun deciding just which herb vinegar or ingredient will bring out the best or will most complement a salad. Elsewhere in the book you will find other recipes for salad dressings which are not based on a vinaigrette.

Basic Vinaigrette Dressing

Ingredients
enough for a salad for 4–6 people

½ **teasp Dijon mustard**
1 **tbs wine vinegar**
3 **tbs olive, groundnut or other oil**
salt and pepper

Either make your dressing in the bottom of your salad bowl (a wooden bowl always seems to help the dressing to emulsify easily) or shake up in a tightly sealed jar. Place ¼ teasp salt and several grinds of pepper in the salad bowl with the mustard. Add the vinegar, stir well until the salt dissolves (it will not dissolve easily in oil) and then gradually add the oil, stirring hard all the time. The mustard helps the dressing to 'take' and become thickly emulsified. Cross your salad servers in the bowl and lay the salad on top of them. When ready to serve, toss all together until every leaf glistens with dressing. Dressing mixed in quantity in a jar will keep for a day or two but tends to taste stale if kept for long.

Vinaigrette Dressings Variations

Walnut Oil Dressing. Walnut oil is delicious but very strongly flavoured. I like to mix it half-and-half with a light oil (sunflower, safflower or ground nut) and make as for Vinaigrette Dressing.

Mustard Dressing. Make as Vinaigrette Dressing, but increase the mustard up to 2 teaspoons and be rather heavy handed with the salt and pepper. This gives you the thick, strong-tasting dressing you sometimes get in France.

Sweet Dressing. 2–3 teaspoons of castor sugar stirred in well with the salt and vinegar give a sweet dressing which many people appreciate.

Shallot Dressing. Add 1–2 tbs very finely chopped shallot to the Vinaigrette Dressing.

Cream Dressing. 1–2 tbs thick cream and a shake of Worcester sauce are added to the Vinaigrette Dressing.

* Whipped Cream Dressing

This is very good with crisp quartered lettuce hearts or with a slightly bitter endive or marigold leaf salad. You can use summer or winter savory for flavour and in place of pepper, as they used to do when pepper was expensive, for savory is quite peppery. Or you can use a little chopped chives or dill or no herb at all, in which case add pepper.

Ingredients
Dressing for a salad for 4–6 people

1½ teasp castor sugar
2 teasp finely scissored winter or summer
    savory (optional)
1 tbs lemon juice
5 tbs whipping cream
good pinch salt
pepper (if necessary)

Mix the sugar, savory, salt and lemon juice, and stir until the sugar and salt dissolve. Then add the cream and whip until light and airy but barely holding its shape. Either keep the dressing fairly flowing and toss the salad in it or, with crisp quartered lettuce hearts, serve the salad on individual plates with a good blob of thick dressing on top.

** Thorpe Mandeville Old English Boiled Dressing

Before olive and other oils found their way so easily to this country, our salads were dressed with a variety of cream dressings, either cooked like a custard or thickened with mashed hard-boiled egg yolks or boiled potato. They were the fore-runners and inspiration of Mr Heinz's perennially popular salad dressing, but have otherwise been rather neglected in favour of vinaigrettes and mayonnaise. On my assumption that we all eat salads a great deal and need many ways of varying them, this dressing, which will keep in the fridge for days, is well worth trying. I have it on a card, bordered in heavy black because of Queen Victoria's death, amongst my great-great-grandmother's manuscript recipes. It came from Thorpe Mandeville, a village close to Farthinghoe but hundreds of miles from great-great-granny who lived in Scotland.

Ingredients

2 eggs
1 tbs made English mustard (actually I
    find this quantity too strong and use
    only 1–2 teasp)
1 tbs sugar
3 tbs wine vinegar
cayenne pepper
¾–1 teasp salt
8 fl oz (225ml) milk
1 oz (25g) butter

Break the eggs into a bowl which can be set over a pan of water. Add the mustard, sugar, wine vinegar, cayenne pepper and salt. Beat in well, then whisk in the milk (you can heat the milk to boiling point before whisking it in if you wish to speed things up). Set the bowl over a pan of water and heat, stirring, until the mixture thickens and coats the back of a spoon thickly. Take off the heat and whisk in the butter. Leave to cool and thicken before using with mixed salads or potato salads.

*   Potted Cheese with Herbs

I find it so useful to be able to turn a tired or deep-frozen bit of cheddar into something delectable for the cheese board. Cheddar Cheese with Walnuts* is a firm winter favourite, but in summer I prefer to pot up my Cheddar with herbs and white wine. Personally I like to serve this soon after it is made, soft and creamy, but of course it will keep in the fridge for a week or so if you wish. In winter, or if you have no fresh herbs, use chopped celery leaves from the top of the sticks or Florence fennel fronds; celery sticks or Florence fennel wedges are good served with this anyway. Chopped watercress can be used too, especially if it's quite strong and peppery, so even without fresh herbs or a garden you can still make this recipe.

Ingredients
Makes about 1¼ lb (550g)

12 oz (350g) mature Cheddar, Leicester or
   Gloucester cheese
4 oz (100g) butter
6 tbs dry white wine
4–5 tbs chopped fresh herbs (chives,
   summer savory, lemon thyme, fennel,
   celery leaf or rocket)
½ teasp paprika

Cream the butter really well until it is very soft and creamy so that it can absorb the wine. Grate the cheese and cream it in with the butter, ideally in a food processor. Warm the wine a little (it combines with the butter and cheese more easily if slightly warm) and gradually beat it in with the herbs and paprika to taste. Mound on to a cheese board or pack into a pot. I sometimes press it into a muslin-lined mould (you could use a *petit coeur à la crème* mould for this) to turn out like a little sand-castle or heart. You can coat with chopped herbs, coarsely crushed peppercorns, halved black olives or paprika, if you wish.

𝒫 ✳✳   Mixed Pickled Vegetables

When tender young vegetables are offered cheaply in the shops or your garden is producing prolifically, you may like to prepare a jar or two of pickled vegetables. I find them very useful to dig out of their jar to serve as part of a mixed hors d'oeuvre or as something colourful to go with a pâté or with salami. It is useful to be able to rustle up an attractive plateful without spending any time or getting involved with any cooking.

In case your nose is wrinkling at the thought of those mouth-searing, throat-burning, voice-stopping pickles, bathed in malt vinegar and often found in pubs, don't worry! I am thinking of something more along the lines of the gloriously attractive jars of mixed baby vegetables, preserved in wine vinegar and olive oil, which you see in Italian shops, though ours probably won't come out in such a carefully arranged pattern! They don't take long to make, though the job must be spread over two days to allow for brining. They can be eaten within a week, though longer will allow the flavours to blend and soften, but will keep, opened, for 6–9 months in the fridge or longer unopened on the shelf. You can use whatever mixture of vegetables you like, and the quantity is equally flexible.

Ingredients
4 large jars approx

some or all of the following

1 bunch carrots
1 cucumber
¾–1 lb (350–450g) French beans
1 cauliflower
1 red pepper
1 green pepper
10–12 little pickling onions
1 head Florence fennel

Brine
for each 1 lb prepared vegetables

2 oz (50g) sea salt
1 pt (600ml) water
sprigs fresh marjoram and parsley
   (optional)

Spiced Vinegar
1 pt (600ml) white wine vinegar
2 cloves garlic
12 peppercorns
3 cardamom seeds
2–3 sprigs fresh or ¼ teasp dried
   marjoram
1–2 teasp sugar
1 head of dill or ½ teasp seeds
6–8 parsley stalks
3 lovage leaves
1 bay leaf

up to 3 pts (1.7l) olive oil or mixed oils

Prepare the vegetables by scrubbing or peeling the carrots; split those as thick as your thumb into four lengthways but leave the babies whole. Cut the cucumber into finger lengths, then lengthways into six segments. Top and tail the beans. Break the cauliflower into small florets. Cut the peppers in half, discard pips and stalks and cut into lengthways strips. Peel any onions, keeping the little ones whole, but the larger ones need cutting in half (or sometimes I use the mild purple onion Brunswick and cut them into thick rounds). Florence fennel needs cutting into lengthways strips.

Brine. Weigh the prepared vegetables and mix up brine at the rate of 2 oz (50g) salt and 1 pt (600ml) water to each 1 lb vegetables. Place the vegetables in a glass or china bowl and cover with brine, topping with a plate to keep the vegetables submerged. Leave in the brine for only 12–24 hours or they will be very salty. They must be brined to draw water out of them, otherwise they would dilute the oil and vinegar so much that it would not preserve them.

Spiced Vinegar. Prepare the spiced vinegar by putting all the flavourings (which you can vary if you wish) and the vinegar in a covered pan and bringing to the boil; leave, covered, until cold. Any spiced vinegar you do not use can be used for salad dressing or to flavour dishes.

Drain the vegetables from the brine (they will taste pretty salty at this stage) and rinse well in cold water. Drain well again and pack tightly and attractively into clean, wide-mouthed jars, adding fresh marjoram and parsley sprigs as you go and distributing the spices from the vinegar between the jars if you wish. Whisk 1 part spiced vinegar with 2 parts oil (all olive oil gives the best flavour, but a mixture of olive and a light oil such as sunflower or safflower is good and cheaper), and pour over the vegetables to cover by one inch. Make sure you get all the air-pockets out of the jars (slip a skewer down inside the jars to release them, and turn the jars this way and that). If you have not used glass preserving jars with rubber and glass lids, cover closely with Bakewell paper and tie down (screw-on lids lined with plastic can also be used).

Keep for a few days, or preferably longer, for the vegetables to mellow. To serve, remove some of the vegetables. They can be eaten as they are with an apéritif, or you can pour a little of the mixed dressing over them, adding chopped herbs to make a salad. Add more oil to the jar if necessary so that the vegetables are always covered by an inch of oil. When your jar is empty, any left-over oil and vinegar can be added judiciously to dressings so that there is no waste of precious oil.

Jam Making

When the shops or our garden are full of strawberries, raspberries, currants and gooseberries, then we know the jam season is upon us. Even a few jars of home-made jam or jelly are a treat and really don't take very long to make.

To make good fresh-tasting and bright-coloured jam, there are several points worth knowing. First, the fruit must be in good condition and, although you can use small and misshapen fruit, it should not be mouldy or too ripe. Secondly, jam only sets and keeps well when it has the right balance of fruit acid, pectin (a natural jell-ing substance) and sugar. The pectin must be drawn out of the fruit in the presence of acid by cooking; then, when it has been fully released and the fruit is soft, the right proportion of sugar is added and the jam boiled to reach a set. If everything is right this should happen very quickly, giving a bright fresh jam. Some fruits have plenty of both acid and pectin, and with these there is no problem. Others may be low in one or the other, and then we have to add it. Acid can be added in the form of lemon juice or tartaric or citric acid (obtainable from chemists), or by including a fruit high in acid such as red or black currant, crab or cooking apple or gooseberries, which are all also high in pectin too. Pectin can be increased by

166

mixing fruits that are low in pectin with those that are high, such as strawberry with red currant and blackberry with apple, or you can add shredded lemon, orange or lime pith to your stewing fruit, as they are also high in pectin. Alternatively, you can add a commercial pectin like Certo to get a set, but this seems to give a blander, more cloying flavour.

All the recipes I have included have taken these facts into account, so that you should get a really good jam. But do remember that, if the fruit is wet on picking, or if it has been a very wet year so that the fruit is watery in content, it needs boiling for longer to evaporate some water, or there won't be enough sugar in the jam to keep it. There should be about 60% sugar in jam to keep it well, which is roughly 3 lb (1.35kg) sugar in 5 lb (2.25kg) of finished jam. Less than this and the jam may grow mould or ferment; more and it will start to crystallise.

** Gooseberry and Elderflower Jelly

A gooseberry jelly, lightly flavoured with elderflower, is one of the most delicious jellies imaginable. The only problem is catching the elderflowers, for their season is quite short, lasting roughly from mid-May to mid-June, but it does vary from year to year and depending on where you live. You can turn the discarded gooseberry pulp into gooseberry cheese by following the Quince Cheese recipe (*see page 221*). It's delicious, keeps for ages, and nothing is wasted.

Ingredients
approx 2½ lb (1.15kg)

2 lb (900g) gooseberries
1 pt (600ml) water
granulated sugar
2–3 heads elderflower

There is no need to top and tail the gooseberries. Place in a pan with the water and simmer very gently until absolutely tender. I prefer to do this in a very low oven (bottom Aga) for about 3 hours, because in this way you get a wonderful amber jelly and more flavour. Turn the mixture into a jelly bag and leave to drain without squeezing. Measure the juice; you should have about 1¼ pts (750ml), and to each pint (600ml) of juice take 1 lb (450g) sugar. Place the sugar and juice in a jam pan, warm, and stir to dissolve the sugar. Tie the elderflowers in muslin and add to the jelly once the sugar has dissolved completely. Boil very fast for about 3 minutes, then test on a saucer for setting (*see page 168*). Boil for a little longer, if necessary, remove the elderflowers, skim, and pot into prepared warmed pots (*see page 168*). Cover, seal, wipe and label.

Strawberry Jam

Strawberry jam is notoriously difficult to make because strawberries are low in both acid and pectin. I either add some red currant juice, which is high in both, or lemon juice and Certo liquid pectin, which never seems quite so fresh. It's an extravagant jam but well worth making, and I usually pot it in little pots which somehow enhances the luxury of it.

Ingredients
5–6 lbs (2.25–2.7kg)

4 lbs (1.8kg) firm dry strawberries	**3½ lb (1.6kg) sugar**
1 lb (450g) red currants	**½ oz (12g) butter**

To Prepare the Jars. Wash in hot soapy water, rinse and dry out completely in a low oven. Fill while warm.

Process the red currants (there is no need to de-stalk them) in a food processor until they are broken up, or crush them well with a potato masher. Strain off the juice, using a large sieve or a soup mouli with fine plate. Alternatively, you can simmer the crushed red currants with 6 fl oz (175ml) of water for about 30 minutes until tender before straining off the juice through a jelly bag.

Place the strawberries, red currant juice, sugar (put the bag of sugar in a low oven to warm and it will dissolve quicker) and butter (which helps keep a clear colour and inhibits scum from forming) in a wide jam pan. The pan should not be filled to more than 3"–4" (7cm–10cm) depth, or insufficient water will boil off quickly enough to make a good jam; by putting the strawberries and sugar together to cook, you stop the strawberries breaking up because they hold their shape in a sugar solution. Stir the fruit, heating gently until the sugar has dissolved completely. Now boil as fast as possible for 5–15 minutes until a set is achieved, then skim, removing scum with a slotted or wooden spoon. Enough moisture must be driven off in this time to leave the jam with a high enough percentage of sugar to keep well and not ferment, but longer boiling will result in a darker colour, a less fresh flavour and sometimes a jam in which the pectin has been destroyed and which remains syrupy for ever.

To Test for a Set. Place a small teaspoonful of jam on a cold saucer and put it in the fridge or freezer, removing the jam pan from the stove so that it does not go on cooking while you wait for the tester to cool. Once cool, push the jam with your finger; the surface should be stiff and it should wrinkle in front of your finger. If it is still thin and sticky, it needs more boiling. A temperature of 220°–222°F (106°C) on a sugar thermometer also indicates setting point, but confirm with the saucer test. Once a set is achieved, leave to stand for 10 minutes or so; this will help to keep the strawberries suspended through the jam, not floating to the top.

To Fill the Jars. Pour the jam (preferably through a jam funnel) into the prepared, warmed jars. Fill practically to the top, for the jam will shrink a little on cooling. Cover with waxed discs and transparent covers immediately so that no mould spores get in. Wipe the jars while hot and label.

To Make with Lemon Juice and Certo Pectin. Increase the sugar to 6 lb (2.7kg). Add 6–8 tbs lemon juice or 2 teasp dissolved tartaric or citric acid to cook with the fruit; then add ½ bottle of Certo once the jam has boiled fast for 2–3 minutes only. Stand and pot up as before, but it will take up to one month to thicken completely.

Raspberry and Red Currant Jam

Raspberries also need additional acid and pectin and can also be made with the addition of red currants.

Ingredients
approx 6 lb (2.7kg) jam

2 lb (900g) raspberries	**3¾ lb (1.7kg) granulated sugar**
2 lb (900g) red currants	**½ oz (12g) butter**

Follow the recipe for Strawberry Jam, processing and sieving the red currants as above. Simmer them together for 15–20 minutes before adding the sugar, warmed, and the butter. Dissolve the sugar fully before boiling for 5–10 minutes to a set. Test, skim and pot.

Sieved Raspberry Jam

This alternative recipe uses lemon juice and lemon pith to add acid and pectin respectively. It also includes sieving the jam, to get rid of the pips some people so dislike, though you can still make it un-sieved if you like.

Ingredients
approx 6½ lb (3kg)

4 lb (1.8kg) firm sound raspberries	**2 lemons**
4 lb (1.8kg) sugar	**½ oz (12g) butter**

Remove and discard the outer zest of the lemon before squeezing out the juice (you need 4–6 tbs) and shredding the white pith finely, for it is a good source of pectin. Place the raspberries, shredded pith and lemon juice in a wide jam pan, rubbed with butter. If you don't want to sieve the jam, put the shreds of pith into a muslin bag so that they can be removed. Simmer gently for 20 minutes until tender, then preferably leave to stand for 30 minutes or so for more pectin to come out of the lemon pith, before sieving. Use a soup mouli with the fine plate for speedy sieving.

Return the purée to the pan and add the sugar, preferably warmed; stir over gentle heat until the sugar has quite dissolved, then boil as fast as possible for 5–10 minutes to achieve a set. Test a little jam on a cold saucer for wrinkling (*see page 168*). Pot into prepared, warmed pots, cover with waxed discs and transparent covers and label.

* Crème Fraîche

Few of us can get thick un-pasteurised cream with that rich, ripened flavour, but have to make do with pasteurised dairy cream, which I find fairly thin and insipid. This cream, or even whipping cream, can be very considerably improved to a thick, tasty cream that needs spooning from the jar by culturing it like yoghurt. You need a fresh pot of crème fraîche from France, from Harrods or any really good delicatessen as a starter, after which you can make batch after batch (or keep some in the freezer to use as a starter). The crème fraîche you make will have a long life, keeping in the fridge for a couple of weeks or longer. I make it in summer to go with strawberries, raspberries and summer puddings, but you can use it in practically all dishes which call for cream, and it will give them a deeper, richer flavour. Cultured buttermilk can also be used as a starter to get practically the same result.

Ingredients
½–1 pt (300–600ml)

**½–1 pt (300–600ml) or more whipping
   cream
1–2 tbs crème fraîche or cultured
   buttermilk**

Very gently heat the cream to lukewarm (not over 85°F/30°C), then mix it with the crème fraîche and turn into a slightly warmed jar or container. Keep this covered with a cloth or muslin in a warm place between 60°F/16°C and 85°F/30°C for about 12–24 hours, by which time the cream will have thickened and ripened in flavour. Keep refrigerated. In summer a draught-proof spot in the kitchen will do to culture the cream, but find a nice warm spot in winter. A yoghurt thermometer and a room thermometer take the guessing out of this recipe.

Use a tablespoon or two of this batch for your next culture.

F * Little Almond Finger Biscuits

Little biscuits to serve with ice creams and sorbets or mousses are always useful. These are easy to make and look good.

Ingredients
approx 25 biscuits

**2 oz (50g) ground almonds
1 oz (25g) self-raising flour
2 egg whites
3 oz (75g) castor sugar
¼ teasp almond essence
1–2 oz (25–50g) flaked almonds
   (optional)**

Sift the ground almonds and flour together. Whisk the egg whites until holding a peak, then gradually whisk in the sugar. Whisk until the mixture is very stiff and shiny, and then carefully fold in the flour and almond mixture and the almond essence. Turn into a piping bag with a large plain nozzle and pipe 3½" (9cm) fingers of the mixture (a little apart for they spread) in a thin layer on to a sheet of Bakewell paper on a baking sheet; use a wet knife to cut off the mixture. Sprinkle heavily with flaked almonds (not essential, but they look pretty) and cook in a slow oven (300°F/150°C/Gas 2) for 10–15 minutes until golden brown. They will still be a little soft as you remove them from the oven, but will crisp up when you put them to cool on a wire rack. When cold, keep in an airtight tin.

You can also pipe the mixture into rounds or use a teaspoon to make small rounds of the mixture; use a wet knife to flatten the top a little, for if the middle is too thick it will not dry out before the edges start to burn.

*   Courgette or Pumpkin Cake

There are many old recipes for bread and cakes which include apples or potato, for when there was a glut it was important not to waste them. If you grow courgettes, there always seems a time when their growing outstrips your eating, or there are times when they are particularly cheap in the shops and it is nice to have this very different way of using them. I only peel them and remove their pippy white fibre if they are large or tough. Nobody will know what is in this moist and more-ish loaf (it's also delicious made with pumpkin), so easy to make for eating fresh or for freezing.

Ingredients
1 × 2 lb (900g) loaf or
2 × 1lb (450g) loaves

1 lb (450g) grated courgette or pumpkin, peeled and de-seeded if necessary	1 teasp baking powder
8 fl oz (225ml) sunflower or light vegetable oil	1½ teasp ground cinnamon
	1 teasp freshly ground nutmeg
12 oz (350g) soft dark brown sugar	5 oz (125g) wholemeal flour
3 eggs	6 oz (175g) broken walnuts
5 oz (125g) self-raising flour	3 oz (75g) sultanas
	1 teasp salt

Mix the grated courgettes with the oil, sugar and whisked eggs. Sift the self-raising flour with the spices and salt and baking powder and mix with the wholemeal flour. Add to the grated courgette mixture with the walnuts and sultanas and mix well. Grease a 2 lb (900g) loaf tin or two smaller ones and pack in the mixture. Bake in a moderate oven (350°F/180°C/ Gas 4) for ¾–1½ hours, depending on size, until a skewer plunged into the centre comes out clean. Turn out and cool on a rack.

Serve plain or sliced with butter. It will keep fresh and moist in a tin for a week or more.

$\mathcal{F}$ *   ## Lemon Squash

Liking fresh natural products, we prefer to make our own lemon squash rather than buy the artificially flavoured, coloured and sweetened commercial variety. Ours keeps for 2–4 weeks in a cupboard or the fridge, rather depending on the weather. It will keep indefinitely if more sugar is added, but we use it fast and don't like it too sweet. You can use grapefruit, lime or orange, or any mixture you wish.

We used to grate in the lemon rind, but when we gave H.R.H. Prince of Wales a glass to quench his thirst at the Game Fair one year, all the grated lemon floated to the top, and as he sucked the squash through his teeth, he asked why we kept plankton in it! Since then we have taken to adding strips of lemon zest, then straining it off as we bottle it.

Ingredients
3 pts (1.7l) approx

6 lemons
2 lb (900g) sugar
1 oz (25g) citric acid
2 pts (1.2l) boiling water

Wash the lemons, then, with a vegetable peeler, take off the outer rind of the lemons (without white pith) in thin strips (or grate the rinds if you prefer). Squeeze the juice and add it to the sugar in a bowl, with the lemon rind and citric acid. Pour on the boiling water and stir until the sugar dissolves. Leave until cold, then strain into screw-top bottles which are clean and have been rinsed in boiling water. Keep in a cupboard or, if possible, in the fridge, especially in hot weather. Dilute to taste with cold water.

AUTUMN'S STORE

Who hath not seen thee oft amid thy store?

—Keats

AUTUMN

Late summer turns suddenly to autumn. The smell of burning stubble is in the air and a feeling of melancholy steals up on one. But it's so easy to miss the full pleasure of these brilliant early autumn days, when the leaves are starting to turn, in the hectic rush that signals the ending of the holidays.

Plum picking is essentially a late summer treat, one of the pre-school pleasures of my childhood. It was wonderful to climb into the Victoria tree and gorge—I'm afraid there really is no other word for it—on warm ripe drops of honey, the stone coming clean and sharp-edged away against the tongue, the risk of a wasp sting or discovery adding spice to the sensation. I still cannot eat a perfectly ripe Victoria plum without a twinge of the stomach-knotting sensation which gnawed one in the last few days of the holidays.

It's a little disheartening to look at the garden, so neat and under control in May, but now ravaged by the exuberance of summer. The courgettes that eluded me as babies bask in the sun like smug, striped cats amongst the prickly leaves—how I detest marrows! The beans I promised myself I'd always pick at little-finger-length hang in bunches like gnarled arthritic hands, though they may have some fresh little haricot beans to offer. And the herb garden! The angelica stands six foot tall, gaunt and bare with sprouting babies under her feet, and the borage is collapsing over everything, strangling my precious thymes and scattering a million unwanted seeds.

The old habits of preparing and stocking up for winter are still natural enough, if a bit submerged by the ease of modern life. I'm sure we should follow these instincts because they are still satisfying (everyone gets a bit of a quiet kick from a well-stocked store cupboard), and it seems a pity if thousands of years of self-preserving instinct are to be lost because of a century of urban living or a generation of freezers.

Bottling fruit is one of the things I try to find time for, because I like to be able to reach for a bottle of plums to open and tip into a bowl, ready to eat immediately and bringing back a breath of summer that's cost me practically nothing. Pears seem, maddeningly, all to ripen at once, but are marvellously good if they are stewed slowly in sugar and brandy to make Brandied Pears, which, even open, keep for a year or more (if they're allowed to). Chutneys, jams and special goodies like Sloe Gin and Japonica Sweetmeats all add a bit of variety to the winter, and mean you can eat just that little bit better and more healthily—at no extra cost. A glut of summer tomatoes will be full-flavoured enough to make into Homemade Tomato Purée, sauces, jams or pizza topping, or Tomato and Tarragon Soup. But one of my autumn dislikes—and I use no stronger word—is for green tomatoes. We always have some of these, and I tried chutney recipe after chutney recipe, but none seemed to catch the sunlight and warmth that a good chutney should bring to cheer up a winter plate. I have now found one that I think good enough to share. The only really useful thing about green tomatoes is that they will continue to ripen, if picked dry and unfrosted and kept in a warm dark place, until Christmas. They may not be quite good enough to eat on their own, but are excellent fried or grilled for breakfast or for adding to salads.

Our autumns are pleasantly long drawn-out seasons, and we avoid the sharp brilliance of the American fall, where everything has to be gathered more quickly, albeit in a blaze of colour. Our trees may not burn and glow quite so strikingly, but then we can enjoy them for rather longer, and it will be the end of October, even early November, before the quinces fall and are ready for use and the sloes are ready to be introduced to the gin. This allows us to do all these things on the fine days spread over a couple of months and more. You can take advantage of any glut that occurs, knowing that you're not missing your only chance to do something else, the freezer acting if necessary as a holding station, especially for your jam-making fruit (but always remember to add 10% extra frozen fruit to your recipe because of the loss of pectin). The microwave can also step into this picture, because it's specially good for making small quantities of jam or jelly, and is the best way to dry small quantities of herbs.

Take advantage of our long autumn season to put up some good things for the winter. Preserving, potting up and storing may be old-fashioned habits, but they are timeless and as relevant as ever, though in the modern way. And autumn is not just the end of a season, it is also the beginning of the winter vegetable season. It is with great pleasure, almost relief, that one turns away from the endless beans and starts on the delicate turnip leaves which make such a delicious purée, or the tiny turnips which glaze to perfection; slim leeks are a treat, and the first sprouts, though not yet frosted and flavourful, are tender and good. Artichokes and celeriac are ready to dig for soup, for a vegetable or as a salad, and calabrese is still there until the heavy frosts come. I'm not sure I don't love the winter vegetables just as much as the summer ones, especially when they have had a frosting and have gained their full flavour. Parsnips, turnips, kale, cabbage—what could be better than these when they are well cooked? They have the added advantage of standing in the garden, ready for use, for several months, quite unlike their impatient little summer cousins, which need constant supervision lest they misbehave and overgrow.

So the seasons change, always with something new to look forward to as one thing comes to an end and another starts.

AUTUMN

First Courses and Supper Dishes

Hot Artichokes with Herb
    Mousseline Sauce
- Smoked Haddock Mousse
Avocado with Salmon and Green
    Peppercorns
Cheese Soufflé
Pasta with Baked Tomatoes
- Cannelloni con Funghi
Little Mushroom Pies
Sauced Mushroom Omelette

Soups

- Tomato and Tarragon Soup
Soupe de Courge
Pumpkin Soup
Cream of Turnip Soup

Fish

Baked Trout with Herb and Lime or
    Lemon Butter
Butter Baked Gurnard
Herrings in Oatmeal

Main Courses

Glazed Loin of Lamb with
    Mushroom Forcemeat Balls
- Lemon Lamb Casserole
Medallions of Pork with Garlic and
    Lemon
Poulet en Cocotte à l'Ail
- Lasagne al Forno
Classic Braised Beef
Roast Fillet of Beef with its own
    Butter Sauce
- Pork with Cider and Apple or Quince
Martinmas Pheasant
Roman Pie

Vegetables

Button Mushrooms with Cream
Aubergines and Onions in Olive Oil
Broccoli Timbales
Sweet-Sour Green Beans
- Risotto Doré
Gratin of Green Beans, Smoky Bacon
    and Mushrooms
Carrots with Coriander and Lime
Lady Farquhar's Beetroot Salad
Cucumber Salad with Shallot and
    Mustard Dressing
Florence Fennel au Gratin

Puddings

Autumn Pudding
Tarte aux Fruits
Damson and Dumpling Pudding
Apple or Blackberry and Apple Pie
- Coffee Apples with Rum
Caramel Rum Cream
Tiny Pear or Apple Vol-au-Vents
Spiced Pear Fool
Brandied Pears
Glace au Raisins

Miscellaneous

Green Tomato Chutney
Home-made Tomato Purée
Piquant Melba Toast
Spiced Courgette and Dried Apricot
    Jam
Quince Jelly
Quince Cheese and Japonica
    Sweetmeats
Bramble Jelly
Damson Jam
Sticky Gingerbread
Sloe Gin

- Also quantities for 25 persons

First Courses and Supper Dishes

**   Hot Artichokes with Herb Mousseline Sauce

The globe artichokes season is from May to November, with fewer around when the weather is dry and hot and a good crop coming on in the autumn. So before we miss them for this year, here is a recipe for serving them hot with a herby mousseline sauce. They are also delicious hot with Hollandaise Sauce* or cold with Vinaigrette*.

> **Ingredients**
> *4–6 people*
>
> **4–6 fine fresh artichokes**
>
> *Herb Mousseline Sauce*
> **6 oz (175g) butter**
> **2 fl oz (50ml) white wine (or water)**
> **1–1½ teasp tarragon vinegar or shallot**
> **   vinegar or lemon juice**
> **1–2 tbs chopped mixed herbs such as**
> **   tarragon, basil, marjoram, chervil and**
> **   parsley**
> **2 egg yolks**
> **2 tbs cold water**
> **salt and pepper**

Twist and break the stems off the artichokes, which will draw out any tough threads. Then, with a serrated or bread knife, saw off the top third of the artichoke leaves (you can then fit more in a pan). Boil in salted water, with a squeeze of lemon juice added, for 35–45 minutes until tender, when a leaf will detach easily. Drain, stalk ends uppermost, then put your fingers into the middle and twist out the inner cone of leaves. Lift out and discard. Take a teaspoon and scoop out all the hairy choke, leaving the hearts exposed.

Set each artichoke on a plate and pour some of the prepared sauce into the centre of the artichoke. The outer leaves are detached and the fleshy base is dipped into the sauce and nibbled from the leaf. Eat the heart at the end with a knife and fork.

Herb Mousseline Sauce. Cut the butter into small cubes. Place the wine or water and vinegar or lemon juice in a saucepan and bring to the boil, add the butter bit by bit and boil the mixture fast, whisking all the time. Once all the butter has been added and has melted to form an emulsified sauce, add the herbs and set aside.

Place a bowl with the yolks and cold water over a pan of hot water and cook, whisking all the time, until the mixture doubles in bulk and becomes moussey. Reboil the butter mixture and add to the egg mousseline, whisking all the time. Continue over hot water until you have a thick velvet mousse, correct seasoning and flavouring and serve at once. Or cover the bowl and leave in a pan of tepid, not hot, water in a warm, not hot, place, where it will keep for an hour or more.

F **   Smoked Haddock Mousse

Process the eggs to an absolutely smooth texture so that you can freeze this mousse if you wish (pieces of hard-boiled eggs go rubbery and uneatable in the freezer). Its delicate flavour and fine texture make it a good first course or light lunch dish. Try making it in a ring mould, filling the centre with a sliced tomato and Florence fennel salad, dressed with a little basil and a good oil and lemon juice dressing.

Ingredients

4–6 people	*25 people*
¾ lb (350g) smoked haddock	3 lb (1.35kg) smoked haddock
¼ pt (150ml) milk	1 pt (600ml) milk
2 eggs	8 eggs
2 tbs white wine	4 fl oz (100ml) white wine
2 teasp gelatine	2 tbs and 2 teasp gelatine
¼ pt (150ml) mayonnaise	1 pt (600ml) mayonnaise
¼ pt (150ml) whipping cream	1 pt (600ml) whipping cream
a squeeze of lemon juice	1–2 lemons
pepper and mace	½–¾ teasp ground mace
	plenty of pepper, salt only if necessary
To Decorate	
sliced cucumber, hard-boiled egg, or a few prawns and parsley	*To Decorate*
	1–2 cucumbers sliced, hard-boiled eggs or prawns and parsley

Hard boil the eggs. Simmer the skinned haddock in the milk until cooked. Drain, remove bones, flake and make the cooking milk up to ¼ pt (150ml), no more.

Sprinkle the gelatine gradually on to the white wine in a small bowl, leave to soak for several minutes, then stand the bowl in a pan of hot water to melt. Process the hard-boiled eggs in a food processor until very smooth, add the fish and process until that is also very smooth (with a liquidiser, process fish, eggs and liquid together). Add the measured cooking milk, gelatine and seasoning, leave to cool, then add the mayonnaise. When just beginning to set, fold in the cream, whipped until it is just holding its shape; correct seasoning and add a squeeze of lemon juice. Turn into a 1 pt (600ml) soufflé dish and chill. Serve decorated with sliced cucumber, hard-boiled egg or a few prawns and parsley.

Variation for 25 people. The cooking milk in which the haddock has been simmered should be made up to 18 fl oz (550ml). You will need 2 × 2 pt (1. 2l) soufflé dishes.

✳✳   Avocado with Salmon and Green Peppercorns

The soft colours of salmon and avocado are very pretty, and the flavour and texture are delicious if spiked with green peppercorns. Very quick and easy to prepare, and if you have any filling left over try it on toast or bread or freeze it.

Ingredients
4–6 people

6–8 oz (175–225g) salmon steak
2–3 ripe avocados
4 oz (100g) cream cheese (Eden Vale
   Somerset soft cream cheese)
2–3 tbs cream
1–1½ teasp green peppercorns in brine
pinch ground mace
squeeze lime or lemon juice
salt and pepper

To Garnish (optional)
wafer-thin slices of lime
sprigs chervil or parsley

Preferably slip the salmon into a boil-in (or roast-in) bag and seal, though you can cook it just in the water. Drop into a pan of boiling water, bring back to the boil, draw off the stove and leave until cool. Remove bones and skin and flake the fish roughly. With a fork, crush the fish and cream cheese together, adding seasoning and green peppercorns, mace, cream and lemon juice to make a soft, thready mixture.

Halve the ripe avocados, remove the stones and season the flesh with a little salt. Fill the cavity with a mound of salmon mixture and garnish with a wafer slice of lime and a sprig of chervil.

✳✳   Cheese Soufflé

You must have well-flavoured cheese for a soufflé, because if you just add a larger quantity of bland cheese it will become too heavy.

I cook soufflés more slowly than chefs who are working 'on command' and therefore wish to get them to their ready-seated customers as soon as possible. Cooked in this way they stay at perfection for longer than if cooked fast, allowing you a little more leeway to get them to the table.

Ingredients
4–6 people

¾ pt (450ml) milk
½ bay leaf
1 slice onion
1 blade mace
2 oz (50g) butter
1½ oz (35g) flour

4–6 oz (100–175g) grated cheese
   (half-Gruyère, half-Parmesan is best,
   or good mature Cheddar)
5 egg yolks
6 egg-whites
salt, pepper and mustard

Heat and infuse the milk with the onion, bay and mace. Melt the butter in a saucepan, add the flour and cook over moderate heat for 2–3 minutes, stirring. Draw off the stove, wait for the sizzling to cease and add the strained milk. Bring to the boil, whisking hard, and simmer 1–2 minutes. Add the cheese, stir until it melts and add the seasoning. Remove from the heat, cool a little and beat in the egg yolks. Whisk the whites until just holding a peak and gently fold into the warm cheese mixture.

Turn into a 2 pt (1.2l) soufflé dish, well buttered, especially around the rim. Smooth the top carefully to the edges and cook in a moderate oven (350°F/180°C/Gas 4) for 30–40 minutes, until well risen, golden and just trembling in the middle when you move the dish. Serve immediately; the outside should be set but the centre should still be like creamy sauce.

*   # Pasta with Baked Tomatoes

This is one of those very nice simple dishes which rely on tasty tomatoes and careful seasoning. The huge pleated continental tomatoes, tasting of southern sunshine, are better than the over-juicy English ones, and home-made or fresh bought pasta, good olive oil and fresh basil make all the difference.

Ingredients
4–6 people

2 lb (900g) fresh tomatoes
1 tin anchovy fillets
3–4 fl oz (75–100ml) fruity olive oil
1 lb (450g) packet spaghetti or about 1½
    lb (675g) fresh or home-made pasta
    (cut as wide noodles)
3–4 tbs roughly chopped parsley or
    parsley and fresh basil
salt and pepper

Skin the tomatoes. Cut in thick slices and layer with the anchovies in a wide ovenproof dish, preferably earthenware. Pour over the oil and bake in a hot oven (400°F/200°C/Gas 6) for about 20 minutes until tender. Meanwhile, cook the pasta in a large pan of rapidly boiling salt water, with 1 tbs oil added. Home-made pasta will take 3–5 minutes, packet spaghetti 15–20 minutes. Cook until tender but still *al dente*. Drain the pasta well and add it to the dish of tomatoes, season highly, add chopped herbs and toss well before serving.

ℱ ✱✱   Cannelloni con Funghi

Even if you don't come across a whole fieldful of mushrooms this is worth making. You can certainly use bought lasagne, but the home-made spinach pasta or fresh bought pasta is very good for this as it is for many other dishes.

If you are making this dish for large numbers, you will probably find it best to cook a dozen or so sheets of pasta at a time, fishing them out of your large pan of boiling water with scissor tongs to refresh under the cold tap, then throwing more into the same water. Make sure the water stays at the boil so that they don't sulk on the bottom and stick together.

Ingredients
4–6 people

Spinach or Plain Pasta
10–12 oz (275–350g) plain strong flour
1 egg and 1 egg-yolk
2 oz (50g) spinach purée
½ teasp salt

or

8–12 squares of green lasagne

Filling
12 oz (350g) cooked ham, chicken, veal or pork
8 oz (225g) mushrooms
2 tbs olive oil
1½ oz (35g) butter
1 large finely chopped onion
1–2 tbs finely chopped parsley (flat leafed for choice)
3–4 tbs of the cheese sauce
salt and pepper
a little extra grated Parmesan

Cheese Sauce
2 oz (50g) butter
1½ oz (35g) flour
1 pt (600ml) milk
1–2 oz (25–50g) freshly grated Parmesan
salt, pepper and nutmeg

25 people

Spinach or Plain Pasta
2–2¼ lb (900g–1.15kg) plain strong flour
3 eggs and 3 yolks
6 oz (175g) spinach purée
1½ teasp salt

or

40–50 squares green lasagne approx

Filling
2–2½ lb (900g–1.15kg) cooked ham, chicken, veal or pork
2 lb (900g) mushrooms
2–3 fl oz (50–75ml) olive oil
4 oz (100g) butter
4 large finely chopped onions
6–8 tbs finely chopped parsley (flat leafed for choice)
8 fl oz (225ml) of the cheese sauce
salt and pepper
2–4 oz (50–100g) extra grated Parmesan

Cheese sauce
8 oz (225g) butter
6 oz (175g) flour
3½–4 pts (2–2.25l) milk
4–6 oz (100–175g) freshly grated Parmesan cheese
¼–½ teasp freshly grated nutmeg
salt and pepper

Spinach or Plain Pasta. If you do not use the spinach add another egg and one teasp olive oil. Mix all the ingredients to a firm dough and knead for 8–10 minutes until the dough is elastic and smooth. Alternatively, process all together in a food processor for 45 seconds, keeping the mixture (by the addition of more flour if necessary) in polystyrene-like granules. Then press together into a dough. Divide the dough into 3 pieces if rolling by hand and roll as thin as possible; otherwise divide into 4–6 pieces and pass through the pasta machine to the thinnest but one setting. Cut into 3″ × 4″ (8cm × 10cm) rectangles. Flour lightly and keep on a cloth on a tray if you are not yet ready to cook it.

Boil the pasta squares in plenty of boiling salted water, with a few drops of oil added, until *al dente*; this takes 2–4 minutes for fresh or 10–15 minutes for dried pasta. Drain, rinse with cold water and keep in the minimum of cold water until ready to use.

Cheese Sauce. Make the sauce next so that it has time to mature while you make the filling. Melt the butter in a saucepan, add the flour and cook over moderate heat, stirring, for 2–3 minutes; then draw the pan off the stove and, when the sizzling has ceased, add the milk. Return to high heat and bring to the boil, whisking hard. Add the Parmesan and season with salt, pepper and nutmeg. If possible, leave over very low heat to mature for half-an-hour.

Filling. Cut the meat into small dice. Heat the oil and butter in a large frying pan, add the onion and cook gently until soft. Turn up the heat, slice the mushrooms and add. Sauté the mushrooms and, when nearly cooked, add the meat and sauté until hot through. Add the parsley, seasoning and 3–4 tbs of the sauce to bind the filling.

To Assemble. Butter a large gratin dish. Remove the pasta from the water, dry and fill with some of the filling. Roll up and place side by side in the dish. Cover with the remaining sauce and scatter with the extra Parmesan. Bake in a moderately hot oven (375°F/190°C/Gas 5) until brown and bubbling; this takes 10–15 minutes if hot or 30–40 minutes if re-heating from cold.

Variation for 25 people. You will need to divide the dough for the pasta into a larger number of pieces.
Filling. The constituents of this will probably have to be fried in several batches. You will need 8 fl oz (225ml) of the sauce to bind the filling.
To Assemble. If you are heating several big dishes of cannelloni at once, allow longer than the times given above, as the oven will take longer to heat a large quantity.

F **   Little Mushroom Pies

These little pies are made with cream cheese pastry and a spiced mushroom filling for a nice first course, picnic dish or savoury. You can keep the uncooked pies or the prepared filling in the freezer.

Ingredients
1 dozen pies

Mushroom Filling

½–¾ lb (225–350g) mushrooms	*Cream Cheese Pastry*
1 oz (25g) butter	**3 oz (75g) soft butter**
2–3 shallots or 1 finely chopped onion	**3 oz (75g) cream cheese**
1 clove finely chopped garlic	**6 oz (175g) plain flour**
1 tbs plain flour	**good pinch salt**

½–¾ lb (225–350g) mushrooms
1 oz (25g) butter
2–3 shallots or 1 finely chopped onion
1 clove finely chopped garlic
1 tbs plain flour
4–5 tbs yoghurt, sour cream or cream
dash tabasco sauce or cayenne pepper
1 tbs finely chopped parsley
a little chopped fresh or pinch dried
   lemon thyme or thyme
freshly grated nutmeg
squeeze lemon juice
egg wash
salt and pepper

Cream Cheese Pastry
3 oz (75g) soft butter
3 oz (75g) cream cheese
6 oz (175g) plain flour
good pinch salt

Cream Cheese Pastry. Cream the soft butter well, beat in the cream cheese, sift in the flour and salt and work to a dough. Knead briefly into a flat disc and rest in a plastic bag in the fridge for about ½–2 hours.

Mushroom Filling. Melt the butter in a frying pan and fry the finely chopped shallot or onion until softened. Slice and add the mushrooms, cutting the slices in halves or quarters if they are large, add the chopped garlic and fry over high heat until lightly cooked, the moisture has evaporated and the butter is again apparent (sometimes mushrooms in autumn can be very watery, and you have to remove them from the pan and boil the liquid away before returning them and continuing). Sprinkle over the flour and cook for a moment or two; then add the yoghurt, spoonful by spoonful, stirring all the time and letting it cook into the dish so that it does not curdle. Season with tabasco or cayenne, nutmeg, seasoning and chopped herbs, add a good squeeze of lemon juice and cook until thick and creamy. Cool the mixture.

Roll the pastry thinly and cut bottoms and lids to fit mince-pie tins. Lay in the bases and fill with a teaspoonful of the mushroom filling. Moisten lids round the edge with cold water and press in place. Prick the tops, brush with egg-wash and bake in a hot oven (400°F/200°C/Gas 7) for 15–20 minutes until crisp and brown. Serve hot or cold.

** Sauced Mushroom Omelette

To make a bit more of a meal and dress it up a little, try saucing this omelette and its creamy mushroom filling with a delicate Sauce Mornay. Use either a large 10″–12″ (25–30cm) omelette or frying pan to make one omelette or else an 8″ (20cm) omelette pan and make individual omelettes.

Ingredients
2–4 people

6 fresh eggs
1 oz (25g) butter
salt and pepper

Filling
4 oz (100g) field or button mushrooms
1 oz (25g) butter
½ teasp plain flour
4 tbs cream
salt and pepper

Mornay Sauce
¾ oz (20g) butter
¼ oz (6g) plain flour
5–6 fl oz (150–175ml) milk
3–4 tbs grated Gruyère cheese
a little cream or milk to thin
salt, pepper and nutmeg

Mornay Sauce. Melt the butter in a small saucepan, add the flour and cook gently, stirring, for 1–2 minutes. Draw off the heat, wait for the sizzling to cease and add the milk. Bring to the boil, whisking hard, and simmer for 2–3 minutes. Season with a little salt, pepper and a trace of nutmeg, add the Gruyère and keep warm.

Filling. Dice the mushrooms and sauté in the butter in a small pan for a moment or two. Sprinkle over the flour, stir well and add the cream. Bring to the boil to thicken. Season, remove from the stove and keep warm, covered.

Omelette. Preheat the grill. Break the eggs into a bowl, season, and whisk with a fork until they are well broken up. Heat the omelette pan over high heat until almost smoking, then add half the butter (put the remaining piece of butter on your warm, not hot, serving dish to melt), and, when melted, lower the heat and pour in the eggs. Shake the pan and stir the eggs with the back of a fork for a moment or two; change to a palette knife or spatula and lit the edges of the omelette while tipping the pan to allow uncooked egg to run under. Once it is nearly cooked but still moist spread with mushroom filling and fold up. Turn on to the serving dish, pour over the Mornay Sauce, thinned with milk or cream to coating consistency if necessary, and pop under the very hot grill to brown lightly. Serve at once.

Soups

F **   Tomato and Tarragon Soup

This is a lovely tasty tomato soup, just right for using up excess autumn tomatoes, and also good and reliable from the freezer. It's also a good soup to make for large numbers.

Ingredients

4–6 people

for 25 people

1½ lb (675g) fresh tomatoes or 1 × 1 lb 14 oz (850g) approx tin of tomatoes
6 oz (175g) onion
1 stick celery
4 oz (100g) carrots
1½ oz (35g) butter
1 tbs olive oil
1 clove garlic
2 tbs tomato purée
½ bay leaf
1–2 tbs fresh or ½–¾ teasp dried tarragon
1¾ pts (1l) chicken stock or stock cube and water
1–2 teasp sugar to taste
1 small strip lemon rind
finely chopped parsley
salt and pepper

makes 10 pts (25 × 8 fl oz (250ml) servings

5 lb (2.25kg) fresh tomatoes or 3 × 1 lb 14 oz (850g) approx tins tomatoes
1½ lb (675g) onion
3 sticks celery
1 lb (450g) carrots
5 oz (125g) butter
3 tbs olive oil
3–4 cloves garlic
6–8 oz (175–225g) tomato purée
2 bay leaves
3–4 tbs fresh or 1½–2 teasp dried tarragon
7 pts (4l) chicken stock or stock cube and water
1–1½ tbs sugar to taste
3 long strips lemon rind
salt and pepper
plenty of finely chopped parsley

Finely slice the onion, celery and carrot (food processor with slicing blade). Melt the butter and oil in a saucepan, add the vegetables and cook gently until softened. Add the skinned and roughly chopped tomatoes (drained and chopped if you are using tinned ones, using the liquid as part of the stock quantity), chopped garlic, tomato purée, tarragon and bay leaf. Simmer for 20–30 minutes on gentle heat before adding the stock, sugar, lemon rind and seasoning. Simmer for 20 minutes longer, then purée, sieve and return to the rinsed-out pan. Check the seasoning, re-heat and serve sprinkled with finely chopped parsley.

Variation for 25 people. The vegetables and tomatoes will need to simmer for 45–50 minutes before the stock is added.

ℱ *   Soupe de Courge

Those naughty courgettes which grow from finger-length to hand-sized while one's back is turned will still make a very nice soup. I like to serve it with fried croûtons and grated Gruyère, as the French serve pumpkin soup.

Ingredients
4–6 people

1½ lb (675g) courgettes
1 onion
1 oz (25g) butter
1 pt (600ml) good stock
½ pt (300ml) milk
a little cream (optional)
salt and pepper

To Finish (optional)
croûtons
grated Gruyère cheese

Soften the onion gently in butter, add the skinned, de-seeded and sliced courgettes, the stock and seasoning and simmer gently for 20–30 minutes until absolutely tender. Purée and sieve back into the pan, add the milk and some cream if you like, and correct the seasoning. Heat the croûtons and hand with a bowl of grated cheese.

ℱ *   Pumpkin Soup

A pumpkin's flavour is delicate, and its greatest contribution to soup is its wonderful velvet texture and golden colour (it is important to recognise and bring out the best points of each ingredient when you are cooking). The dark green Table Ace pumpkin is quite small and not nearly as impressive as those great golden Cinderella pumpkins which, once cut, are so difficult to cope with. But will keep in a frost-free shed throughout the winter.

Ingredients
4–6 people

2 lb (900g) pumpkin flesh
2 oz (50g) butter
1 finely chopped onion
1 finely chopped stick celery
8 oz (225g) tomatoes
1½ pts (900ml) chicken stock or water
    and 1½ stock cubes

½ pt (300ml) milk
salt and pepper

Garnish
2–3 rashers streaky bacon, diced and
    gently fried until crisp, or finely
    chopped parsley

Melt the butter in a large saucepan, add the onion and celery and soften gently over low heat without colouring. Cut the peeled and de-seeded pumpkin flesh into large dice and roughly cut up the tomatoes. Add the pumpkin and tomato to the saucepan and pour over the chicken stock. Season lightly and simmer for 20–30 minutes until the pumpkin is absolutely tender. Purée and sieve the soup, add milk and correct the seasoning. Heat and serve with a garnish of crispy bacon dice or chopped parsley. Piquant Melba Toast is good with this.

F **   Cream of Turnip Soup

The rather distinctive flavour of turnip seems to blend particularly well with a game stock so, if there should be a pot of pheasant or wild duck stock on the go, pull a few turnips and try this. Diminish the quantity of turnips and adjust the thickening if you prefer a soup less obviously flavoured with turnips.

Ingredients
4–6 people

12 oz (350g) peeled turnip
2 shallots or 1 small onion
1¼–1¾ oz (35–45g) butter
½ teasp castor sugar
1¾ pts (1l) game or chicken stock
1 tbs potato flour
3–4 fl oz (75–100ml) cream or milk
little fresh chopped parsley
salt and pepper

Finely chop the onion and cut the turnip into thin slices. Sweat in ¾ oz (20g) of the butter in a heavy pan, sprinkle with sugar and cook gently, without browning, for 20–30 minutes (add a tablespoon or so of stock if the pan gets too dry). Season, add the stock and simmer for 20 minutes, or until completely tender, then purée and return to the rinsed-out pan.

Mix the potato flour with the cream or milk, add to the pan and bring to the boil, stirring. Correct the seasoning and simmer for a minute or two before drawing off the stove. Stir in the remaining butter in little bits and serving with a sprinkle of parsley.

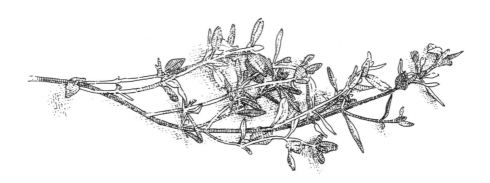

Fish

*   Baked Trout with Herb and Lime or Lemon Butter

Good quality frozen trout or really fresh trout are ideal for this dish, which can be all prepared and left ready for the oven. Lime is good with fish, so do use it if you can find it. You can use various fresh herbs in the butter, such as fennel, dill, tarragon or chervil, or you can even use just parsley or watercress.

Ingredients
4–6 people

**4–6 good trout weighing about 11 oz
    (300g) each**
¾ oz (20g) butter
1 lime or lemon
salt and pepper

Herbs and Lime or Lemon Butter
3 oz (75g) soft butter
1 tbs finely chopped green herbs
1 lime or lemon
salt and pepper

Wipe the trout with kitchen paper, gut if necessary and wipe out inside. Season inside and out with salt and pepper and lay in a generously buttered shallow baking dish; cover loosely with very well buttered paper or tinfoil. Cook in a hot oven (425°F/220°C/Gas 7) for about 14–18 minutes, until the eye has gone white and the flesh at the thickest part no longer feels soft and 'squishy' but just resilient. Remove the paper for the last few minutes if the trout are not already going a nice golden brown.

Decorate the fish with thin slices of lime or lemon and serve with the herb and lime or lemon butter.

Herb and Lime or Lemon Butter. Have your butter really soft so that it creams easily. Cream the butter well, adding herbs until it is speckled a nice green. Season and gradually beat in squeezes of lime or lemon juice until it's quite sharp. Roll it in tinfoil into a cylinder, chill until firm and cut into discs the thickness of a peppermint cream. Or let it firm a little in the fridge, then roll into balls with butter patters which have been well soaked in cold water before use. Chill until firm in iced water in the fridge. Pile in a little dish and serve with the trout.

* Butter Baked Gurnard

The grey or pink skinned gurnard is quite often to be seen on the fishmonger's slab these days. It is a fairly fearsome looking fellow with a spiny backbone which the fishmonger will normally trim off for you (I should get him to remove the head too!). It's not a great fish, but when good and fresh the flesh is very sweet and rather nice and firm between the teeth. I like to bake it with shallots, butter and a little white wine, a way that is also good with monkfish.

Ingredients
4–6 people

4–6 small or 2–3 larger gurnard or monkfish (approx 1½–2 lb (675–900g) headless, trimmed fish)
2–3 oz (50–75g) butter
2–4 finely chopped shallots or sweet onions

4–6 tbs dry white wine
1 sprig thyme
salt and pepper

Place the chopped up butter, shallots or onions, wine and thyme in a shallow oven-proof dish and heat in a hot oven (425°F/220°C/Gas 7) for 5–6 minutes until the butter is melted and bubbling. Add the headless, trimmed and wiped fish, back uppermost, season with salt and pepper, spoon over the butter and cover the fish lightly with butter paper. Bake in the oven for about 10–20 minutes depending on size, basting once or twice, until just cooked and coming away from the backbone. If all the wine reduces away, add a tablespoon or so more (or a little water). If too much juice remains (this can happen with frozen fish), remove the fish and boil the juices fast until reduced. Serve from the dish with the buttery juices.

* Herrings in Oatmeal

Good fresh herring may be in at any time of year, so watch out and grab them when you see them sparkling and fresh. Split and fried in oatmeal is one of the best ways of having them.

Ingredients
4–6 people

4–6 good herring, boned and split
a little milk
some medium oatmeal

2–3 tbs light oil
salt and pepper

Wipe the prepared herring, season, then dip briefly in milk and roll in oatmeal, patting it on firmly. Heat a thin layer of oil in a wide frying pan, and when very hot lay the herrings in, flesh side down. Once browned on one side, turn over carefully and fry the other side. Remove from the pan and drain on kitchen paper before serving.

Main Courses

✱✱ Glazed Loin of Lamb with Mushroom Forcemeat Balls

A well-grown autumn lamb will furnish a generous loin that makes a lovely dish for entertaining when boned and rolled for easy carving; you can if you prefer get your butcher to do this for you. Surround it with mushroom forcemeat balls in the old fashioned way, the bread diced rather than crumbed for a light open texture.

Ingredients
4–6 people

3 lb (1.3k) loin of lamb, boned but keep
   the bones
1 little sprig rosemary
2–3 tbs olive oil
1 teasp honey
¼ pt (150ml) red wine or stock
salt and pepper

Mushroom Forcemeat Balls
8 oz (225g) mushrooms
3 oz (75g) butter
1 small onion
½ clove garlic
4 oz (100g) stale white bread
3 tbs finely chopped parsley
1 teasp finely chopped rosemary
grated lemon rind
1–2 eggs
2–3 tbs oil or dripping
salt and pepper

Warm the olive oil with the bruised sprig of rosemary and leave to steep. Bone out the loin of lamb; if the skin is tough, carefully cut or rip it off, then lightly cut the fat in a criss-cross lattice fashion. Brush all over with rosemary oil and tie 3–4 times into a good roll. Set aside to bring to room temperature (you can lay it on a sprig of rosemary in the roasting tin if you like). Roast in a hot oven (425°F/220°C/Gas 7) for 45–50 minutes. Mix the honey with the remaining rosemary oil and brush the joint with it from time to time to achieve a crisp golden skin, but not so lavishly that it runs into the roasting tin and burns. When cooked, set the joint aside to keep warm and rest for ½ hour or longer. Pour off the fat from the roasting tin, add the wine or stock to the pan and boil up, scraping off all crusty brown juices. Season and strain into a gravy boat. Serve the loin surrounded by the mushroom forcemeat balls and hand red currant jelly. Don't let the forcemeat balls slip into the meat juices so that they become soggy.

Mushroom Forcemeat Balls. Melt the butter in a frying pan and gently fry the chopped onion for several minutes. Cut the mushrooms into fairly large dice, add to the pan and sauté briskly until tender and the liquid has gone. Add the finely chopped garlic and cook for a minute without browning. Turn into a bowl with the bread, cut into tiny cubes, the herbs, grated lemon rind and seasoning. Fork all together lightly and bind with the eggs. Take tablespoons of the mixture and roll and squeeze into balls with wet hands. Heat the oil and sauté the forcemeat balls to a light brown on all sides. Keep warm or reheat in the oven with the roast for 10 minutes or so.

$\mathcal{F}$ * ## Lemon Lamb Casserole

A simple and tasty lamb casserole that is one of my favourites. It gets its flavour from the browning of the lamb as well as from the lemon and a touch of curry and spices.

Ingredients
4–6 people

25 people

2–2½ lb (900g–1.15kg) boned shoulder of lamb	10–12 lb (4.5–5.4kg) boned shoulder of lamb
1 pkt or a good pinch saffron stamens	2 pkts or 2 good pinches saffron stamens
½ pt (300ml) hot stock	1–1½ pts (600–900ml) hot stock
1 clove garlic	2–3 cloves garlic
3 tbs oil	3–6 tbs oil
1 teasp curry powder	1–1½ tbs curry powder
½ teasp ground cinnamon (or cook ½ stick with the lamb, then discard)	1 teasp ground cinnamon (or cook 1 stick with the lamb then discard)
1 thin-skinned lemon	2 thin-skinned lemons (10–12 thin slices)
¼ teasp garam masala (optional)	½–1 teasp garam masala
salt and pepper	salt and pepper

Cut the lamb into generous 1½" (4cm) cubes, discarding excess fat. Steep the saffron in the hot stock. Heat the oil in a frying pan and brown the meat well all over (you will probably have to do it in several batches), then return all to the pan. Sprinkle with curry powder and cinnamon and fry gently for another minute or two. Turn into a casserole, de-glaze the frying pan with the hot saffron stock, and add to the meat with the seasoning, garlic, and 5–6 slices thinly sliced lemon, discarding the ends. With a thick-skinned lemon, you will have to take off a thin layer of skin and shred it finely; then cut off and discard the white pith, which can spoil the dish with its bitterness, before slicing the lemon flesh.

Cook gently either on top of the stove or in a very moderate oven (325°F/170°C/Gas 3) for about 1½ hours or until the meat is very tender. De-grease the sauce a little if necessary and sprinkle with garam masala, a mixed spice powder which adds fragrance to the dish. Cover and leave for 5–10 minutes before serving, possibly with rice.

* ## Medallions of Pork with Garlic and Lemon

This is a quick and favourite way with pork fillet. It's just right for a supper for 2–3 people, and the children beg for it as a special treat. French bread or Stovie or boiled potatoes for the buttery juices are a must. If you cook more than one fillet, do not increase the butter and garlic proportionally.

Ingredients
2–3 people

1 fillet of pork (pork tenderloin) weighing about 12 oz (350g)	1 tbs olive oil
1–2 cloves garlic	½ lemon
1½–2 oz (35–50g) butter	salt and pepper

Trim all fat, skin and bluish membrane from the pork fillet, then cut into ½″ (1.5cm) slices, on the slant to increase their surface area. Bat out thinner with the heel of your hand and season generously with pepper. Chop the garlic finely. Heat the oil and ½ oz (12g) butter in a frying pan and, when very hot, fry the pork medallions briskly until golden, then turn over and add the garlic to the pan. When the second side has sealed, add the remaining butter to the pan in little pieces and season the pork. Remove the pork when just cooked, fry the butter for a moment longer (the garlic should be only faintly golden), add a squeeze of lemon juice and pour the buttery juices over the pork medallions. Serve at once.

* Poulet en Cocotte à l'Ail

A true French bourgeois dish and just right for the season's fresh garlic, either bought or your own grown. You can get this all prepared and leave it ready for the oven. Then pop it in and forget it until ready to serve. The garlic is surprisingly delicate treated in this way, so please don't be afraid of it.

Ingredients
4–6 people

3½ lb (1.6k) chicken
1–2 heads garlic
4–5 tbs olive oil
¼ teasp pernod
3–4 slices stale French bread
a good bunch of herbs (3 sprigs fennel, 2
    sprigs rosemary, 3 sprigs thyme and a
    little marjoram)
1 bay leaf
salt and pepper

Huff Paste
8 oz (225g) plain flour
5 fl oz (150ml) water
½ teasp salt

Whisk together 2 tbs oil and the pernod. Dry the bread until crisp in a low oven. Use 1–2 cloves of garlic, cut in half, to rub over both sides of the bread, then moisten them with the pernod-oil, season with salt and pepper and pop inside the chicken. Rub the dry chicken all over with the remaining pernod-oil.

In a casserole (preferably earthenware) place 2–3 tbs olive oil just to cover the bottom. Make a bed of herbs on this and scatter over the cloves of garlic, separated but un-peeled. Lay the chicken on this, breast up, season with salt and pepper and cover with the lid. Seal the lid in place with huff paste. Set the casserole to cook in a hot oven (450°F/230°C/Gas 8) for 1¼ hours. Remove the lid of the casserole at the table so that you catch the wonderful trapped aroma and carve the chicken. Serve 2–3 of the cloves of garlic with each serving. Pressed from its paper skin, the purée is mild and delicious.

Huff Paste. Mix the flour, salt and water to a stiff paste, knead until smooth and use to seal the casserole.

F **   Lasagne al Forno

A dish of baked lasagne is always very popular but can be quite a business to make with all its different components. So I have written a recipe for more than the usual quantity, either enough to feed 8–10 generously or to make two smaller dishes, one for now and one for the freezer. 'No-cook pasta' (packets of bought pasta that are supposed not to need cooking before baking) is a boon when you are in a hurry, but not as good as home-made, bought fresh or dry pasta cooked before assembling.

Ingredients
8–10 people

1 batch home-made spinach or plain
   pasta *(see page 183)* **or 12 oz (350g)**
   'no-cook' or packet lasagne
2–3 oz (50–75g) freshly grated Parmesan
   or rather more Cheddar

Meat Filling
4–8 oz (100–225g) diced salami
8 oz (225g) diced cooked ham
1 lb (450g) diced cooked chicken or cold
   roast meat
or use
1¾–2 lb (775–900g), or a
proportion, of raw beef mince
1–2 tbs olive oil
1 oz (25g) butter
1 large onion
2 cloves garlic
½–1 teasp freshly grated nutmeg
¼–½ teasp ground allspice
¼ teasp chilli or cayenne pepper
4 fl oz (100ml) dry white wine
salt and pepper

Tomato Sauce
1 × 1 lb 14 oz (850g) tin tomatoes
2 large onions
1 carrot
1 stick celery
2 cloves garlic
3 tbs olive oil
1 oz (25g) butter
4 oz (100g) tomato purée
8 fl oz (225ml) stock *or* water and ½
   chicken stock cube
1 bay leaf
salt and pepper

White Sauce
4 oz (100g) butter
4 oz (100g) plain flour
1½ pts (900ml) milk plus a little extra
freshly grated nutmeg
salt and pepper

25 people

2–2½ times the quantity, depending on
   appetites

Start with the tomato sauce, which should simmer for an hour or so; next prepare the meat and make the white sauce; lastly cook the lasagne (or soak the 'no-cook' lasagne) and assemble the dish.

Tomato Sauce. Finely chop the onions, carrot, celery and garlic and soften in the butter and oil, without browning, for about 10 minutes. Add the tomato purée and fry for several minutes before adding the roughly chopped tomatoes with their juice and the stock, bay leaf and a light seasoning. Simmer for about 1 hour until well reduced and tasty.

Meat Filling. Chop the onion and fry in the butter and oil in a wide pan for about 10 minutes until golden. Add the chopped garlic, diced salami, ham and cold meat (or beef mince) and sauté, stirring frequently, for 5–10 minutes until browning. Add the nutmeg, allspice, chilli and the wine with a light seasoning of salt and pepper. Simmer uncovered for 10–15 minutes or until almost all the liquid has gone. If using all raw minced beef add a little water and cover the pan, for the meat will need to cook until tender.

If using a mixture of raw and cooked meats, fry and simmer the raw meat, then sauté and add the cooked meats 10–15 minutes before the end of the cooking time.

White Sauce. Melt the butter in a saucepan, add the flour and cook, stirring, over moderate heat for 2–3 minutes. Draw the pan off the stove, wait for the sizzling to cease and add the milk. Bring to the boil, whisking hard, and simmer for 3–4 minutes. Season with nutmeg, salt and pepper and leave, covered, on the side of the stove to mature.

Lasagne. Cook the lasagne in plenty of boiling salted water with a tablespoon of oil added. The secret is to 'post' the lasagne in gradually, keeping the water boiling. If it stops, the pasta sulks on the bottom and sticks together. Cook home-made or fresh bought pasta for 3–5 minutes until just *al dente* (firm to the bite), or packet pasta for 15–20 minutes. 'No-cook' pasta is best thrown into boiling salted, oiled water just to soften and become flexible. Drain and rinse in cold water and keep in the minimum of cold water until ready to use (easier than spreading it on cloths all over the kitchen).

To Assemble. Butter a 9″ × 14″ (24cm × 36cm) gratin dish. Mix the meat filling with half the tomato sauce and 2–3 good tablespoons of the white sauce. Place a layer of plain tomato sauce over the bottom of the dish to stop the pasta from sticking. Layer with a quarter of the cooked, drained, lasagne, then cover with one third of the meat. Sprinkle with Parmesan and add the next layer of lasagne. Continue until you have four layers of lasagne and three of filling and cheese. Now pour the remaining tomato sauce over the lasagne and top the dish with the white sauce and a good sprinkle of Parmesan. Bake in a moderately hot oven (375°F/190°C/Gas 5) for ½–¾ hour until brown and bubbling. Alternatively, leave to stand for 12–24 hours, then bake in a moderate oven (350°F/180°C/ Gas 4) for 1–1¼ hours until brown and bubbling.

Variation for 25 people. You will need several gratin dishes, and 5–6 tablespoons of white sauce for mixing with the meat filling.

ℱ *** Classic Braised Beef

To produce a braise fit for a dinner party, so that your husband won't say afterwards 'That was a nice stew' (and how daunting is faint praise!), means taking quite a lot of trouble in the preparation and cooking of the dish, particularly with the sauce at the end. Anything served from a casserole, awash with insipid sauce, deserves to be labelled stew, delicious as it may be for a winter's lunch. But for a dinner party you need really generous chunks of good meat, bathed in a small quantity of really rich, smooth sauce in which are suspended nicely cooked mushrooms and lardons of smoked bacon (though many other garnishes can be used). Our old English cookery books have many recipes for this type of dish, often highly seasoned with spices, which I prefer to use more discreetly nowadays.

The joy of this sort of dish is that all the care and attention can be given ahead, for braises taste even better when given time to blend and mature. You then have nothing to do but carefully reheat it, cook any separate garnish and serve it up, preferably piled on a serving dish and surrounded by glazed carrots, baby turnips, cucumber or forcemeat balls. No one can then call it a stew!

Ingredients
4–6 people

2½–3 lb (1.15–1.35kg) *thick* cut chuck or braising beef
4–6 oz (100–175g) pork skin in one piece
½ lb (225g) onions
½ lb (225g) carrots
1 stick celery
1 oz (25g) butter ⎫ *or* 3 oz (75g) good
4 tbs olive oil ⎬ dripping
1 oz (25g) flour ⎭
½ pt (300ml) beefstock or ½ stock cube and water
½ pt (300ml) good red wine
bouquet garni of 3–4 parsley stalks, 2–3 sprigs thyme, 1 bay leaf, a little marjoram and 2 cloves
1–2 cloves garlic
any stalks from the button mushrooms
1–2 tbs mushroom ketchup
salt and pepper

Larding Strips

2 oz (50g) back pork fat
pinches of ground cloves, allspice, mace and nutmeg
salt, pepper and cayenne pepper

Garnish
4–6 oz (100–175g) thick cut smoked streaky bacon cut in ½" (1cm) slices
½ lb (225g) button mushrooms
¾ lb (450g) segments of lightly cooked carrots glazed in butter with a little sugar and chervil
1 cucumber, segmented, boiled and glazed in butter with tarragon *or* Glazed Turnips (*see page 256*)

Larding Strips. Start by cutting the back pork fat into narrow strips and sprinkling with the seasoning and spices. Lay these lardons straight and freeze for a few minutes until firm.

Cut the meat into 2 oz (50g) cubes and lard each with a seasoned lardon (make a hole with a fine bladed knife and push in a frozen strip).

Bring the pork skin to the boil in plenty of cold water, skim and simmer for 20–30 minutes.

Slice the onion, carrot and celery and soften and brown gently in the butter with 1 tbs oil (or dripping) added. I use a heavy casserole which will hold all the braise.

Heat the remaining oil in a frying pan and fry the cubes of meat until browned on all sides; then sprinkle over the flour and allow that also to brown very lightly. Turn all into the casserole and de-glaze the pan with some of the stock or wine. Add to the casserole with the remaining stock and wine, the bouquet garni and the cloves of garlic, lightly flattened with the skins removed; also add the drained pork skin in one piece, mushroom ketchup and any mushroom stalks. Season very lightly, for the sauce will be reduced later, and bring just to the simmer. Cook in a very slow oven (250°F/130°C/Gas 1) for 2½–3 hours until tender.

Remove the meat from the sauce and set aside. Strain the sauce into a wide pan, pressing the vegetables and débris well (they can make a delicious soup). Leave to stand a few minutes, then de-grease and reduce the sauce, skimming off any scum that rises. When only about 10–15 fl oz (300–450ml) remains, correct the seasoning, and return the meat cubes.

Garnish. Meanwhile de-rind the streaky bacon and cut into oblong lardons, blanch if salty, then fry gently, adding a little butter, if they are very lean, until golden. Remove and add to the beef. Keep the braise hot or set aside to reheat. Briskly sauté the mushrooms in remaining fat and add to the beef.

To Serve. Remove the meat, bacon and mushrooms to a hot serving plate and spoon the thick rich gravy over them (there should be just enough to moisten but not swamp the meat). Garnish around with carrots and cucumber or turnips. Fried forcemeat balls or glazed pickling onions could also be served around the braise.

**   Roast Fillet of Beef with its own Butter Sauce

When you can afford or can get hold of a fillet of well-hung, fresh (not frozen) beef, this is a gem of a dish. Prepare and seal the beef, then leave ready for the oven. Prepare the thickened egg-yolk sauce base. Then, at the appropriate moment, cook the beef in its butter sauce, no watching or basting really needed. Once cooked, it can rest, then it is the work of a moment to whisk the buttery cooking juices into the egg-yolk base to make a béarnaise style sauce with all the flavour from the beef. Adjust the timing only on the thickness of the fillet, not on its weight or length.

Ingredients
6–8 people

2½–3 lb (1.15–1.35kg) centre cut fillet of
   beef
3 tbs olive oil
7 oz (200g) butter
4–6 thin cut rashers streaky bacon
1–2 tbs white wine
1 finely chopped shallot
1 sprig fresh or ¼ teasp dried tarragon
2 bay leaves
pepper

Sauce Base
3 egg yolks
1 tbs tarragon vinegar
1 oz (25g) butter
salt and pepper

Trim the fillet, which should be a nice thick centre cut (Châteaubriand) of meat, well marbled with fat, removing all external fat and bluish membrane. Bring to room temperature and pat quite dry. Season with pepper only and tie with string in 2–3 places to keep a good shape. Heat the oil in a frying pan or roasting tin and brown the beef all over. Lay it in a roasting tin, in which you have melted the butter and cover with rashers of streaky bacon. Add the wine, shallot, tarragon and bay leaves and cook in a very hot oven (425°F/240°C/Gas 9) for 10 minutes, then baste and lower the temperature to moderate (350°F/180°/Gas4) for a further 15–25 minutes until cooked to your liking. Check once or twice during the cooking that the butter is not burning and add a spoonful of wine if necessary.

Remove the beef and rest somewhere where it will keep warm but *not* go on cooking (turned-off oven, warming drawer or hostess trolley). This allows the meat fibres to relax and the juices to spread back through the meat. Pour off the butter juices, remove the sprig of tarragon and the bay leaves and cool a little before adding to the sauce.

Sauce. Whisk the egg yolks well with a wire whisk, then beat in the tarragon vinegar. Place the bowl over a pan of hot, not boiling, water so that the bowl does not touch the water. Add half the butter and stir until the yolks thicken enough for you to see the bottom of the bowl when you draw your whisk across. Remove the bowl from the pan quickly before they cook further and curdle, and whisk in the remaining piece of cold butter to cool the mixture and stop it cooking. This can now wait covered, just keeping warm over tepid water.

When you are ready to finish the sauce, gradually whisk in the slightly cooled butter roasting juices as if making a béarnaise or mayonnaise sauce. Stop when the sauce has the right consistency, thickly flowing, for it may not need all the meat juices from under the butter. Correct seasoning, add a little more chopped fresh or dried tarragon if necessary and serve in a sauce boat with the beef. Once made it will keep warm in a pan of lukewarm water.

𝓕 ** Pork with Cider and Apple or Quince

It's a very old and good custom to cook pork with apple. This makes an extremely nice casserole, especially if you can use quinces or just include a small proportion of quince.

Ingredients

4–6 people	*25 people*
1½–2 lb (675–900g) boned shoulder of pork	8–10 lb (3.6–4.5kg) boned shoulder of pork
2½ oz (65g) pork fat, dripping or butter	4–6 oz (100–175g) pork fat, dripping or butter
1 tbs oil	2–3 tbs oil
2 sliced onions	8 sliced onions
2 tbs calvados or brandy	6–8 tbs calvados or brandy (optional)
1 oz (25g) flour	4 oz (100g) flour
8 fl oz (225ml) dry cider	1 pt (600ml) dry cider
8 fl oz (225ml) stock	1 pt (600ml) stock
bouquet garni of parsley stalks, sage and bay leaf	bouquet garni of 6–8 parsley stalks, 4–6 sprigs sage and 2 bay leaves
1 clove garlic	2–3 cloves garlic
2 teasp paprika	3 tbs paprika
4 medium cooking or eating apples or quinces or quince and apple mixed	12 medium cooking or eating apples or quinces or quince and apple mixed
salt and pepper	salt and pepper

Remove the skin from the pork and cut into 1½" (4cm) cubes. Cut some of the pork skin into very fine dice to add later to give richness to the dish.

Heat the oil and half the pork fat, dripping or butter in a large frying pan and fry the onions until soft. Add the pork cubes and fry until they are lightly browned on all sides and the onion is brown. Flame with calvados or brandy, sprinkle with flour and toss. Turn into a casserole and de-glaze the pan with cider and stock. Add to the casserole with the cubes of pork skin, the flattened clove of garlic and the bouquet garni, paprika and seasoning.

Meanwhile melt the remaining fat or butter in a frying pan and add the peeled, cored and thickly sliced apple or quince. Fry until light golden on each side, then add to the casserole. Cover and simmer gently or cook in a slow oven (300°F/150°C/Gas 2) for 1½–2 hours until the pork is absolutely tender and the sauce rich and tasty.

This dish tastes even better re-heated, and freezes beautifully.

Variation for 25 people. Brown the onions and remove before frying the meat in batches and flaming. Before serving, you may need to remove the meat from the casserole and reduce the sauce or thicken it a little more.

**   Martinmas Pheasant

St Martin's Day is 11 November, when you might have a pheasant nicely hung and ready for the pot! I find this sealed-pot way of cooking it one of the few ways of keeping a pheasant (or chicken) really succulent, so kick the roast pheasant habit and try it.

Ingredients
3–4 people

1 plump pheasant
2–3 rashers streaky bacon
1–2 sprigs rosemary
¼ teasp ground cinnamon
2 oz (50g) butter
1 thickly sliced onion
2 peeled, cored and thickly sliced apples
8 fl oz (225ml) cider
1 oz (25g) raisins or sultanas
¼ chicken stock cube
5 fl oz (150ml) double or whipping cream

½–1 teasp potato flour (or arrowroot or
  cornflour)
2–3 tbs cold water
up to 2 oz (50g) butter (optional)
salt and pepper

Huff Paste
8 oz (225g) plain flour
5 fl oz (150ml) cold water
½ teasp salt

Place the apple cores and seasoning inside the pheasant and wipe dry. Melt the butter in a frying pan and use a little to rub the pheasant all over vigorously. Add the onion to the butter and fry until golden. Remove it and fry the apple slices until golden on both sides. Take a reasonably large casserole (preferably earthenware) and place the onions and apples with any remaining frying butter in the bottom, adding the sprig of rosemary and the cinnamon. Lay the buttered pheasant on its side on this, season and cover with the rashers of bacon. Cover with the lid and seal in place with huff paste. Place in a hot oven (425°F/220°C/Gas 8) for 1 hour, or 50 minutes for a small bird. Meanwhile, simmer the raisins in the cider with the bit of stock cube added, until the liquid has reduced by half and the raisins are well plumped; set aside. Boil the cream for several minutes to reduce and set aside, covered. Mix the potato flour with a little cold water.

When the pheasant is ready, break off the huff paste and discard. Remove the pheasant to keep warm, being careful not to spike or prod it with a knife or fork prong, which would let the juice out. Remove and discard the rosemary, and turn the rest of the contents of the pan into a food processor or liquidiser and process until very smooth. Sieve into a small pan, then add the cider and raisins, the cream and the slaked potato flour. Bring to the boil to thicken the potato flour and correct the seasoning. If you wish, you can whisk in little bits of butter just as you take the sauce off the stove, but once the butter is added it will not wait.

Carve the pheasant (it is all the better for resting in a warm place for 20–30 minutes before carving so that the flesh relaxes and re-absorbs the juices) and cover with the sauce, or hand the sauce separately. The carved pheasant, covered in sauce, can be re-warmed carefully later.

Huff Paste. Mix the flour, salt and water to a stiff paste, knead until smooth and use to seal the pot.

**   Roman Pie

This recipe comes from an aunt who says they often used to have it in Scotland during her childhood. I also have it in my old manuscript book as Roman Pudding. Recipes for this pop up here and there in old books, but it does not seem very widely known. Since our rabbits are not as tasty as the wild ones, I include some ham, which is not authentic. You can make this pie with puff pastry (bought does well enough) or it could be made with shortcrust, but here we use cheesy flaky pastry, which I find is excellent. It can be served hot with brown gravy, made from the rabbit bones, or cold, which many consider even better, and is excellent for picnics.

Ingredients
6–8 people

the meat from 1–2 cooked rabbits *or* 1
   chicken or pheasant *or* 1½lb (675g)
   cooked veal
6 oz (175g) cooked ham
4 oz (100g) macaroni or little shells (1 lb
   (450g) cooked)
4 oz (100g) Parmesan or strong Cheddar
   cheese
4–6 fl oz (100–175ml) cream
egg wash
salt, pepper and cayenne pepper

Cheesy Flaky Pastry
8 oz (225g) plain flour
6 oz (175g) butter
2 oz (50g) grated cheese
iced water
½ teasp dry mustard
salt and pepper

Cheesy Flaky Pastry. Sieve the flour with the salt, pepper and mustard into a bowl or food processor and add the grated cheese and firm butter, cut in hazelnut-sized pieces. Rub in or process, adding iced water as you go and stopping as the mixture draws together. Knead briefly into a ball and roll to a 5″ × 10″ (12cm × 25cm) rectangle. Fold the bottom third up, top third down, press the edges together and turn the pastry half a turn to the right. Roll and fold the pastry twice more, then rest in a plastic bag in the fridge for 1–2 hours.

Cook the macaroni or shells in boiling salt water for 18–20 minutes or until well cooked; drain and cut macaroni into ¼-finger lengths (if cooking ahead, leave to cool in a little water).

Dice the rabbit meat and ham into ¼–½″ (½–1cm) dice and mix with the macaroni and cheese. Season highly and stir in the cream. Roll two thirds of the pastry thinly and line a 9″ (23cm) pie dish or removable base cake tin or 2″ (5cm) deep tart tin. Turn the mixture into the pie, damp the edges with water, cover with the remaining pastry and press the edges together. Make a small hole in the top, decorate and brush with egg wash.

Cook in a hot oven (425°F/220°C/Gas 7) for 10–20 minutes until well browned, then turn down to moderate (350°F/180°C/Gas 4) for a further 45 minutes or so. You may like to remove the outer ring of the cake tin for the last 20–30 minutes so that the sides of the pie can brown well. Turn out and serve hot or cold.

Vegetables

* Button Mushrooms with Cream

This is extravagant but lovely, and can almost be used as a sauce with something like a steak or grilled chops.

Ingredients
4–6 people

¾–1 lb (350–450g) button mushrooms
2 oz (50g) butter
1 clove finely chopped garlic
1 tbs plain flour

8 fl oz (225ml) whipping cream
½ lemon
2 tbs finely chopped parsley
salt and pepper

Cut any large mushrooms into halves or quarters. Heat the butter in a frying pan or sauté pan and, when hot, toss in the mushrooms and sauté over high heat for 3–5 minutes. Sprinkle over the finely chopped garlic and cook a minute or two more until the mushrooms just start browning, but don't burn the garlic. Sprinkle over the flour and cook for a moment or two before adding the cream. Shake and stir over the fire until the cream thickens, then add seasoning and a squeeze of lemon juice to taste, and stir in the parsley. Serve at once or keep warm in a *bain marie*.

** Aubergines and Onions in Olive Oil

Aubergines are good in autumn, and you may even grow your own. They are wonderful when cooked slowly with lots of oil to accentuate their suave texture and spicy flavour. Garlic and onions should be well ripened now, but still retaining their summer sweetness; you may have some throaty onions, which don't make a good round shape and won't store well, so use them for this with sun-ripened tomatoes and lavish quantities of good olive oil for the very taste of captured summer sun. This dish can be eaten hot or cold as a vegetable with cold meat; it can have ½ lb (225g) pasta, cooked *al dente*, tipped into it and tossed with more basil and grated Parmesan; or it can be topped with breadcrumbs and cheese and baked until brown in a hot oven.

Ingredients
4–6 people

1–1½ lb (450–675g) aubergines
1 lb (450g) onions
4–5 fl oz (100–150ml) good fruity olive oil
2 cloves garlic
1 lb (450g) ripe tomatoes or 1 × 14 oz (400g) tin

½ teasp sugar
1–2 tbs fresh chopped basil *or* basil in butter or oil from the freezer *or* ½ teasp dried basil
salt and pepper

Start by setting the oil to warm in a heavy casserole, earthenware for choice. Peel and cut the onions into quarters if small or into thick lengthways slices if large. Add them to the oil with the garlic cloves, flattened slightly, and allow them 30 minutes to stew gently but not brown. Slice the aubergines, sprinkle heavily with salt in a colander and leave to de-gorge their juices under a plate and weights for 30 minutes. Process and sieve the fresh tomatoes or drained tinned tomatoes, or you can put them through the fine plate of the soup mouli. Boil with ¼ teasp salt and ½ teasp sugar in a wide pan until reduced by half.

Wash and dry the aubergine slices, drain the golden but unbrowned onions from the oil and set aside. Heat the oil until very hot, then fry the aubergine slices until light golden on both sides; do them in several batches, pressing and draining well when you remove them from the pan. Try not to use more oil or the dish will be greasy, for a lot of oil will come out of the aubergine later. When all are soft and browned, return them to the pan with the onions and reduced tomato, add chopped basil and seasoning, and leave to simmer very gently for 30 minutes or so until rich, soft and tasty. Correct seasoning, add a little more basil and serve hot or cold, or mix with cooked pasta and freshly grated Parmesan.

This dish can also be baked, perhaps topped with breadcrumbs and cheese.

✳✳   Broccoli Timbales

These delicate little broccoli custards can be used either as a first course or as a vegetable. The superbly flavoured autumn broccoli Romanesco is perfect for this.

Ingredients
4–6 people

6–8 oz (175–225g) broccoli
2 eggs
4 fl oz (100ml) milk
4 fl oz (100ml) whipping cream
½ oz (12g) butter
salt, pepper and nutmeg

Break the broccoli into florets and cook in plenty of boiling salt water until just tender. Drain and refresh under the cold tap, draining really well.

Purée the broccoli in a food processor or liquidiser, adding the eggs, cream and milk. Season with salt, pepper and nutmeg and sieve if necessary. Generously butter 4–6 ramekin dishes and fill with the mixture. Set them in a roasting tin with boiling water to come halfway up the outside of the ramekins and cook in a very moderate oven (325°F/170°C/Gas 3) for about 20–25 minutes until set. Leave for a few moments before turning out, because they will then come out more easily. Turn out the broccoli moulds and serve.

You can also cook the mixture in a buttered shallow gratin dish, set in a *bain marie*, and serve it straight from the dish.

✳✳   Sweet-Sour Green Beans

This Middle-European way with beans is rather nice and a little different. It reheats well and is good for entertaining, especially with hot ham or roast game, which the sweet-sour taste will complement.

Ingredients
4–6 people

1½–2 lb (675–900g) French beans,
    broken into 2″ (5cm) bits
12 fl oz (350ml) boiling water
1 clove garlic
1 thinly sliced onion
1 bay leaf
3 tbs brown sugar
3 tbs tarragon vinegar
pinch ground cloves
1 teasp potato or cornflour
1½ oz (35g) butter, diced
2 tbs chopped parsley

Add the whole peeled and lightly crushed garlic clove, the sliced onion and the bay leaf to the lightly salted boiling water in a saucepan. Simmer gently, covered, for 15 minutes before adding the prepared beans. Cook until just tender, then drain, reserving the cooking liquid. Discard the garlic and bay leaf. Add the sugar, vinegar and ground cloves to the cooking liquid and boil fast to reduce to ¼ pt (150ml). Add the potato flour, mixed with a little cold water, and boil to thicken. Then stir in the diced butter, beans and parsley, correct seasoning and reheat before serving.

✳✳   Risotto Doré

Risottos are always useful, whether made with white rice, brown rice or saffron flavoured rice. This one includes peas and sultanas, and I sometimes cheat, especially for large numbers, by using a pinch of turmeric for colour rather than the much more expensive saffron.

Ingredients

4–6 people	*25 people*
8–10 oz (225–275g) long grain rice	2–2½ lb (900g–1.15kg) long grain rice
¾–1 pt (450–600ml) chicken stock	3–3½ pts (1.7–2l) chicken stock
1 pkt saffron or pinch turmeric	2 pkts saffron or ½ teasp turmeric for colour
1 oz (25g) butter	
1 finely chopped onion	3 oz (75g) butter
2–3 oz (50–75g) fresh or frozen peas	3 finely chopped onions
1 tbs sultanas	8–10 oz (225–275g) fresh or frozen peas
1 teasp tomato purée	3–4 tbs sultanas
salt and pepper	1 tbs tomato purée
	salt and pepper

204

Soak the saffron, if used, in a little of the hot stock for 15–30 minutes. Melt the butter in a casserole and gently cook the onion until transparent. Add the unwashed rice and cook for 2–3 minutes or until the rice looks milky and glistens with butter. Add the hot stock, peas, sultanas, tomato purée and soaked saffron (or turmeric if used). Season with salt and pepper, bring to the simmer and place in a moderate oven (350°F/180°C/Gas 4) for 18–20 minutes or until ready. Lightly loosen the rice with a fork; each grain should be separate and perfectly cooked. Serve from the casserole or as a border round a dish, or it can be packed into a greased mould, then turned out after 10 minutes in a slow oven.

Variations for 25 people. Fry the rice for rather longer and allow more cooking time.

** Gratin of Green Beans, Smoky Bacon and Mushrooms

When the French beans are getting larger, they can be used in this lightly bound gratin, flavoured with smoked bacon to make a good supper dish or to serve with cold meat.

Ingredients
4–6 people

1½ lb (675g) French beans
3 oz (75g) smoked streaky bacon, cut thick
4 oz (100g) field or button mushrooms
1½ oz (40g) butter
1 tbs potato flour
5 fl oz (150ml) cream or milk or a mixture
10 fl oz (300ml) bean cooking water
2 teasp finely chopped summer savory or parsley
4–6 tbs grated cheese
4–6 tbs breadcrumbs
salt and pepper

Toss the prepared beans into lightly salted boiling water and cook until just tender. Drain, reserving the cooking liquid.

Meanwhile, dice the bacon and fry in 1 oz (25g) butter until lightly golden (I use a wok or large frying pan which will eventually hold all the ingredients). Slice the mushrooms thickly, add, and sauté until just done. Mix the potato flour with the cream and/or milk, add to 10 fl oz (300ml) of the reserved bean cooking water and combine in the pan with the bacon and mushrooms. Bring to the boil, stirring, and simmer for 1–2 minutes. Stir in the cooked beans, seasoning and herbs, and toss to coat with sauce. Turn into a buttered gratin dish, top with grated cheese, breadcrumbs and flakes of butter and pop under the grill to brown. It can also be set aside and reheated in a hot oven (400°F/200°C/Gas 7) for about 30 minutes.

* ## Carrots with Coriander and Lime

This is one of my favourite vegetable dishes because the subtle flavours complement each other beautifully. It is good enough to be served on its own or is nice with something simple like a grilled chop, when it can be fully appreciated.

Ingredients
4–6 people

1 lb (450g) young carrots
1 teasp whole coriander seeds
½–1 oz (12–25g) butter
1½ teasp castor sugar
grated lime or lemon rind
1½ teasp lime or lemon juice
fresh chopped coriander or parsley
   (optional)
salt and pepper

Scrape or peel the carrots and cut into quarters or sixths lengthways, then across into 2" (5cm) segments. Parboil in plenty of salted boiling water or steam for about 5–7 minutes until nearly tender. Drain.

    Crush the coriander with a pestle and mortar.

    Heat the butter in a wok or large frying pan until sizzling, toss in the drained carrots and sprinkle with sugar, coriander and seasoning. Toss and turn over high heat until glazed, then add grated lime or lemon rind and juice. Toss a moment or two more and serve scattered with fresh herbs, if desired.

** ## Lady Farquhar's Beetroot Salad

This is an old recipe from my great-great-grandmother which I rather like. I usually cut the beetroot, once cooked, into 'chips' rather than slices, and the caraway is my addition. The recipe says that a few sliced potatoes may be added.

Ingredients
4–6 people

1–2 lb (450–900g) beetroot
3–4 tbs tarragon vinegar (or shallot
   vinegar)
½ teasp caraway seeds (optional)

Dressing
1 egg yolk
1 teasp Dijon mustard
1 teasp sugar
1–2 teasp Worcester sauce
2 tbs oil
3 tbs cream
1 teasp capers
salt and pepper

Boil the beetroot, unpeeled and with the leaf stump left on, in plenty of boiling salt water until tender and the skins rub off. Peel, slice (food processor with chipper blade), season and sprinkle with the vinegar and caraway seeds and leave to cool.

Dressing. Combine the egg yolk, seasoning, mustard, sugar and Worcester sauce, beat in the oil and cream and add the capers. Pour over the beetroot, toss and serve chilled.

** Cucumber Salad with Shallot and Mustard Dressing

Summer ridge cucumbers or winter long ones all make good salads. I like them de-gorged with salt, then dressed with a mustardy shallot dressing. A scattering of roasted sesame seeds or little black onion seeds makes a change.

Ingredients
4–6 people

1 large or several smaller cucumbers
salt
1–2 tbs toasted sesame seeds or onion
  seeds or finely chopped chervil

Dressing
1½ teasp Dijon mustard
1 tbs finely chopped shallot or onion
1 tbs wine vinegar
4 tbs light oil
few drops sesame oil (optional)
salt and plenty of pepper

Slice the peeled (or unpeeled) cucumbers, remove any large seeds and lay in a colander. Sprinkle with salt and leave under a plate and weights to degorge for 30 minutes. Drain, rinse and dry well. Mix with the dressing, turn into a bowl and serve scattered with toasted sesame seeds or onion seeds or chopped herbs. Toast the sesame seeds, if used, in a heavy dry frying pan until fragrant, browning and jumping. Onion seeds are just scattered over.

Dressing. Mix the mustard, shallot or onion, pepper and vinegar until the salt dissolves; gradually beat in the oil and, if you like, a few drops of sesame oil to make a thick dressing.

* Florence Fennel au Gratin

Florence fennel, with its succulent white swollen stems and strong flavour of aniseed, is a great favourite of mine and I wander round the garden crunching its juicy stems. For some, though, it is too strongly flavoured, so instead of a salad recipe I give you a milder cooked dish of fennel, topped with garlic *beurre noisette*, breadcrumbs and cheese.

Ingredients
4–6 people

2–4 bulbs Florence fennel
1½ oz (35g) butter
1 clove garlic
a handful brown or white breadcrumbs
½–1 lemon
½–1 oz (12–25g) freshly grated Parmesan
   cheese or 2 oz (50g) grated strong
   Cheddar cheese
salt and pepper

Cut the Florence fennel into quarters or sixths, lengthways so that the wedges are held together by the core, and cook in boiling salted water, to which you have added a good squeeze of lemon juice, until just tender. Drain and lay in a shallow buttered gratin dish.

Meanwhile melt the remaining butter and cook until brown and smelling nutty. Add the breadcrumbs and the garlic, chopped very fine, and toss for a few moments until the breadcrumbs are browning. Season the fennel and squeeze a little lemon juice over it before scattering with grated cheese and the fried breadcrumbs. Pop under the grill or into a hot oven until the cheese has melted and the top is browned.

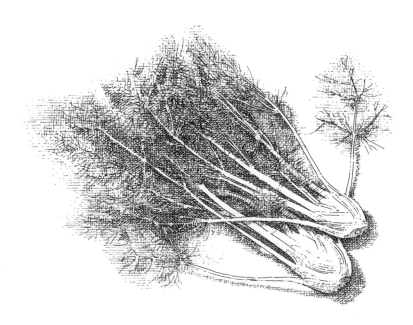

Puddings

$P F$ ** **Autumn Pudding**

Everyone knows Summer Pudding, that wonderful bread-encased cornucopia of summer fruit, but how many people make an Autumn Pudding? The flavours are softer and mellower, like the season, and the colour is more tawny. Bread for Summer or Autumn Pudding should ideally be a sandwich loaf from a good baker, left to go dry for 4–6 days so that its texture is short rather than soggy.

Ingredients
6–8 people

1 loaf *stale* white bread or brioche
1–1½ lb (450–675g) apples
¾–1 lb (350–450g) pears
2 quinces *or* 4–5 tbs quince jelly
12 oz (350g) blackberries
1 lb (450g) plums
4–8 oz (100–225g) mulberries (optional)
any autumn raspberries and late
   strawberries or *fraises de bois*
sugar
2 tbs rum or brandy (optional)

a mixture weighing approx 3–4 lb (1.35–1.8kg)

Peel, slice and core the apples, pears and quinces (or use quince jelly). Cook gently in a very little water with sugar to taste until the quinces and apples are tender, adding stoned plums, blackberries then finally the mulberries, raspberries and strawberries for the last few minutes or so. Check the sweetness, and stir in rum or brandy if used. The mixture should be quite juicy.

Line a 2½–3 pt (1.5–1.7l) pudding bowl or soufflé dish with crustless slices of white bread or brioche loaf, about ⅜" (1cm) thick. Stand the bread-lined bowl on a large plate to catch drips. Fill with fruit and juice until tightly packed. Cover the top with more bread slices and cover with a plate or saucer that just fits the top. Weight with a brick or heavy weights and keep in a cool larder or fridge for at least 24 hours. Turn out the beautiful firm pudding and serve in slices with thick cream or Crème Fraîche.

✳✳✳   Tarte aux Fruits

A tart of rich sweet pastry, layered with crème patissière and filled with whatever varieties of fruit are at their best, is a lovely pudding. Apple or pear make suitable autumn fillings, peach and grape are an attractive combination, and strawberry or raspberry are favourites in summer.

Ingredients
4–6 people

Pâté Sucrée

6 oz (175g) plain flour
2 oz (50g) icing sugar
4 oz (100g) soft butter
a few drops orange flower water
   (optional)
1 egg yolk
1 tbs cold water
pinch salt

Crème Patissière
3 oz (75g) vanilla sugar
3 egg yolks
8 fl oz (225ml) milk
1 vanilla pod
1¼ oz (30g) plain flour (*or* half flour and
   half rice flour *or* cornflour)
½ oz (12g) butter
vanilla essence to taste

Filling
¾–1 lb (350–450g) mixed fresh fruit:
   strawberries, grapes, sliced kiwi fruit
   or any other fruit in season: poached
   and drained apricots, peach, apple or
   pear halves

Glaze
4–5 tbs red currant jelly or apricot jam,
   whichever colour is appropriate

Pâté Sucrée. Sift the flour on to a board and make a well in the middle. Put in the middle the sifted sugar, well softened butter, salt, orange flower water and the egg yolk mixed with the water. Pinch and mix these together without the flour to make a soft paste; then draw the flour into it, kneading the paste as little as possible. Form into a flat disc and rest in a plastic bag in the fridge for 2 hours.

If making in a food processor, cream the soft butter with the sugar, salt, egg yolk and water and orange flower water, just enough to mix thoroughly. Sift in the flour, process until just incorporated, form into a flat disc and chill.

Roll the pastry to fit a 9″ (23cm) flan tin, press into the corners well, roll off excess, prick base, line with tinfoil and baking beans and bake in a hot oven (400°F/200°C/Gas 6) for 7–10 minutes. Once the pastry has set, remove the tinfoil and baking beans and continue to bake in a moderately hot oven (375°F/190°C/Gas 5) until fully cooked and a light golden brown. You should see tiny bubbles of butter on the pastry when you take it from the oven. Cool on a rack.

Crème Patissière. Heat and infuse the milk with the vanilla pod. Beat the egg yolks and vanilla sugar for 2–3 minutes until pale yellow and forming a 'ribbon'. Beat the flour into the egg mixture. Pour the boiling milk on to the yolks gradually in a thin stream, whisking hard all the time. Pour into a heavy enamel or stainless steel (*not* aluminium) saucepan and bring to the boil, whisking all the while. Simmer for 2–3 minutes or until the flour is cooked, still whisking all the time. Remove from the heat, beat in the butter and vanilla essence and turn into a bowl. Press cling film or wet greaseproof paper on top of the custard and keep refrigerated, or freeze, thaw and beat well before using.

Glaze. Very gently melt the red currant jelly but do not boil. Sieve the apricot jam first.

To Assemble. Spread the base of the pastry with a layer of Crème Patissière, which you may need to thin with cream or milk to a spreading consistency, or into which you can fold a little whipped cream if you like. Cover with whole hulled strawberries or fruit of your choice, carefully draining poached fruit. Brush them lightly with the appropriate glaze.

*   Damson and Dumpling Pudding

You can use damsons or plums for this. Real suety dumplings are rather heavy, so we make butter dumplings and literally pop them on top of the stewing plums to steam for 15 minutes. It is quick and easy and a real proper pudding. It is best when just cooked.

Ingredients
4–6 people

1½–2 lb (675–900g) damsons or plums
a little water
sugar to taste

Dumplings
5 oz (125g) plain flour
1½ teasp baking powder
1½ oz (35g) butter
2–3 fl oz (50–75ml) milk
tiny pinch salt

Just cover the bottom of a wide pan with water and add the plums and sugar to taste. Cover and cook gently for about 5 minutes.

Dumplings. Sift the flour, salt and the baking powder into a bowl, add the diced butter and rub in to the breadcrumb stage. Bind the mixture to a soft scone dough with the milk, and press out on a floured board to a disc about ½" (1.5cm) thick. Cut into 1" (2–3 cm) diamonds or squares and lay on top of the plums. Cover the pan and simmer for 15 minutes, by which time they will be cooked and spongy. Serve at once with pouring cream.

F **   Apple or Blackberry and Apple Pie

Apple pies are perfect autumn fare, and good for using up windfalls. Russets, pippins or other quite acid apples were always considered to be superior and were generally cooked under a puff pastry crust. Nowadays we are more likely to use a light, rich short crust, but no reason not still to use the traditional seasoning of powdered cinnamon, cloves and lemon rind? And is there any reason why we should not reinstate the old habit of 'buttering' an apple pie by dropping in a piece of butter when the pie is opened? This habit came to be considered un-genteel and was abandoned, but how good it is! Blackberries, scattered in with the apples to add colour and flavour, make this one of the most evocative of autumn dishes. Quince jelly or cheese or 2–3 tbs diced candied peel can be used instead of the lemon or spices, and honey can take the place of sugar for a change.

Ingredients
4–6 people

Pastry
6 oz (175g) plain flour
1–1½ oz (25–35g) icing sugar
3–4 oz (75–100g) firm butter
1 egg yolk
1–2 tbs iced water
pinch salt
a little egg white
a little sugar

Filling
2½ lb (1.15kg) russets, pippins or
   cooking apples
8–12 oz (225–350g) blackberries
   (optional)
1 tbs flour
2–4 tbs brown sugar or to taste
2 pinches ground cinnamon
little pinch ground cloves
grated rind ½ lemon
½ oz (12g) butter to 'butter' the pie
   (optional)

Pastry. Sift the flour, sugar and salt into a bowl or the food processor. Add the firm butter, cut into hazelnut-sized cubes, and rub in or process to the breadcrumb stage. Mix the egg yolk with a tablespoon of water, sprinkle over and work up to a dough, using another tablespoon of water if necessary. Form into a flat disc and chill in a plastic bag in the fridge for ½–2 hours.

Filling. Mix together the flour, sugar, spices and lemon rind. Peel, core and slice the apples to fill a 2 pt (1.2l) pie-dish, layering with blackberries if used, and sprinkle each layer with some of the flavouring mixture. Mound the fruit well up into a dome.

Roll the pastry into an oval, rather larger than the pie-dish, and cut a ½" (1cm) wide strip from the edges. Moisten the rim of the pie-dish with cold water and stick the strip in place. Moisten this strip with water and set the pastry over the pie. Seal the edges and decorate the pie, cutting a small hole in the centre to let out the steam. Bake it in a hot oven (400°F/200°C/Gas 6) for about 20–30 minutes until the pastry has set and browned. Brush the pastry with a little whisked white of egg and sprinkle generously with sugar. Then continue cooking at a lower temperature (375°F/190°C/Gas 5) for a further 15–30 minutes so that the apple is properly cooked, covering the pie if it is getting too brown. Serve the pie, 'buttered' if you wish by dropping in the butter through the central hole or when you open it.

This pie is also very good served just warm with thick cream.

F *   Coffee Apples with Rum

When there are masses of apples in the autumn, this is a lovely and slightly unusual way to cook them. They also freeze well like this, and can be very welcome in the late winter. The Caramel Rum Cream is a wonderful sauce and makes the apples rather special.

Ingredients
4–6 people

25 people

4–6 people	25 people
1½ lb (675g) cooking or eating apples, preferably ones which keep their shape	8–10 lb (3.6–4.5kg) cooking or eating apples, preferably ones which keep their shape
6 oz (175g) sugar	1¼ lb (550g) sugar or to taste
grated rind and juice 1 lemon	grated rind and juice of 2–3 lemons
1 oz (25g) butter	3 oz (75g) butter
3 tbs rum	5 fl oz (150ml) rum
1½–2 tbs Camp or 1½–2 teasp powdered coffee	6–8 tbs Camp coffee or 6–8 teasp powdered coffee

Peel, core and slice the apples and cook them with the sugar, grated lemon rind and juice, butter, half the rum and the coffee until they are well cooked and reduced (they should be a deep umber brown colour). Leave to cool, then stir in the remaining rum. Serve warm or cold with Caramel Rum Cream.

**   Caramel Rum Cream

Serve this with the Coffee Apples for which it was created, but also try it with ice-cream and steamed or baked puddings. Made with double cream in double quantities, it becomes a lovely sort of syllabub or cream, served in individual glasses with Little Almond Finger Biscuits (*see page 170*).

Ingredients
4–6 people

25 people

4–6 people	25 people
3 oz (75g) granulated sugar	8 oz (225g) granulated sugar
1 fl oz (25ml) cold water	2 fl oz (50ml) cold water
3 fl oz (75ml) boiling water	8 fl oz (225ml) boiling water
½ lemon	1–1½ lemons
1 tbs rum	3–4 tbs rum
6–8 fl oz (175–225ml) whipping cream	1 pt (600ml) whipping cream

Place the sugar and cold water in a saucepan and heat gently, stirring, until the sugar has completely dissolved. Turn up the heat and boil fast to a good brown caramel. Add the boiling water carefully (the caramel will spit and bubble), and shake and boil until the caramel dissolves and you have a nice thick caramel syrup. Leave to cool.

Stir the caramel syrup, the rum and lemon juice to taste into the cream. If necessary thin to pouring consistency with milk, and turn into a jug.

𝓕 ✳✳✳   Tiny Pear or Apple Vol-au-Vents

Michel Guérard's tart apple tarts are a perfection, sharp buttery caramelised apple in puff pastry that is light as air—they cannot be bettered. The only trouble is that I can never get them to absorb quite as much butter and sugar as he recommends. But such a brilliant dish sets one thinking, and I hope you might like to try these, filled with lemony pears in cinnamon sugar and topped with quince jelly and rum. The pastry is carefully scored ½" (1cm) in from the edges so that it can rise to make the vol-au-vents, whilst the filling sits cooking in the middle. They can all be prepared and frozen for a day or two, ready to pop straight into the oven for a special occasion.

Ingredients
6–8 people

Puff Pastry

2 lb (900g) good, small eating pears or apples	8 oz (225g) 'strong' flour
1 lemon	8 oz (225g) butter
4 oz (100g) unsalted or lightly salted butter	squeeze lemon juice
	4 fl oz (100ml) water (approx)
	pinch salt

2 oz (50g) castor sugar ⎫
1 teasp ground cinnamon ⎬ mixed to make cinnamon sugar
quince jelly or apricot jam ⎭
6–8 teasp rum

Puff Pastry. Sift the flour and salt into a bowl and add a quarter of the butter, diced, and a squeeze of lemon juice. Rub in the butter and add water to make a medium firm dough known as *la détrempe*. Do not overwork the dough or it will become too elastic. The remaining butter should be of the same consistency as *la détrempe*, firm but spreadable. Make it into a square flat cake. Roll the pastry into a rectangle, place the butter on one half and fold the other over to encase the butter, sealing the edges. Roll carefully to a rectangle (stop at once if the butter shows signs of coming through), brush off excess flour, then fold up the bottom third of the pastry and fold down the top third over it. Press the edges together and rest for 20 minutes in a plastic bag in the fridge. Repeat two more 'rolls' and 'turns', rolling only in a longwise direction as slantwise rolling will produce an uneven rise, and rest again for 20 minutes. Repeat this twice more so that the pastry has seven 'turns' and four rests in all. The pastry is now ready to be kept until needed.

Peel, core and cut the pears or apples into ½" (1cm) sections, discarding the top thin bit of pear. Sprinkle with lemon juice to stop them discolouring, toss well and leave for 5–10 minutes to sharpen.

Roll the pastry to about $^1/_{16}$" (2mm) thickness and cut out eight saucer-sized 5" (13cm) circles. Turn these over on to a damp baking sheet and carefully score a circle ½" (1cm) in from the edge with a sharp knife, cutting only halfway through the pastry. Arrange pear or apple overlapping slices in a circle on the inner part of the pastry only. Dot each with about ¼ oz (6g) butter, sprinkle with lemon juice and scatter generously with cinnamon sugar.

Bake in a hot oven (425°F/220°C/Gas 7) for ten to fifteen minutes. Once the outer edge of pastry has risen, dot each with another ¼ oz (6g) butter and a teaspoonful of rum mixed with a teaspoonful of quince jelly or apricot jam. Return to the oven and turn down to (400°F/200°C/Gas 6) for a further 15 minutes. Serve at once, golden brown, with the pear or apple faintly caramelised—though they also taste marvellous when luke warm.

** Spiced Pear Fool

Pears that are not perfect or are bruised can be made into this spiced fool. You can either fold the cream into the pear or serve it on top as we have it below.

Ingredients
4–6 people

6–8 pears
1 lemon
6 oz (175g) sugar
5 fl oz (150ml) water
3 cloves
½ stick cinnamon
1½ tbs gelatine
2 tbs water
a little ground cinnamon and cloves
    (optional)
8 fl oz (225ml) whipping cream
a little vanilla sugar
1–2 tbs eau-de-vie of pear or Kirsch
    (optional)
flaked browned almonds

Take julienne strips of lemon rind and blanch in a pan of boiling water for about 10 minutes. Melt the sugar in 5 fl oz (150ml) water and boil for 1–2 minutes, add the lemon juice, julienne strips, cloves and cinnamon.

Peel, core and slice the pears. Poach in the syrup until tender, and remove the cloves and cinnamon stick. Purée the pears and lemon with the syrup (pears and syrup should not come to more than 2 pts (1.2l), so boil the syrup down if they do). Sprinkle the gelatine on to the cold water in a small bowl and leave to soak for several minutes. Stand in a pan of hot water to melt, and add to the purée (with a food processor, put powder gelatine in with hot pears and process together). Adjust the flavour, adding a little ground cinnamon and cloves if necessary, turn into a 2 pt (1.2l) soufflé dish and chill until set.

Whip the cream, sweeten with a little vanilla sugar, and flavour with a little eau-de-vie of pear or Kirsch, if used. Pile on top of the pear fool, scatter with browned almonds and serve.

** Brandied Pears

This is a wonderful preserve. The sugar and brandy keep the pears indefinitely, and you can just dig into the jar whenever you want them. The pears shrink a lot in size, and of course the syrup is very sweet, so you only want a little in a glass, served with cream. The recipe is very old and comes from a friend in Northumberland. Make it when pears are plentiful in late autumn. Conference are good, and are not so prone to discolour as some others.

Ingredients

20 firm pears (preferably Conference)	3 cloves
sugar	½ stick cinnamon
rind of 1 lemon	¼ pt (150ml) brandy

Peel, core and quarter the pears, then weigh them and take ¾ lb (350g) sugar for each 1 lb (450g) pears. Place the pears, sugar, strips of lemon rind, cloves and cinnamon in a pan or large casserole and cook, covered, stirring from time to time, in a very slow oven (250°F/130°C/Gas 1) until the pears go pinkish-red and soft but do not break up, probably for 6 hours or more. Add the brandy and keep the pears in a jar for up to a year or more, removing what you need. Serve with cream or Yoghurt Whip (*see page 108*) without sugar.

F ** Glace aux Raisins

This is a lovely ice cream for any time of year, but late autumn is often a moment when you see the freshly shipped, large succulent raisins. Those that need stoning often have the best flavour.

Ingredients
4–6 people

3 oz (75g) large raisins	4 fl oz (100ml) water
6 tbs sweet Malaga wine or Marsala	3 egg whites
6 oz (175g) sugar	8 fl oz (225ml) double cream

Macerate the stoned raisins in the wine for 12–24 hours. Melt the sugar in the water in a small saucepan and, when completely melted, boil fast for about 4–6 minutes to 238°F/116°C (long thread stage) on the sugar thermometer.

While the syrup is cooking, whisk the egg whites until just holding a peak, then pour the boiling syrup in a fine stream over the egg whites, beating with a whisk constantly (an electric hand-held whisk makes this part easier). Beat until smooth and very stiff, then cool.

Whip the cream until stiff, adding the wine from the macerated raisins, then fold into the cold egg white meringue with the raisins. Turn into individual glasses or a bowl and freeze for at least 4–6 hours. Allow to mellow in the fridge for 15 minutes for individual glasses, or up to 1 hour for a large bowl, before serving with little biscuits.

Miscellaneous

Green Tomato Chutney

When the frosts approach and tomatoes will no longer ripen outside, you know it is time to make green tomato chutney. This has a nice, mellow, warm flavour without being too powerful.

Ingredients
approx 8½ lb (3.8kg)

4 lb (1.8kg) green tomatoes
1 lb (450g) onions
1½ lb (675g) apples
8 oz (225g) sultanas
1 oz (25g) garlic cloves
1 oz (25g) peeled fresh root ginger
1½ teasp carraway seeds
5–6 fresh or dried chillies or 1–1½ teasp
   cayenne pepper
1½ pts (900ml) wine or malt vinegar
1½ lb (675g) brown sugar
2 tbs salt

Do not use a brass, copper or iron pan for chutney making because it reacts with vinegar.

Wash and slice the tomatoes, peel and chop or slice the onions, peel, core and dice the apples. Place in a wide pan with the sultanas, chopped garlic, grated root ginger, carraway seeds and chopped chillies (without their seeds if you don't want it too hot) or cayenne. Just cover with vinegar (keep some back to mix with the sugar) and simmer gently, covered, for about 1½ hours until very soft. Dissolve the sugar in the remaining vinegar and add to the mixture, then continue to boil with the lid off until the chutney is thick enough. Remember it will thicken with keeping. Pot up in warm prepared jars (*see page 168*) and cover, seal, label and wipe the jars. Keep in a cool, dark and dry place.

The chutney is best left for 2–3 weeks before eating, but is often better still after a year.

**   Home-Made Tomato Purée

If you have too many tomatoes, especially the fleshy continental varieties, you can make your own tomato sauce and purée; it's delicious, but takes time to simmer down. Keep it in the freezer to use as you require. It won't be as concentrated as bought purée, and it will tend to freeze hard and will be more difficult to chop up when you need it.

Ingredients

4 lb (1.8kg) ripe tomatoes
3 tbs olive oil
1 finely chopped clove garlic
1 finely chopped onion
sugar
salt
1–2 teasp chopped fresh basil or lemon
    thyme (optional)
pepper (optional)

Put the roughly cut up tomatoes in a wide pan or casserole (earthenware is ideal) with the oil, onion and garlic. Simmer gently for 1–2 hours until completely tender and most of the watery liquid has evaporated. Press through a sieve (or fine blade vegetable mouli) to separate skins and pips, and measure the resulting tomato pulp. There will be about 2 pts (1.2l), so add approximately 1 teasp salt and 1 teasp sugar per pt (600ml) and return to the wide pan to simmer down and concentrate further. Add some finely chopped basil or lemon thyme and a little pepper if you like. Reduce down to 1 pt (600ml); you can concentrate it more if you wish, but stir frequently so that it doesn't 'catch' when it gets thick.

    Freeze in boxes to use as required. I believe you can also keep it unfrozen in small pots in the fridge, topped with a film of oil.

*   Piquant Melba Toast

Melba toast is quite easy to make and often solves the difficult problem of last-minute toast making. This piquant version is very 'moreish'; hand it to accompany and add contrast to soups, mousses and first course salads such as the Salade Composée or Fruits de Mer en Salade. Plain melba toast is made in the same way without any of the seasoning or butter.

Ingredients
4–6 people

6–8 thin slices brown or white bread
2 oz (50g) butter
¾–1 teasp curry paste
1 teasp grated fresh root ginger
1–2 teasp chopped parsley or other herbs
salt and pepper

Toast the bread on each side until golden brown but not dry and crisp. Cut off the crusts, and with a sharp knife cut the bread through its soft middle into two thin pieces, each piece toasted on one side but untoasted on the other. Remove any little rolls of soft crumb.

Meanwhile heat the butter with the curry paste, grated ginger and parsley until sizzling. Paint the melba toast on the untoasted side with the piquant butter and lay on a rack. Season with salt and pepper and bake in a moderate oven (350°F/180°C/Gas 4) until it is golden brown and quite crisp and curled.

Keep in an airtight tin and re-warm if necessary before serving, but it's nicest served fresh. Serve in a pile from a napkin-lined basket.

$\mathcal{P}$ ** Spiced Courgette and Dried Apricot Jam

To find another use for too many overgrown courgettes, I add them to this continental *confiture* in place of melon or pumpkin. It is delicious and tasty, but it's perhaps wiser not to reveal its humble contents till people have had a chance to taste and enjoy it! In this recipe, lemon pith is used for pectin, and lemon juice, tartaric or citric acid for the necessary acidulation to get a set.

Ingredients
approx 3 lbs (1.35kg) jam

2 lb (900g) courgettes (quite large ones will do)
½ lb (225g) dried apricots
1 pt (600ml) water
squeezed juice and shredded pith and skin of 1 lemon
3 more tbs lemon juice *or* 1 teasp tartaric or citric acid

1 vanilla pod
1 cinnamon stick
3 cloves
6–8 whole almonds
2 lb (900g) granulated sugar

Dice the apricots into little finger-nail-sized cubes and, if they are hard and dry, soak them in the water overnight. Then drain it off and make the liquid up to 1 pt (600ml) again. If they are the squishy sort, they need no soaking.

Peel the courgettes and, if large, cut into four lengthways and remove any fibrous pulp and seeds. Dice the courgettes and place in a pan with the water and shredded lemon pith and skin and all the lemon juice or juice and tartaric or citric acid. Simmer gently for about ¾–1 hour until the courgette is completely tender, adding more water if it boils away too soon. Sieve the courgettes (a soup mouli with the fine plate is quickest for this job, and will remove the lemon shreds). Return the pulp to a wide jam pan, add the apricots, the vanilla pod and the cinnamon stick, both broken into two, the cloves and the almonds, cut into shreds. Stir in the sugar and heat gently, stirring, until the sugar has completely dissolved; then boil fast for about 10–15 minutes to get a set. Test on a saucer, where the cooled jam should wrinkle in front of your finger when you press it (*see page 168*). Remove the vanilla pod, cinnamon stick and whole cloves. Pour into warm, clean jars, cover and label.

**   Quince Jelly

The ornamental Japanese quince *Chaenomeles specïosa* often carries a number of small golden fruit, and these can be used to make delicious jelly. Wait until they ripen and drop in October before gathering them, then, on a blustery day when it's good to be inside, treat yourself to making not only the tart and fragrant Quince Jelly but also Quince Cheese and Japonica Sweetmeats.

Strangely enough, both ripe and unripe quinces have a low acid content, so we need to add lemon juice. Their pectin content is adequate, but I often toss in the squeezed lemon shells, without their yellow zest, to increase the pectin.

Ingredients

quinces
water
lemon juice
granulated sugar
tiny bit of butter (optional)

Chop up and weigh the quinces, place in a stainless steel or enamel pan or casserole. Cover with the water (1½ pts (900ml) to each 1 lb (450g) quince), add the lemon juice (1 tbs to each 1 lb (450g) quince) and cook for 1½ hours at a steady simmer or in a low oven, uncovered, for 4–6 hours until very tender. A low oven gives a clearer juice as the fruit does not get broken up. I find a low Aga oven overnight is very good, but the long cooking gives a more amber coloured jelly.

Turn the fruit and juice into a jelly bag and hang up to drain. Do not press or squeeze the bag, and do not be alarmed if the juice looks milky and opaque because it will clear on boiling. Measure the juice and put it in a wide jam pan with warmed sugar (1¼ lb (550g) sugar for each 1 pt (600ml) juice). Stir over gentle heat until the sugar has dissolved, then boil fast for 10–20 minutes until a set is achieved, testing by the wrinkle test on a saucer (*see page 168*).

Skim if necessary, adding a tiny bit of butter to help clear the scum. Pot up in warmed, prepared jars (*see page 168*), and cover at once with waxed discs and cellophane covers. Wipe the jars clean, if necessary, and label.

The pulp in the bag may be used to make Quince Cheese and Japonica Sweetmeats (*see next recipe*).

F   # Quince Cheese and Japonica Sweetmeats

Ingredients

**the pulp in the jelly bag after making
    quince jelly
sugar**

Quince Cheese. When the jelly has drained, turn the quince pulp out of the jelly bag and purée and sieve it. The soup mouli with the finest disc is best for this job, but you can process the pulp in a food processor and then sieve it. To each 1 lb (450g) pulp use 1 lb (450g) sugar. Place pulp and sugar in a very deep, roomy pan and heat gently until the sugar has dissolved; then boil gently, stirring from time to time, until the mixture is very thick. When it becomes thick, you will find it plopping and bubbling like a pool of molten lava, and dangerously hot. It's best then to keep stirring all the time, reaching all over the pan, for it can catch and burn very easily at this stage.

You can cook the mixture to various thicknesses, depending on your time and patience. I sometimes cook it just to a thick purée, which I store in the freezer to serve with yoghurt, whipped cream or rice pudding. If you boil it further, so that a wooden spoon drawn across the base of the pan leaves a clear channel for several seconds, it will set to a cheese or cuttable quince cake. Turn it into plastic boxes or an oiled, round-bottomed bowl to turn out when set. Serve cut into slices to accompany cheese, like the Spanish mombrilla. It will keep, covered, for a year on the shelf at this stage.

Japonica Sweetmeats. If you like, you can go even further and boil it until very stiff, being careful because it burns very easily. Then turn it out in a ½" (1cm) layer on Bakewell paper and dry it off in a slow oven or on the back of the stove or in the airing cupboard until it is firm enough to cut into diamonds. Roll them in granulated sugar (or toasted sesame seeds), and dry on a rack in a warm place until dry enough to store in boxes.

This makes a lovely natural sweetmeat for Christmas or parties.

✳✳ Bramble Jelly

One of my friends makes the most delicious bramble jelly, and this is roughly what she does. Don't forget that early blackberries may be low in pectin and later ones low in acid, so add a few apples or crab apples, or even apple peelings and cores. I like to sieve the brambles, so it is really neither jam nor jelly.

Ingredients

brambles
water
sugar
apples

Just cover the ripe, dry brambles with water, using roughly 1 pt (600ml) water to each 1 lb (450g) fruit and adding in washed and chopped up but unpeeled apples, roughly two to each 1 lb (450g). Simmer gently until absolutely tender, then process and sieve the mixture (a soup mouli with a fine plate can be used). Measure the purée, and to each pint (600ml) add 1 lb (450g) sugar.

Place in a wide jam pan and heat gently, stirring, until the sugar has completely dissolved. Boil fast for 5–10 minutes, then test on a saucer for a set (*see page 168*). Pot into prepared warmed pots (*see page 168*), cover, seal, wipe and label.

✳✳ Damson Jam

This is a lovely jam. Its fresh, sharp flavour is much enjoyed by all, and being high in pectin and acid it sets very easily. The only trouble is the stones, which have to be fished out once the damsons are cooked.

Ingredients

**To each 1 lb (450g) damsons add ¼ pt
(150ml) water and use 1¼ lb (800g)
sugar**

For example:
approx 6 lb (2.7kg) jam

3 lb (1.35kg) damsons
¾ pt (450ml) water
3¾ lb (1.7kg) sugar

Wash and warm the jam jars (*see page 168*)

Wash the damsons and place in a wide pan with the water. Simmer gently, stirring and crushing from time to time, for 30–35 minutes or until tender and the stones are floating loose. Warm the sugar while the fruit cooks. Fish out the stones and discard. Add the warmed sugar and stir over gentle heat until the sugar has quite dissolved. Boil fast for about 5–15 minutes until a set is achieved. Test on a cold saucer for wrinkling (*see page 000*).

Turn into the prepared jars, insert waxed discs and top with cellophane covers. Wipe the jars with a wet cloth whilst still warm, and label.

F *   Sticky Gingerbread

A dark sticky gingerbread that keeps well is a traditional favourite, especially if spread with a little butter. This is an old Cox family recipe, and I usually make two while I'm about it, because you can always freeze one. I make it in a 2 lb (900g) loaf tin, and it turns out looking like a sticky, sunken topped brick. Store in a tin for several days before eating, and it will keep on getting better and better.

Ingredients
Approx 2 lb (900g) cake

8 oz (225g) plain flour	4 oz (100g) butter
½ teasp bicarbonate of soda	4 oz (100g) castor sugar
2 teasp ground cinnamon	12 oz (350g) black treacle
1 tbs ground ginger	3 eggs
1½ teasp mixed spice	good pinch salt

Line a 2 lb (900g) loaf tin with Bakewell or buttered greaseproof paper. Heat the oven to slow (325°F/170°C/Gas 3). Sift the flour, soda, spices and salt into a bowl. Heat the chopped up butter, sugar and treacle in a heavy pan. (The best way to measure treacle is to weigh your pan, then add warmed runny treacle until the weight has gone up by the required amount.) Bring to the boil. Whisk the eggs to a froth, then pour on the boiling treacle mixture whilst whisking. Pour this mixture into the dry ingredients and mix very thoroughly before turning into the prepared tin.

Bake in a slow oven (325°F/170°C/Gas 3) for about 1½ hours for a really sticky cake, or 1¾ hours for one with a drier consistency. Leave to cool in the turned-off oven if possible.

✳✳ Sloe Gin

I have picked sloes from October to December, depending on the year. If they hold on the trees until December, they will have taken a few frosts, the skins will have softened and they hardly need pricking. People go to great trouble turning or shaking the bottles daily, but I find that by standing the bottles on top of the fridge they get enough vibration and I don't have to worry too much. Culpeper stores stock natural bitter almond essence.

Ingredients

⅓–½ **gin bottle full of sloes**
4–8 oz (100–225g) **white or Demerara**
   sugar
2 **drops bitter essence of almond**
   (optional)
gin to fill the bottle

or you can make it in any large glass
   container that can be stoppered
   tightly.

Prick the sloes with a darning needle and put them into the bottle (late sloes need only to be gently squeezed so as just to break the skin), add the sugar and almond essence, if used, fill up with gin and cap tightly. Keep in a fairly warm place and shake occasionally.

After 3 months, strain off the gin through flannel or a paper coffee filter, return to clean dry bottles, and preferably keep for 3–6 months or more before drinking. For a sweeter gin, often more appreciated on a cold day in the open, you can add up to 12 oz (350g) sugar to each bottle of gin.

An alternative method is to take 1¼ pt (750ml) gin or vodka for each 1 lb (450g) sloes and add between 6–12 oz (175–350g) of sugar and 3–4 drops bitter almond essence.

THE CHRISTMAS SEASON

At Christmas play and make good cheer,
For Christmas comes but once a year

—Thomas Tusser, 1557

THE CHRISTMAS SEASON

The pleasant task of preparing for Christmas used to start early, as the dark months drew on after the plenty of summer and the 'putting up' of autumn. The first thing to think about, on the arrival of the season's freshly dried fruit from Smyrna and Corinth, was the Christmas pudding. Not, I hasten to explain, for the coming Christmas but for the one after that, to allow proper time for it to mature! Such was the confidence of the Victorians' stately progress, their steady and orderly march into the future. As well as the pudding, there was mincemeat to make, and how slow and laborious that was. All the fruit had to be washed, dried, de-stalked and picked over, and then chopped by hand before mixing, stirring and finally packing into jars. There was fruit to candy, sweetmeats to prepare, beef to spice, cakes to bake and pies to fill. It all took an unconscionably long time, but it was part of the routine of life, and the excitement and anticipation mounted as the preparations neared completion.

Today we seem to rush hither and thither, our noses against the window-pane, barely able to see the day after tomorrow, let alone the Christmas after next. We are prepared for Christmas by strings of tinsel and rows of Christmas trees outside shops, and sugary Christmas musak is piped at us wherever we go. Is it a wonder that we feel surfeited with Christmas even before it arrives, turn our backs on it, fight against it and try to pretend it will never happen? I believe that Christmas is still a wonderful time, in spite of its garish veneer, if it is grasped and fashioned to your taste, by adapting old traditions and creating new ones. You have to put a lot of thought and planning into it, but it should turn out to be a family occasion that everyone will enjoy.

Because we are a large family, we like to visit one another and gather together for Christmas. Sometimes we stay away, which is lovely, and all we have to do is to take some goodies, select a few contributions from the cellar, and make sure that all the presents and stockings, dogs and children get into the car. When it's here we may be anything up to twenty for Christmas lunch, and will probably have five or six staying for a few days. In this case I like to get as organised as possible, and I find this means starting to plan it all quite a long way ahead. The freezer is invaluable, of course, for all the stuffings and soups and some of the puddings, but there are the plum puddings to make (not for next year, though make an extra one if you can and see how you like it well matured), the Christmas cake to bake and ice, the goose to order for Christmas Eve and the other goodies I try to find time to make, such as Japonica Sweetmeats, Crystallised Grapefruit and home-made Preserved Chestnuts in Syrup, perhaps not so perfect as from Fortnum's but cheap to make, and they seem to disappear quickly enough. I think the smell of baking mince pies and the fun of preparing gingerbread decorations for the tree mean a lot to children in later life, and for me they put Christmas back into perspective after the radio, shops and television have set our teeth on edge.

My planning is a mixture of the precise and the general. I normally know how many we shall be for the main occasions, so I can plan these in some detail. As far as the rest, I never quite know who will be at home or asked out to a party at the last minute, who will drop in, what impromptu outings we may plan or what everyone will be feeling like. So I usually have a large, locally cured ham and a piece of Spiced Beef*, and they come out again and again. With unusual pickles, spiced jellies and mustards and good winter salads, they make the final preparations very easy. I find that after several days of rich Christmas food everyone enjoys the clean saltiness of ham and beef, the piquance of pickles and the freshness of the salads.

Christmas Eve has become a very important tradition for us as our own private Christmas party. Just the children and us, with no outsiders except any family who are staying. A candlelit dining room, best silver and china, and everyone dressing up madly and being very grown up. This is when we have the goose, which isn't usually big enough for Christmas lunch but is just right and suitably special for Christmas Eve. How good it seems, the first cut at the Christmas goodies, with the apple sauce, red cabbage with chestnuts and a rich gravy, and clean ripe pineapple to follow. It's a very special, close family moment and, to me, typifies the way good food and wine can help to make a great family occasion.

The traditional Christmas lunch is a marathon, even for the experienced cook, but it's no good heaving a deep sigh and wishing it could be simpler; tradition dictates what we should have, so we must plan carefully, cook ahead and enjoy it.

Make the stuffing well in advance and keep it in the freezer if you like. Stuff the turkey on Christmas Eve and have it at room temperature, ready to go into the oven. Cover the breast with muslin, which will have a self-basting effect, use a fairly gentle oven, and you can go happily off to church without fear of a ruined turkey. The potatoes can be peeled and waiting in their water (and this recipe for Roast Potatoes really is one of the best), and the sprouts are prepared. The breadcrumbs are ready for the bread sauce, the onion and milk can be on the simmer, and your good stock is standing by to augment the gravy. The plum pudding is the easiest part, and only needs a long morning's boiling. The brandy butter was prepared days ago, and mince pies, if you have them, only need heating up.

Perhaps the worst moment, with a large family anyway, is getting everyone actually sitting down with a plateful, because it's no good relaxing till then. The carving knife has got to be sharp and your husband briefed to go on for a record time without stopping and turning round to tell that frightfully funny story. Tell him which stuffing is at which end, and make sure the rest of the gang know exactly what they have to do. There will be seating to organise and cushions and high-chairs for the very small. There will be a fire to make up, empty glasses to clear, a new bottle to pour, and vegetables and gravy to hand round. It will be bedlam, with granny the only calm island in a storm of chatter.

The plum pud is easy, and the only thing to look out for is not to let it boil dry. However euphoric your guests, a burned pudding that looks like an extinct volcano and tastes of lava will really stop the party in its tracks. One little trick is to put a marble in the boiling water so that you will hear it bouncing madly about if the water gets too low. On the other hand, you probably won't hear it through the din unless you're in the kitchen, so it's worth checking finally before you bring in the turkey. Now is not the time to ransack everyone's pockets in search of 5p or 10p pieces which should be ready scrubbed to insert with the point of a knife when you turn out the pudding, or they could be put in before its second boil. We know someone who still has the old silver threepenny pieces which are

* *Good Food from Farthinghoe*

used every Christmas and then gathered in again—another family tradition and rather a nice one. All you've got to do now is to stick in the sprig of holly (no, it's too late to run into the garden!), pour over the brandy and set it alight. Then make your entrance into a darkened room to loud applause, and, if at any stage you swore that you'd never do another Christmas, just look at the younger children's faces and see the sparkle of joy and excitement which makes it all worth while.

It's all a downhill run from now on, enjoying the Stilton and the fruit, the glass of port and the nuts and sweetmeats.

After the main Christmas meals are over, it's nice to be able to eat conveniently, to fit in with all the different things individual members of the family are doing, and fairly simply and cheaply after all the richness and expense of Christmas. As I've said, I rely a lot on cold cuts and salads (and it's surprising what good value these are), but I also like to be able to use up the remains of Christmas lunch as interestingly as possible—toasted turkey sandwiches, for instance, sometimes larded with a bit of Stilton to give it a bit more kick.

The Stilton will go on for weeks, and this is the best season for proper frosted, field-green celery—the stuff that's grown in a nasty dirty field and actually has some taste! It will keep, unwashed, for weeks in a cool larder, and its spicy flavour revives jaded appetites and goes superbly with cheese. Still on the subject of Stilton, there is a great divide between cutting round or scooping in. If you scoop, you get an awful lot of dried Stilton round the edge, and even if you commit the other wickedness, feeding it with port, you still get a lot of wastage. So we cut round, and nothing is wasted but the base. When it starts to get a bit dried out, you can always turn it into Potted Stilton (*see page 61*), and it will keep for ages.

I find Stir Fried Turkey a great favourite, and I keep the wherewithal for this in the store cupboard. Hot-Sour Soup is another popular one, a good pick-me-up for New Year's Day, and excellent when made with turkey stock. Ham can be made up in innumerable ways, and the empty New Year purse appreciates a thick Ham Bone Bean Soup made with ham bone stock, a most satisfying lunch or supper dish. Or a curry lunch can be just the thing on New Year's Day to tickle up the palate and drive away the cobwebs.

That brings us to the end of the country year, and so round we go again! In spite of all our good intentions, we've probably missed the asparagus or been on holiday when we should have been making Seville Orange Marmalade or could have been making Brandied Pears, but there's always next year to look forward to.

THE CHRISTMAS SEASON

First Courses and Supper Dishes

Terrine de Foies de Volailles
Salade Sylvestre
Goose or Duck Salad
Goose or Duck Pâté
• Smoked Haddock Pâté
Spiced Fish Turnovers

Soups

• Celery and Almond Soup
Chicken or Turkey Soup
Hot-Sour Soup
Creamy Onion Soup
Hot Crab Soup

Fish

Truite Farcie au Beurre Ecrémé

Main Courses

Boned Roast Duck with Wild Rice
    Stuffing
Raised Poultry or Game Pie (after
    Mrs Beeton)
Roast Turkey
Turkey Breasts à la Savoyarde
Stir-Fried Turkey with Garlic and
    Water Chestnuts
Sweet Glazed Ham
• Beef Cheese
Tongue with Almond and Raisin
    Sauce
• Civet of Venison

Vegetables

Roast Potatoes
Creamy Mashed Potatoes

• Sweet-Sour Beetroot
Spiced Roast Parsnips
Glazed Turnips
Brussels Sprouts with Walnuts
Red Cabbage with Sultanas and
    Cider Vinegar
Braised Celery
• Chicory and Apple Salad with
    Walnut Dressing
• Christmas Salad

Puddings

Christmas Honours Tart
Superlative Mincemeat Pies
Mocca Roulade with Praline Cream
Plum Pudding
• Chestnut Yule Log
Nesselrode Pudding
• Prune and Whisky Mousse with
    Whisky Snow Cream
• Christmas Ice and with Hot
    Mincemeat Sauce
Apricot and Banana Flambé
Brandy Wine Sorbet

Miscellaneous

Special Turkey Stuffing
Bread Sauce
Cumberland Sauce
Brandy Butter
Gingerbread Christmas Tree
    Decorations
Christmas Cake
An Excellent Lemon Mincemeat
Praline Truffles
Preserved Chestnuts in Syrup
Crystallised Grapefruit

• Also quantities for 25 persons

First Courses and Supper Dishes

P ***   Terrine de Foies de Volailles

Foie gras tends to be the monopoly of the top restaurants and great chefs. You can bring tins or jars back from holidays in France, even sometimes finding the semi-conserved variety in glass jars which is better than the tinned. But foie gras really needs to be eaten fresh, and although you can occasionally buy it at Christmas it's always extremely expensive. I sometimes sat and talked to Madame, our farmer neighbour in France, as she force-fed her ducks in late autumn; she would explain how you can open one duck up and find a beautiful 14oz (400g) liver, blond and beautiful, but another duck would only have a silly little 4 oz (100g) liver, and there is no knowing. She told me how to cook the foie gras and the appropriate marinade and seasoning, which is very little and very delicate. Well, there is really no point my giving you a recipe for foie gras, but perhaps a smooth and delicate pâté with the self-same seasoning may be useful; it's certainly quite easy, can be prepared several days ahead, and will keep for a week or more. Sometimes at Christmas you will come across large pale duck, capon, chicken or turkey livers, and they are particularly good for this. I add a little bit of bacon or ham so that the saltpetre in it keeps the pâté pinkish. Truffles could, of course, be included, but I don't think they are worth the expense of using unless they are fresh. I have successfully added English truffles which I find keep well in the freezer.

Ingredients
12–16 people

1 lb (450g) best pale duck, goose, capon,
    turkey or chicken livers
4 tbs port
2 tbs cognac (or armagnac is often used)
½ teasp castor sugar
good pinch quatre épice or allspice
scrap garlic (optional)
pinch thyme (optional)
1 tbs chopped parsley (optional)
1 oz (25g) butter
1 finely chopped shallot
2–3 oz (50–75g) diced streaky bacon
15 fl oz (450ml) double cream
salt and pepper

Pick over the livers, very carefully removing threads and any sacks of green bile; also cut off any green-tinged flesh (this is very bitter, and even a little bit can spoil a whole dish). Soak the livers for 1 hour in milk or water at blood heat. Then marinate with port, cognac, quatre épice, sugar, garlic, thyme and parsley (if used) and salt and pepper. Leave to marinate for 12–24 hours.

Melt the butter in a small pan and gently cook the shallot and bacon until soft and golden. Scrape into a food processor or liquidiser and process until smooth. Add the livers and the marinade and reduce to a smooth purée, then add the cream and switch off at once.

Pass the mixture through a fine sieve into one or two terrines in a layer no deeper than 2″ (5cm); add shavings of truffle to the mixture at this stage. You can cook a little, to taste the seasoning, in the bottom of a cocotte standing in a pan of boiling water. Place the terrines in a roasting pan with hot, not boiling, water to nearly the full depth of the pâté. Cook in a slow oven (250°F–300°F/130°C–150°C/Gas 1–2) for about 45–60 minutes until the mixture sets (the water in the *bain marie* should never rise above (170°F/75°C) for a really delicate pâté). Leave to cool and keep in a cool larder for 1–2 days.

Cover with a layer of melted butter. Use clarified butter (*see page 134*) quite deep if you wish to keep the terrine for up to a week before eating, and serve with melba toast, brioche loaf or brioche toast and unsalted butter.

* Salade Sylvestre

This makes a nice little Christmas time first course, either using up left-over turkey or chicken breast or with chicken breasts cooked as in the Salade Composée (*see page 124*).

Ingredients
4–6 people

8 oz (225g) cooked turkey or chicken breast	*Mayonnaise Sauce* 2 egg yolks
4 oz (100g) grapes	½ teasp mustard
3–4 sticks celery	½ lemon
1 bunch watercress	8 fl oz (225ml) olive oil or mixed oils
½–1 oz (12–25g) toasted flaked almonds	1 teasp Worcester sauce
	1 teasp tomato ketchup
	salt and pepper

Pour boiling water over the grapes, leave for about ½ minute, then plunge into cold water before skinning and de-seeding.

Dice the turkey or chicken and the celery and fold into the mayonnaise with the grapes, adding a dash of lemon juice or water if the sauce is too thick. Pick over the watercress and remove any tough stalks. Line individual glasses or dishes with a few sprigs of watercress and pile in the salad. Serve topped with flaked browned almonds.

Mayonnaise Sauce. Place the yolks with the salt, pepper, mustard and a little grated lemon rind and juice in a bowl. Whisk for a minute or so, then gradually add the oil, drop by drop to start with, later in a fine thread and whisking all the time to make a mayonnaise. Finally, correct the seasoning, adding lemon juice to taste and the Worcester sauce and tomato ketchup.

*   Goose or Duck Salad

A duck goes a long way if roasted and served cold in a salad. You can also use leftover duck or goose meat, particularly the thighs. This makes a pleasant fresh salad around Christmas, and the crispened strips of skin add a nice touch.

Ingredients
4–6 people

½–¾ lb (225–350g) cold cooked goose or
   duck
goose or duck skin (if available)
2 eating apples ⎫
1 clementine, satsuma or orange ⎭ *or* use 3 oranges
1 head celery or Chinese leaves

Dressing
1 teasp Dijon mustard
1 teasp red currant or mint jelly
1 tbs sherry *or* wine vinegar
good squeeze lemon juice
a little grated orange rind (optional)
3–4 tbs best olive oil
salt and pepper

Take any piece of goose or duck skin and cut into strips. Season highly and roast in a hot oven, or under the grill, for 3–5 minutes, until the fat renders out and the strips are crisp. Set aside to sprinkle over the salad.

Cut the meat into thumbnail dice. Core, quarter and cube the apple, and add de-pithed clementine segments or orange segments, cut out from the skin. Slice the celery or Chinese leaves.

Combine all the ingredients, season and toss with dressing. Scatter with crispy skin if available.

Dressing. Make the dressing by mixing the mustard, jelly and vinegar with the lemon juice, grated orange rind and seasoning. Mix well, and energetically stir in the oil to make a thick dressing.

F *   Goose or Duck Pâté

Any little scraps of meat you can winkle off the carcass can be made into a little pot of pâté. Use some goosefat, if you have it, as well as butter, for it gives a lovely texture and flavour to the pâté.

Ingredients
6–8 people

½ lb (225g) cooked scraps of goose or
    duck meat and fat without skin, bone
    or sinew
2–3 oz (50–75g) soft butter, or mixed
    goosefat and butter
2 tbs Madeira or sherry
salt, pepper and mace

Process, mince or pound the meat until smooth, then work in the butter, fat, seasoning and Madeira or sherry. Pack into pots. Serve at room temperature with hot toast and lemon wedges.

F *   Smoked Haddock Pâté

One of the simplest yet nicest of smoked haddock pâtés, which freezes well and is also popular at parties.

Ingredients

4–6 people	*25 people*
8 oz (225g) smoked haddock fillet	2 lb (900g) smoked haddock fillet
4 tbs milk (approx)	6–8 fl oz (175–225ml) milk
4 oz (100g) soft butter	1 lb (450g) soft butter
½ bay leaf	1 bay leaf
1" (3cm) thick slice crustless white or brown bread made into breadcrumbs	4 × 1" (3cm) thick slice crustless white or brown bread made into breadcrumbs
½ teasp anchovy essence	1½–2 teasp anchovy essence
½ lemon	1½–2 lemons
salt, pepper, paprika and ground mace	½ teasp ground mace
	1–2 teasp paprika
	salt and plenty of pepper

Skin the haddock fillet and put in a saucepan with the milk, half the butter, the bay leaf, a little sprinkle of mace and salt and rather more pepper and paprika. Cook over gentle heat until the fish will just flake, but do not over-cook.

Pour the milk from the fish over the breadcrumbs in a food processor or liquidiser, add the flaked fish, anchovy essence and lemon juice. Process, and add the remaining soft butter. Adjust seasoning and pack into pots, where it will firm up a bit on cooling.

Serve cold with hot toast and lemon quarters.

$\mathcal{F}$ ∗∗   Spiced Fish Turnovers

Little spicy fish parcels in a cheesy flaky pastry are greatly enjoyed when handed round hot with drinks. They also make a nice first course or savoury. They will freeze and can be cooked from frozen, and any left-over filling is nice cooked under a baked egg.

Ingredients
36 turnovers

Filling	*Cheesy Flaky Pastry*
12 oz (350g) haddock fillet	**8 oz (225g) plain flour**
½ pt (300ml) milk	**6 oz (175g) firm butter**
1 bay leaf	**2 oz (50g) grated strong cheese**
1½ oz (35g) butter	**3–4 tbs iced water**
1 small finely chopped onion	**½ teasp dry English mustard**
2 teasp curry powder	**a little black pepper**
1 oz (25g) plain flour	**good pinch salt**
1 egg yolk	
pinch ground mace	
black pepper	
egg wash	

Cheesy Flaky Pastry. Sieve the flour into a bowl or the food processor with the salt, pepper and mustard. Add the grated cheese and firm butter, cut into hazelnut-sized cubes. Rub in, or process, as you add the water, and stop the moment the mixture draws together. Lightly knead together and roll out on a well-floured board to an oblong 10″ × 5″ (25cm × 12cm). Brush off excess flour, fold the top third down and the bottom third up and give the pastry a turn to the right. Roll and fold the pastry twice more, then rest in a plastic bag in the fridge for 1–2 hours.

Roll the pastry very thin and cut out 36 or so 3″ (8cm) circles of pastry. Place a small spoonful of cold filling on each round, moisten the edges with water, fold over and seal the pastry together to form turnovers. Brush with egg wash, make a tiny slit in the top, and bake in a hot oven (425°F/220°C/Gas 7) for about 15 minutes until crisp and golden. Serve piping hot.

Filling. Place the skinned fish in a saucepan with the milk, bay leaf, a turn or two of pepper and a pinch of mace. Bring to the simmer and cook gently until the fish will just flake. Drain and reserve the liquid.

    Melt the butter in a saucepan, add the onion, curry powder and another pinch of mace and cook gently until soft and golden. Off the stove, stir in the flour, egg yolk and cooled fish milk all at once. Whisk and just bring to the boil. Fold in the flaked fish and correct the seasoning; the mixture should be fairly stiff and highly seasoned. Turn out on to a plate, cover and leave until cold.

Soups

𝓕 ** **Celery and Almond Soup**

The carefully fried ground almonds add a nice nutty flavour to this winter soup, which is good for winter parties.

Ingredients

4–6 people	*25 people*
1 medium head celery	3 large heads celery
1 medium onion	4 onions
1 medium potato	4 large potatoes
2½ oz (60g) butter	9 oz (225g) butter
2–3 parsley stalks	4–6 parsley stalks
small sprig thyme	2–3 sprigs thyme
½ bay leaf	2 bay leaves
1½ pts (900ml) chicken stock	6 pts (3.4l) chicken stock
1 oz (25g) ground almonds	4 oz (100g) ground almonds
1 oz (25g) flour	4 oz (100g) flour
½ pt (300ml) milk	4 pts (2.25l) milk
¼ pt (150ml) cream or some flakes of butter	½–¾ pt (300–450ml) cream or 2–4 oz (50–100g) flakes butter
2–3 tbs flaked browned almonds	good handful flaked browned almonds
salt and pepper	salt and pepper

Slice the celery, onion and potato. Melt 1½ oz (35g) butter in a heavy pan and add the vegetables, parsley stalks, thyme and bay leaf. Cook very gently, covered, without browning for 15–20 minutes until soft and golden. Add the stock, bring to the boil and simmer for 30 minutes until completely tender. Remove the bay leaf, purée, and sieve.

Melt the remaining butter, add the ground almonds and brown very gently. Add the flour and cook together for 2–3 minutes. Draw off the stove, wait for sizzling to cease, and add the milk. Bring to the boil, whisking hard. Stir in the celery purée. Correct seasoning, heat through carefully and add the cream or whisk in a few flakes of butter. Serve sprinkled with the flaked almonds.

Variation for 25 people. You will need 4 oz (100g) butter for cooking the celery, onion and potatoes. Sweat them for 30–45 minutes before adding the stock.

ℱ * Chicken or Turkey Soup

There are many styles of chicken soup, but I find this one is simple and quick and really tastes of chicken. It is the generous quantity of butter that gives it its smooth texture and lovely flavour.

Ingredients
4–6 people

2½ oz (60g) butter
1½ oz (35g) plain flour
1½ pts (900ml) chicken or turkey stock
½ pt (300ml) milk
½ chicken stock cube (optional)
any scraps of cooked chicken or turkey,
  cubed
chopped parsley
salt and pepper

Melt the butter in a saucepan, add the flour and cook over moderate heat, stirring, for 2–3 minutes. Draw the pan off the stove, wait for the sizzling to cease and add the stock, stock cube (if used) and milk. Bring to the boil, whisking with a wire whisk (use a wooden spoon round the edge of the pan so that no flour sticks there) and simmer for 2–3 minutes. Add any cubed cooked chicken or turkey and the chopped parsley, correct the seasoning, re-heat and serve.

* Hot-Sour Soup

This appetising, piquant soup has a rather Chinese character. Whenever you have some good stock, it can be quickly put together with whatever of the ingredients you happen to have. A packet of dried cèpe or Chinese mushrooms pre-soaked in warm water heightens the flavour. For crunchy contrasting textures serve the moment it is made.

Ingredients
4–6 people

2 pts (1.2l) good chicken, turkey or game
  stock
½ small clove garlic
½ onion or 2 spring onions
½ chicken stock cube (optional)
2 oz (50g) finely sliced cooked chicken
  (optional)
2 oz (50g) sliced button mushrooms
  or 2 dried Chinese mushrooms
  or a few bits of dried cèpe soaked in
  warm water for ½ hour

a little grated root ginger
3 oz (75g) frozen green peas
1 teasp sugar
2 tbs soy sauce
2 tbs vinegar
½ teasp chilli sauce
2–3 teasp cornflour
2 oz (50g) frozen prawns
finely chopped chives, parsley or
  coriander (optional)
a few drops sesame oil (optional)
salt and pepper only if necessary

Cut the garlic into tiny slivers and the onion into wafer thin slices and add to the stock with the stock cube, chicken, sliced mushrooms, grated ginger and peas. Add the sugar, soy, vinegar and chilli sauce and bring to the boil. Stir in the cornflour, slaked in a little cold water. Boil for just another minute or two until thickened and clear, then add the prawns, chopped herbs and a few drops of sesame oil (if used). Test for seasoning and serve at once.

$\mathcal{F}$ ** Creamy Onion Soup

It's a help to have recipes using ingredients which are usually around. This creamy white soup, which is nicest with a generous hint of nutmeg or mace, can be finished with cream, or not, as you please.

Ingredients
4–6 people

1 lb (450g) roughly chopped onions
1½ pts (900ml) stock
1½ oz (35g) butter
1½ oz (35g) flour
½ pt (300ml) milk
¼ pt (150ml) cream (optional)
½–1 oz (12–25g) butter to finish
freshly grated nutmeg or pinch mace
salt and pepper

Simmer the onions in the stock with the seasoning for 30–40 minutes or until tender; drain and reserve the liquid. Melt the butter, add the flour and cook over moderate heat, stirring, for 2–3 minutes; then draw the pan off the stove, and when the sizzling ceases add the milk. Bring to the boil, whisking hard, and simmer for 2–3 minutes.

Purée the onions and add. Thin with the reserved onion stock, correct the seasoning and add a good grate of nutmeg or pinch of mace. Finish with the cream, if used, and add flakes of butter stirred in off the stove.

* **Hot Crab Soup**

Very quick and easy to make, but quite rich and powerful. Just the thing to precede the cold Duck Salad.

Ingredients
4 people

8 oz (225g) white and brown crab meat
1 oz (25g) butter
1 onion
½ oz (12g) flour

¼ teasp mace
5 fl oz (150ml) white wine
15 fl oz (450ml) milk
7 fl oz (200ml) cream
squeeze lemon juice
finely chopped parsley, chervil or chives
salt, pepper and cayenne

Melt the butter and cook the finely chopped onion. Add the flour and mace and cook, stirring, for several minutes; then draw the pan off the stove and add the wine, milk and cream. Season and bring to the boil, whisking hard. Simmer for several minutes, then stir in the crab meat and heat through. Correct the seasoning, add a good squeeze of lemon juice and serve, sprinkled with finely chopped parsley and a trace of cayenne pepper.

Fish

✳✳   Truite Farcie au Beurre Ecrémé

The sauce for this is so good, and so quick and easy to make, that I think you will find yourself using it for vegetables such as asparagus, broccoli or beet stems as well as with all sorts of fish. Try also making it with crème fraîche. The trout can be plain, but is nice filled with this fresh green stuffing.

Ingredients
4 people

4 good trout
4 tbs breadcrumbs
4 tbs chopped parsley and watercress
    with a little fennel or chervil
grated rind ½ lemon
1 egg yolk
salt, pepper and nutmeg

Beurre Ecrémé

4–6 tbs thick double cream
4 oz (100g) lightly salted soft butter
1 lime or lemon
salt and pepper

Combine the breadcrumbs and chopped herbs with a little grated lemon rind, the egg yolk and a seasoning of salt, pepper and nutmeg. Stuff each fish with a little of the mixture and lay in a well-buttered, shallow baking dish. Rub the fish with a drop of oil, cover lightly with butter paper or greased tinfoil and bake in a hot oven (400°F/200°C/Gas 6) for about 15–18 minutes until done, when the eye goes white and the flesh feels firm. Serve with a little of the creamy butter sauce poured over the fish, with the rest in a sauceboat.

Beurre Ecrémé. Heat the cream in a small saucepan and boil for several minutes to thicken; then whisk in the soft butter in small pieces until a creamy sauce forms. Do not boil. Add seasoning (preferably rather coarse ground pepper) and a little grated lime or lemon rind with a good squeeze of juice. Serve at once, or it will keep warm, covered.

Main Courses

P ✳✳✳   **Boned Roast Duck with Wild Rice Stuffing**

Wild rice is expensive. But this aquatic grass from the great lakes of Canada and America partners duck or game so well that I can't resist using it (though you can use half brown rice if you like). The address of a good supplier is given on page 279. This dish can be prepared and left ready to roast, but allow a little longer if cooking from chilled.

Ingredients
4–6 people

4–5 lb (1.8–2.25kg) duck
¼–½ pt (150–300ml) duck stock or wine

Wild Rice Stuffing
4 oz (100g) wild rice *or* 2 oz (50g) wild
**   rice and 3 oz (75g) brown rice**
the duck liver
2–3 tbs rendered duck fat or butter
1 finely chopped onion
4 oz (100g) mushrooms (optional)
½ oz (12g) sultanas
1 egg
salt and pepper

To Garnish
1 bunch watercress

Wild Rice Stuffing. Wash the rice and soak overnight in cold water. Alternatively, toss into plenty of boiling water, simmer for 5 minutes, then draw off the stove and leave for 1 hour.

Whichever way you have prepared it, add 1 teasp salt to the pan and boil for 20–30 minutes until the rice is nearly tender. Drain, refresh under the cold tap and drain again thoroughly.

Dice the duck liver and sauté in the hot duck fat until just firm. Remove, add the onion to the pan and cook gently until golden and remove. Turn up the heat, add the thickly sliced mushrooms and sauté lightly. Add all to the drained rice with the sultanas, egg and seasoning, and fork together.

Bone out the duck, starting by cutting straight down the back with a sharp boning knife. Then carefully work your way round to the breast bone, cutting the skin and flesh off the carcass and easing the legs and wings from their sockets. When the flesh is detached on both sides except along the breast bone, pick up the carcass so that the weight of the flesh hangs down and cut along the breastbone, being careful not to pierce the skin or leave a gristly strip of breastbone in the meat. Cut off the two end wing joints from each wing and bone out the third. Cut carefully round the joint to detach the ligaments and tendons, and then you should be able to pull out the bone quite easily, drawing the wing skin through to the inside. Remove the thigh bones but leave the drumsticks in so as to have a good ducky shape. Leave a bit of the lower leg bone on or the flesh will draw up the drumstick, making it look naked. Should there be any holes in the skin, do not despair, but sew them up, leaving a generous end of thread to pull out later.

You may like to make rich duck stock with the carcass and wing tips, etc, for gravy at the end.

Pile the stuffing in the centre of the duck, making sure you get plenty between its legs, then sew up, using a big darning needle and button thread and large oversewing stitches, cutting off the tail (so that you are sure the preen glands are removed) and any excess skin from the neck end. Turn over and pat into shape (it does not need to be too tightly stuffed, for it will draw together in the cooking). Set on a rack in a roasting tin and cook in a hot oven (425°F/220°C/Gas 7) for 30–40 minutes, covering lightly with tinfoil when the skin is a good brown. Remove the duck and keep warm.

Drain most of the fat from the roasting pan, add a little strong duck stock or wine and boil up, stirring in all juices and brown crusty bits. Reduce until strongly flavoured, season and strain into a sauce boat.

Serve the duck cut across in generous slices and garnished with watercress. The gravy is handed separately.

✳✳✳   Raised Poultry or Game Pie (After Mrs Beeton)

Typical old English flavourings are used in this pie, which can be made with chicken, pheasant, grouse, partridge or what you will, by adjusting the quantities to suit. The jellied stock is not essential and, had the pie been destined for keeping or sending to someone, would have been omitted, as would the fresh herbs, and the pie would have been filled up after cooking with good lard, and would then have kept for quite some time. Truffles or mushroom might have been included; truffles (I have made it with truffles gathered locally in England) certainly add a great taste and aroma. Although it is not an easy or quick dish to make, both this and my Raised Game Pie* are well worth doing for a special occasion.

Ingredients
8–12 people

Filling
1 chicken, plump pheasant or other
 available game
8 oz (225g) pie veal
8 oz (225g) cooked ham
nutmeg
allspice
mace
salt and pepper
egg-wash

Jellied Stock
chicken or pheasant carcass and bones
pork skin, pig's trotter or bacon rinds
 (optional)
1 sliced onion
1 sliced carrot
1 stick celery
bouquet garni of parsley stalks, thyme
 and bay leaf
1 teasp vinegar
water to cover
1–2 teasp gelatine ⎫
1–2 tbs cold water ⎭ if necessary
salt and pepper

Pastry
1 lb (450g) plain flour
8 oz (225g) butter
2 egg yolks
5 fl oz (150ml) cold water (approx)
½ teasp salt

Forcemeat
¾ lb (350g) pie veal
4 oz (100g) green or smoked bacon or
 cooked ham
½ lb (225g) back pork fat
grated rind ½ lemon
a little chopped fresh or good pinch
 dried marjoram, savory and basil
1 tbs chopped parsley
2 eggs
salt, cayenne pepper, nutmeg and mace

Pastry. Sift the flour and salt into a bowl, rub in the butter and work up to a very pliable paste with the egg yolks and some water. Form into two flat discs, using a little more than ⅔ for the base and a little less than ⅓ for the top. Rest the pastry for 1–2 hours, or preferably 24 hours. Remove from the fridge a little while before rolling.

Forcemeat. Mince or finely chop together (or use a food processor with metal blade) the veal, the bacon or ham, pork fat, herbs and grated lemon rind. Season with salt, cayenne pepper, mace and a tiny bit of freshly grated nutmeg. Combine with the beaten eggs and beat well.

Filling. Cut the veal and ham into thumb-nail-sized cubes. Bone the chicken or game; start by cutting the skin down the backbone and carefully cutting round to the breastbone, removing wings, legs and flesh from the carcass. Cut off the two end wing joints and bone the remaining joint. Bone out the thigh and drumstick. Season the bird on the flesh side with salt, pepper, mace and allspice. Spread with a layer of forcemeat, then some cubed veal and ham, cover with more forcemeat, and reform the bird so that the skin meets at the back. If you prefer, cut all the meat off the bird and dice it up with the veal and ham.

To Assemble. Butter a raised pie mould (a 9″ (22/23cm) mould is about right, measured lengthways internally) or a removable base cake tin of about 8″ (20cm) diameter. Take the larger piece of pastry and roll out, keeping the middle thicker than the edges. Flour well and fold in half, edges towards you. Roll into a bag shape by drawing the edges towards you and rolling out the thicker centre. Turn over and roll the other side or the bottom pastry will be thicker. Fit into the mould, pressing well into all the corners and pressing out the thick central ridge. Make sure no holes appear. Leave a 1″ (2–3cm) overhang all round the mould. Line the pastry with forcemeat, then lay in the stuffed bird, packing round it the remaining seasoned veal, ham and forcemeat. Mound well up on top. Cover with the rolled pastry lid, wetting the edges and sealing well. Decorate, make a hole for escaping steam by inserting a tinfoil chimney, and set in your meat thermometer, if used. Glaze with egg wash and bake in a hot oven (400°F/200°C/Gas 6) for about 20–30 minutes until the pastry is set and a good brown. Continue baking in a moderate oven (350°F/180°C/Gas 4) for a further 2½–3 hours (or to a meat thermometer reading of 180°F/80°C). Pour the prepared warm stock through a funnel into the still warm pie a little while after it has come out of the oven.

Keep the pie for several days in a cool larder for the flavour to develop before eating.

Jellied Stock. While the pie cooks, make a good strong stock with the carcass and bones of the bird, porkskin, blanched pig's trotter or bacon rinds if available to give gelatine, the vegetables, herbs, vinegar and seasoning and water to cover. Simmer for 3 hours or more, then strain and reduce until very strong and only about 15 fl oz (450ml) remain. Test a little for setting in a saucer in the fridge, and if necessary add a little gelatine soaked in cold water and dissolved; the stock must set to a firm jelly.

$\mathcal{P}$ ✳✳　　Roast Turkey

When choosing a bird for Christmas, it's nice to have a large one so that there is plenty left to eat as cold turkey or for sandwiches. Allow at least 1 lb (450g) weight per head for eating hot, and don't forget that frozen birds are sold 'oven weight', ready for roasting and including their giblets, whereas fresh birds are sold 'dressed weight'; this means that although they have been plucked, they still have head, feet and innards, accounting for about $^1/_5$ of their weight, though the butcher will draw and prepare them before delivery if asked to do so.

An 8–10 lb (3.6–4.5kg) 'oven weight' hen-bird is not too large if you are 6–8 for Christmas day; it will be very tender and tasty and should still leave plenty over. When roasting a turkey, the great thing is to keep it moist and succulent during the cooking. To achieve this, we cover it with muslin or a bit of clean tea towel (or you can even use a new, rinsed out J cloth) soaked in butter, which you keep basting as the turkey cooks. A fairly moderate oven and some liquid in the roasting tin ensures that the butter does not burn and you do not have to watch it too closely. My mother-in-law always kept the skin of the ham to lay over the turkey breast, and of course it makes a wonderful, self-basting protective layer.

When your turkey arrives, take out the giblets to make some stock. The well-cooked gizzard can be diced and added to the stuffing, or it will make the cat a magnificent Christmas dinner.

Ingredients
8–10 people

8–10 lb (3.6–4.5kg) turkey (oven ready)
4–6 oz (100–150g) butter
4 tbs olive oil
1 pt (600ml) turkey stock or water
　　(approx)
salt and pepper
a double layer of muslin, a clean piece of
　　sheet or tea towel or a new, rinsed out
　　J cloth to cover the turkey

Turkey Stock and Gravy (to make 1¼–1¾
　　pts (¾–1l))
neck, gizzard and heart from the giblets
wing tips from the turkey
1 onion
1 carrot
1 stick celery
1 bouquet garni of parsley, thyme and
　　bay leaf
1 chicken stock cube
1¾–2 pts (1–1¼l) water to cover
¼ teasp salt and 8 peppercorns

Allow a frozen bird to thaw very thoroughly and slowly, preferably in the larder or bottom of the fridge for 2–3 days.

Make the turkey stock in advance, as you will need this for cooking the turkey.

Stuff the bird only shortly before cooking it, say on Christmas Eve, stuffing the body cavity with about 2 lb (1kg) perhaps Special Turkey Stuffing (*see page 000*) stuffing and, if you wish, the crop or neck end with another ½ lb (250g) of a different stuffing. It is better not to stuff large turkeys in the body cavity with an uncooked meat stuffing. The heat may not penetrate to cook it properly, so use a chestnut or some other already cooked stuffing. If possible leave the turkey out of the fridge to come to room temperature before roasting (one should do this for all meat roasting). Heat the oven to moderately hot (375°F/190°C/ Gas 5). Melt the butter in a small saucepan. Set the turkey breast down in a roasting tin and cover it completely with the cloth. Spoon over the oil and the butter (leaving behind the white sediment, which would otherwise burn) so that the whole cloth is saturated. Add about 5 fl oz (150ml) stock to the pan and place in the oven. Baste by spooning over the buttery juices every 20–30 minutes, and add a little more stock or water if the juices in the pan get too reduced and brown. After 1 hour, cover loosely with tinfoil. Allow about 15 minutes to each 1 lb (450g) weight and 15 minutes over. Turn breast upwards for last 30 minutes cooking time.

When the turkey is cooked remove from the roasting pan and allow it to rest in a turned off or very low oven for ½–1 hour before serving; this allows the meat fibres to relax and the juices to re-enter the meat tissue so that it will be much more succulent and easier to carve.

Turkey Stock and Gravy. Wash the neck, gizzard and heart well under running water, then place in a pan with the other ingredients. Cover and simmer very gently for 4–6 hours or for 8 hours in a slow cooker or low oven. Drain and use for cooking the turkey.

Once the turkey is cooked and resting, spoon off some of the buttery fat from the roasting pan and add enough stock to make your gravy. Stir in all the crusty brown bits round the edge (these give your gravy its flavour and colour), season and strain into a sauceboat.

If you like a thickened gravy, add some flour to the spooned-off roasting fat in a separate pan and cook until light brown, then cool a little before adding the pan juices (having stirred in all the brown tasty bits) and stock if necessary. Bring to the boil, whisking. Simmer for 5–10 minutes and strain into a gravy boat.

✳✳   Turkey Breasts à la Savoyarde

Fresh turkey escalopes should be available all the year now, from good stores, and they make a lovely dish for a dinner or supper party. You can also use this sauce to make left-over cold turkey quite special.

Ingredients
4–6 people

1½–2 lb (675–900g) boneless turkey or chicken breast	*Sauce*
little flour	8–10 fl oz (225–300ml) good turkey or chicken stock
4–6 tbs stale white breadcrumbs	1 teasp dried tarragon
½ oz (12g) butter	1 oz (25g) butter
1½–2 oz (35–50g) clarified butter (*see page 134*)	1 oz (25g) flour
1 tbs olive oil	6–8 fl oz (175–225ml) double cream
salt and pepper	1 teasp Dijon mustard
	½ oz (12g) grated Gruyère cheese
	salt and pepper

Make the sauce first.

Sauce. Heat the stock and tarragon in a saucepan and boil down to 5 fl oz (150ml). Strain out the tarragon and discard. Set the stock aside.

Melt the butter in a saucepan, add the flour and cook over moderate heat for 2–3 minutes. Draw off the stove, wait until the sizzling ceases before adding the prepared stock. Bring to the boil, whisking well, and simmer for 1–2 minutes. Gradually add the cream, season with salt, plenty of pepper, mustard and the cheese.

Set on a heat-diffuser mat or in a *bain marie* at the side of the stove for 20–30 minutes for the sauce to cook and mature (flour-based sauces with a high proportion of cream should not be boiled as they may separate).

Fry the breadcrumbs in ½ oz (12g) butter until golden. Cut the turkey breasts into the required number of thick serving pieces (escalopes). When ready to serve, season and sprinkle them very lightly with flour. Heat the clarified butter and oil, and when very hot sauté the turkey escallops briefly on both sides. Cook very lightly, so that they still feel slightly squishy under your finger, for they are delicate and can toughen if overcooked.

Spoon a little of the sauce into a flat gratin dish, lay the turkey escalopes on the sauce, mask with the remaining sauce and sprinkle with the fried breadcrumbs. Grill until brown and serve at once.

The sauce is also good with leftover cold turkey. Heat the meat through carefully, then sauce it and brown it in a hot oven or under the grill. A prolonged period in a hot oven may cause the sauce to separate.

*   # Stir-Fried Turkey with Garlic and Water Chestnuts

This is what I call an 'up-my-sleeve' recipe. If I have some cold turkey or leftover chicken, I know I can rustle up this extremely popular, Chinese style dish in a moment, because I usually keep a tin of water chestnuts and a jar of yellow bean sauce in the store cupboard for just this reason. In fact, it's so popular that I often cook a large chicken, use half of it for this, and keep half to eat cold or in pancakes. Make sure you get Sharwood's Yellow Bean *Stir Fry* Sauce, not just their yellow bean sauce.

Ingredients
4–6 people

1 lb (450g) cold cooked turkey or chicken
2 medium onions
2–3 cloves garlic
2–3 medium carrots
2 sticks celery
½ green pepper
½" (1cm) fresh root ginger
8 oz (225g) tin water chestnuts
4 tbs corn or groundnut oil
pinch of Chinese 5 spices powder
    (optional)
1 × 5 fl oz (150ml) jar Sharwood's Peking
    Yellow Bean Stir Fry Sauce
1 tbs soy sauce
salt and pepper if necessary

Cut the turkey into ½" (1cm) dice, finely slice the onion and garlic, cut the carrots, celery and green pepper into julienne strips and shred or grate the ginger. Drain and slice the water chestnuts.

Heat 2 tbs oil in a wok or large frying pan and stir-fry the turkey for 2 minutes; remove. Add another 2 tbs oil to the wok, and when very hot add the onion, garlic, carrot and ginger and stir-fry for about 30 seconds. Add the celery, green pepper and water chestnuts and stir fry for about 1 minute longer before returning the turkey to the pan and adding a pinch of 5 spices powder, if used, the yellow bean sauce and soy sauce. Heat and stir until bubbling and hot. Season if necessary and serve at once.

P **   Sweet Glazed Ham

Can we still say 'We hold a Westmorland or Yorkshire ham, well-fattened and properly cured, against all the hams in the world' as Mr Touchwood of the celebrated Cleikum Club did? To me, the important words are well-fattened and properly cured. Who now feeds their pigs on acorns or beech mast, which imparted 'great sweetness and solidity to their flesh', and made the hams of Buckinghamshire and Hampshire justly famous? Who carefully finishes the fattening process by feeding peas, beans and potatoes? Where will you find hams smoked over dried seaweed for a delicious flavour? Who uses the old and excellent pickling mixture which included beer, spices, sugar and treacle?

We once had an excellent ham from our local butcher. It was all of twenty pounds weight with a generous coating of delectable fat and such sweetness of flavour in the meat. (The coating of fat is essential for flavour in the meat, but just look at modern Danish and English hams; the fat layer is kept to a minimum at the mistaken insistence of the customer.) It was a joy to eat and lasted for weeks. Every year since I have begged and badgered him for a home-cured ham, but he says he doesn't have time to prepare them. What a sad state of affairs.

Our local farmer neighbours in France cure their own *jambon cru*, eaten raw and with a wonderful honey flavour in the fat and lean alike. Their hams are packed in salt for 40 days, then air-dried, but the maize, skimmed milk, greens and beet which have fed these great porkers have all added to the quality. When we dine with French or German friends, they will frequently produce some home-produced or local ham, and the conversation often gets heated about how much salt, which herbs and spices, how long to cure it, over which wood to smoke it—it is all of intense interest and importance to them.

I can't find you a ham of quality, but I can tell you how to cook it. Having given a recipe for a Fig Baked Ham in *Good Food from Farthinghoe*, I am now giving a recipe for simmering a ham. Should I find a superior home-fed and cured ham I would not insult it with a sweet glaze, but dignify it with a coating of home-made breadcrumbs and a frill. But for the run of the mill Danish or English ham or gammon, you will find this method answers well and looks very fine for a party.

Ingredients

a fine ham
water to cover generously
1 ham frill (optional)

To finish with Spiced Marmalade Glaze
2 tbs marmalade
2–3 tbs Demerara sugar
⅛ teasp ground cloves
whole cloves (optional)

To finish with Breadcrumbs
dry breadcrumbs

Enquire from your supplier and soak your ham accordingly; well hung, home-cured and Bradenham hams may need up to four days, whereas fresh, commercially produced hams may need only a few hours. If it needs days, change the water frequently (one was usually advised to put them in the trough under the yard pump!).

To Cook. Place the ham in a large pan so that it is not touching the bottom (set on a trivet, upturned plate or some such). Cover it generously with fresh clean water and bring gently to the boil, taking 1–2 hours, depending on the size of the pan. Start timing once the water boils, and keep it at the merest tremble. Calculate the weight of the ham and allow 20 minutes for each 1 lb (450g) and 20 minutes over for joints up to 10 pounds (4.5kg); or 15 minutes for each 1 lb (450g) and 15 minutes over for hams between 10 lb (4.5kg) and 15 lbs (6.75kg); those over 15 lbs (6.75kg) will not need the extra 15 minutes.

To finish with breadcrumbs. Cook the ham for the prescribed time, then remove from the heat and leave to cool a little in the water. Skin and cover with breadcrumbs (it's easiest to pat these on whilst still warm, for they then stick to the warm fat).

   Slip a ham frill on to the knuckle bone before serving.

To finish with spiced Marmalade Glaze. Remove the ham ¼ hour before the end of its cooking time. Carefully cut off the skin while still hot, and score the fat lightly into diamonds, then rub with the glaze and spike each diamond with a clove. Bake in a hot oven (400°F/200°C/Gas 6) for 20–30 minutes, watching carefully, until nicely browned and glazed.

Spiced Marmalade Glaze. Mix the marmalade, Demerara sugar and ground clove together and use to rub into the prepared fat of the cooked ham.

** Beef Cheese

This old English dish, tasty and salty, will keep for several weeks and is an excellent addition to the Christmas board. Of course, it's just as useful in summer when you can serve slices of it day after day with different salads. A double quantity would be a sensible amount to make.

Ingredients
4–6 people

25 people

1½ lb (675g) lean braising beef
½ lb (225g) uncooked fat bacon or ham
¼ lb (100g) back pork fat or good beef dripping
¼ teasp ground mace
⅛ teasp ground cloves
good shake cayenne
½ teasp dried thyme (or fresh if you are not trying to keep the cheese for long)
1 tbs Worcester sauce
1 tbs brandy
½ clove garlic
½ lb (225g) thin-cut streaky bacon
salt and pepper

Huff Pastry (to seal)
8 oz (225g) plain flour
5 fl oz (150ml) water
½ teasp salt

6 lb (2.7kg) lean braising beef
1½ lb (675g) uncooked fat bacon or ham
¾–1 lb (350–450g) back pork fat or good beef dripping
1 teap ground mace
¼–½ teasp ground cloves
⅛ teasp cayenne pepper
1–1½ tbs fresh or 1 teasp dried thyme
3 tbs Worcester sauce
3 tbs brandy
1 clove garlic
1½ lb (675g) thin-cut streaky bacon
salt and pepper

Huff Pastry
1½ lb (675g) plain flour
¾ pt (450ml) cold water (approx)
1½ teasp salt

Mince together (or chop in a food processor) the beef, free from gristle, the bacon or ham and the pork fat or dripping. Season fairly highly with salt and pepper, cloves, mace and cayenne pepper, and stir in the thyme, Worcester sauce and brandy.

Rub a 2 pt (1.2l) terrine or several terrines (a long loaf shape is the best) with a cut clove of garlic and line with strips of streaky bacon. Carefully turn the meat mixture into the terrine and pack down tightly. Cover the terrine with a thick layer of the rolled huff pastry, sealing it with cold water carefully round the outer edges of the terrine. Bake in a very moderate oven (325°F/170°C/Gas 3) for 5–6 hours. The same time will do for either quantity. If you turn the oven off after the cooking period and leave the terrine to get completely cold without opening the oven door, it will be sterile and hermetically sealed, and will keep unopened for quite a while.

Huff Pastry. Mix the flour, salt and water to a stiff dough. Roll out thickly and use to cover the terrine.

To Serve. Remove the crust and discard, or give it to the dog as a Christmas present! Turn out the beef and serve in thin slices with gherkins, salad and mustard, Cumberland sauce (*see page 272*) or hot toast or bread.

The mixture can also be turned into potted beef, either whilst still hot or to use up the remainder. The meat is pounded or processed until smooth, with a little melted butter (about 3–4 oz (75–100g) for the smaller quantities given above). The jelly or gravy can also be added, but the potted meat will not keep so long with the liquid in. Pack into little pots and serve with toast or bread, or in sandwiches.

$\mathcal{P}$ **   Tongue with Almond and Raisin Sauce

A pickled tongue, cooked and served hot with this slightly unusual sauce of almonds, raisins, chocolate and peel, is certainly a little different. For summer a cold tongue with salads is nice for a change.

Ingredients
6–8 people

3–4 lb (1.35–1.8k) pickled tongue
2 carrots
2 onions
1 stick celery
1 bay leaf
bouquet garni or parsley stalks and
   thyme
6–8 peppercorns

Sauce
2 oz (50g) butter
2 chopped onions
1 oz (25g) flour
1 tbs tomato purée
1 pt (600ml) stock
1 tbs sugar
2 tbs wine vinegar (rosepetal or
   raspberry is good)
2 tbs chopped flaked almonds
2 tbs raisins
2–3 teasp grated chocolate
1 tbs chopped candied peel
salt and pepper

Soak the tongue in fresh water for about half-an-hour, or however long recommended by your butcher, then curl round into a circle and fit into a pan. Cover by 2 inches with cold water, add the vegetables and herbs and simmer very gently for about 4–6 hours until the little bones can be easily removed. (They used to say the tongue should be pierced with a straw to check if it was ready.) Leave to cool for 1 hour, remove from the water, skin, and remove all the little bones.

To serve hot. Slice while still hot, slicing up from the tip towards the root. This is a little more wasteful than when curled round and sliced cold, as the very tip and the root tend to be wasted, but of course they can always be potted. Or you can let the tongue cool, then slice it and reheat in the sauce.

To serve cold. Curl the tongue round into a 9″–10″ (23cm–25cm) cake tin with a removable base, turn the cake tin upside down on to a wooden board or plate and weight the base with a 7 lb (3–4kg) weight. Leave overnight. Two tongues in a larger tin fit together even better.

Sauce. Melt the butter in a saucepan, gently fry the onions until golden, add the flour and cook for 2–3 minutes. Draw the saucepan from the stove, add the stock and tomato purée, bring to the boil, whisking hard, and simmer for about 30 minutes to reduce, skimming if necessary. Add the sugar, vinegar, almonds, raisins, chocolate and peel, correct the seasoning and simmer for 10–15 minutes, until of a good coating consistency. Pour over the hot sliced tongue or serve in a sauceboat.

251

P F *** **Civet of Venison**

Marinated venison, gently braised with little cubes of fat to keep it succulent and with pork rinds to enrich the sauce, has been one of our great Fillafreeze favourites. I get my young fallow deer locally from a deer park—the shoulder or haunch is best.

Ingredients
4–6 people

2½–3 lb (1.15–1.35kg) boneless haunch or shoulder of venison
2 oz (50g) plain flour, seasoned
2 oz (50g) streaky bacon cut thick
2 oz (50g) back pork fat (optional)
1 onion
1 carrot
1–2 oz (25–50g) bacon rinds or pork skin
1½ pts (900ml) venison or beef stock approx
bouquet garni of parsley stalks, sprigs thyme, 3 juniper berries, 1 bay leaf and 1 clove
strip orange rind (Seville when possible)
1 teasp black treacle
2 tbs port
squeeze Seville orange or orange and lemon juice
salt and pepper
croûtes of bread fried in butter and olive oil (optional)

25 people

10 lb (4.5kg) boneless braising venison
8 oz (225g) plain flour, seasoned
8 oz (225g) streaky bacon cut thick
8 oz (225g) back pork fat (optional)
1 lb (450g) onion
1¼ lb (550g) carrots
6–8 oz (175–225g) bacon rinds or pork skin
3–3½ pts (1.7–2l) venison or beef stock approx
bouquet garni of 6–8 parsley stalks, 3–4 sprigs thyme, 9 juniper berries, 2 bay leaves and 3 cloves
4 strips orange rind
1–1½ tbs black treacle
4 fl oz (100ml) port
juice 2 Seville oranges or 1 orange and ½ lemon
salt and pepper
croûtes of bread fried in butter and olive oil (optional)

Marinade
1 finely chopped onion
1 finely chopped shallot
1 finely chopped stick celery
1 clove garlic
2–3 juniper berries
2 tbs olive oil
1 tbs wine vinegar
¼–½ pt (150ml–300ml) red wine
1 sprig thyme
2–3 parsley stalks
1 bay leaf
salt, pepper and cayenne

Marinade
2–3 finely sliced onions
2–3 finely sliced shallots
2 finely sliced carrots
3 finely chopped sticks celery
2 cloves garlic
6 juniper berries
6 tbs olive oil
3 tbs wine vinegar
2–3 sprigs thyme
6 parsley stalks
2 bay leaves
salt, pepper and cayenne

Cube the meat into generous 1″ (2–3cm) cubes and marinate with all the marinade ingredients for 12–24 hours.

Drain the meat and toss in seasoned flour.

In a casserole, gently fry the cubed streaky bacon and pork fat until the fat runs and the bacon browns; remove. Slice the onion and carrot and brown in the fat, and return the meat and bacon to the pan. Add the bacon rinds or pork skin cut into tiny pieces (I sometimes boil the rinds for ½ hour to soften them). Pour over the strained marinade, and enough stock just to cover. Tuck in the bouquet garni and orange rind, add the black treacle and cook in a slow oven (300°F/150°C/Gas 2) until tender for 4–6 hours, depending on your venison.

Remove the meat and vegetables to a serving dish and keep warm, removing the bouquet garni and orange rind. Boil the gravy down fast to reduce well, skimming if necessary. Add the port and the orange and lemon juice, correct the seasoning and strain over the meat.

Serve surrounded by croûtes of fried bread and accompanied by a purée of Creamy Mashed Potatoes or Red Cabbage with Sultanas and Cider Vinegar.

Vegetables

*   Roast Potatoes

Crunchy roast potatoes are not always easy to produce. We always par-boil them before roasting, and this helps to give a crusty finish.

Ingredients
4–6 people

2–2½ lb (1–1.15kg) potatoes
4 oz (100g) dripping or lard

Peel and cut the potatoes into even sizes; keep in cold water in a cool place until ready to cook.

Bring the potatoes to the boil in fresh, salted water and boil for 3–4 minutes. Turn into a colander and leave to drain. Take a fork and scratch the potatoes all over so that they have a ridged surface. Melt the fat in a roasting tin but do not get it very hot (too hot and the potatoes seal at once and don't absorb any of the fat which gives them that nice crunchy outside). Turn the potatoes in the fat so that they are coated, then put them into a hot oven (400°F/200°C/Gas 6) for at least 1 hour (sometimes even 1½ hours), turning them from time to time until they are golden brown and crisp. Drain off the fat for the last ¼ hour if they are not crisping nicely.

Potatoes will wait for ½ hour or so in a moderately hot oven just getting browner and crisper, but don't put them in a low oven or food warmer or they will go soft very quickly. If you are cooking them in the same oven as the turkey or a large joint of meat, allow them plenty of time, because with a full oven they will take longer.

Creamy Mashed Potatoes

Craggy lumps of stiff mashed potato are easily resistable, but a smooth, light and moussy mixture that drops easily off the spoon is quite another story. A potato ricer makes all the difference, and I picked mine up for 2p at a jumble sale; it forces the cooked potato through tiny holes and guarantees no lumps. The smooth mixture then has chopped butter and milk beaten in to lighten it and is seasoned with masses of pepper and some salt. Nice floury potatoes like Maris Piper, Pentland Ivory or Crown, the lovely Scots Golden Wonder, the Kerr's Pink or the excellent modern all-rounder Désirée are some smashing mashers.

Ingredients
4–6 people

1½–2 lb (675–900g) peeled potatoes
2 oz (50g) butter (approx)
6 fl oz (175ml) milk (approx)
a little freshly grated nutmeg (optional)
salt and pepper

Cut the potatoes into even sizes and cover generously with water. Add salt and bring to the boil. Boil gently for about 20–30 minutes until the potatoes, stuck with a knife, feel tender; then drain well and press back into the saucepan through the potato ricer or a large sieve (failing that, use a potato masher or fork, but this is much more difficult). Return to the stove and add the cut up butter and seasoning and then gradually add the milk, beating all the time with a masher, fork or wooden spoon until the mixture lightens and becomes a very soft purée.

Make sure the potatoes are hot, and serve as soon as possible, for mashed potato is impatient and doesn't like to be kept waiting.

If you are making a largish quantity or wish to keep the potatoes hot for a while, beat them in a mixer with butter, hot milk and pepper. The potatoes will then wait happily for a considerable time in a cool oven, covered with foil.

*   Sweet-Sour Beetroot

This is one of my favourite ways with beetroot. Cook them whenever you wish, then, when ready to eat them, just toss them up in a wok or large frying pan with a Chinese style sweet-sour sauce. If you do the larger amount, you will need several big pans.

Ingredients
4–6 people

1½ lb (675g) cooked beetroot	
3 tbs oil	
1 teasp fresh chopped or ¼ teasp dried dill or dill seed	
salt and pepper	

25 people

6–8 lb (2.7–3.6kg) cooked beetroot
9 tbs oil
1–1½ tbs fresh chopped or ¾–1 teasp dried dill or dill seed
salt and pepper

Sauce
2 teasp cornflour
2 tbs sugar
3–4 tbs vinegar
1 tbs soy sauce
shake chilli or tabasco sauce
3 tbs undiluted lemon or orange squash

Sauce
3 tbs cornflour
4 oz (100g) sugar
6–8 fl oz (175–225ml) vinegar
4 tbs soy sauce
several shakes chilli or tabasco sauce
6 fl oz (175ml) undiluted lemon or orange squash

Peel and dice the beetroot into generous thumb-nail-sized cubes.

Heat the oil in a wok or large frying pan until just smoking, then add the beetroot. Stir and toss round until hot through, pour on the sauce and stir until it boils, thickens and coats each cube of beetroot in a shiny glaze. Season with plenty of salt and pepper and add more sugar or vinegar if necessary. Sprinkle with the dill, toss and serve.

Sauce. Mix all the sauce ingredients together.

* Spiced Roast Parsnips

Parsnips are naturally very sweet and, though delicious boiled or mashed, I think are best roasted. A sprinkling of cinnamon, sugar, cayenne and orange rind seems to enhance their natural flavour.

Ingredients
4–6 people

1½–2 lb (675–900g) peeled parsnips
2 oz (50g) dripping, lard or oil
2 teasp castor or brown sugar
¼ teasp ground cinnamon or cardamom
grated rind of one orange
a little cayenne pepper
salt

Cut the parsnips into quarters or eighths lengthways, depending on size, and then into segments, removing any woolly or woody core if necessary. Add them to a pan of boiling salted water and parboil for about 4–6 minutes. Drain well.

Heat the fat in a roasting pan, add the drained parsnips and sprinkle over the sugar, cinnamon or cardamom, grated orange rind, cayenne pepper and a little salt. Toss well and roast in a hot oven (425°F/220°C/Gas 7) for 40–60 minutes, turning from time to time until well browned. Drain from the fat, sprinkle with salt and serve.

*   Glazed Turnips

If you planted your turnip seed in the last few days of July, that moment when you catch the first heavy dews to help germination but while there is still plenty of the growing season ahead, you will have tender leaves for Creamed Turnip Tops and fine, golf-ball-sized turnips by October or November. These are quite delicious glazed whole, with a tuft of stalk left on *à la Michel Guérard*, and I like to use them where suitable for autumn dinner parties. Later on, when the turnips are larger, cut them into little finger batons and cook them the same way; they are meltingly tender with a wonderful flavour. Of course, young turnips can be cooked as in this recipe at any time, but I think they are really a winter flavour.

Ingredients
4–6 people

1–2 lb (450–900g) tender turnips
1 oz (25g) chicken fat, dripping, butter or
    oil
1 teasp castor sugar
approx ¼ pt (150ml) stock
1 sprig thyme (optional)
salt and pepper

Either leave even, golf-ball-sized turnips whole with a ½" (1cm) tuft of stalk left on or, if larger, peel and cut into ½" (1cm) slices, then across into batons.

Melt the fat in a wide-based sauté pan, big enough to take the turnips in one layer. Add the turnips, sprinkle with sugar and sauté gently, shaking the pan frequently for about 5–10 minutes until they brown lightly. Add a few tablespoonfuls of the stock, the thyme and a light seasoning and cover. Cook gently, shaking the pan frequently, and adding more stock if necessary, until the turnips are glazed and tender and the stock has all gone (this may take only another 5 minutes).

These turnips are particularly good to serve with beef, venison or lamb.

*   Brussels Sprouts with Walnuts

We all know about Brussels Sprouts with chestnuts, especially at Christmas, but chestnuts are a fag to do and have only a short season. Try your sprouts with walnuts prepared in the Chinese way (the walnuts are also very good on their own with drinks), and use some walnut oil to toss the sprouts. You might also try roasted hazelnuts and hazelnut oil or fried almonds and almond oil as a change.

Ingredients
4–6 people

2 tbs walnut oil
squeeze lemon juice (optional)
salt and pepper

Prepare the sprouts by peeling off loose, discoloured or dirty leaves. Do not cut a cross in the base, as it only lets the water in and they go mushy. Throw into plenty of boiling salted water and boil fast, uncovered, until they are just tender but still crisp. Drain well in a colander.

Meanwhile throw the walnuts into boiling water and boil for 5–6 minutes, drain well and dry. Heat the butter or oil and the walnut oil in a frying pan and sauté the walnuts over high heat for about 5 minutes until they are crisp and golden, before removing with a slotted spoon. Add sprouts to the hot oil and toss and heat until lightly glazed. Season and add a squeeze of lemon juice if you like.

Turn into a serving dish, scatter over the walnuts and serve at once or, if keeping warm, top with walnuts only on serving.

*   Red Cabbage with Sultanas and Cider Vinegar

Long slow cooking with spices and apple is usually the favourite way of cooking red cabbage but this recipe is for when one would like a fresher flavour and a vegetable that will cook in a shorter time, and it's just as good in its way. For real speed, try the Sweet and Sour Red Cabbage* cooked in the Chinese style.

Ingredients
4–6 people

1½ lb (675g) thinly sliced red cabbage
4–5 tbs cider vinegar (wine vinegar
**   would do)**
1 oz (25g) butter
1 finely chopped shallot or small onion
2 cloves
6 whole allspice

1 oz (25g) sultanas
¼ teasp carraway seeds
pinch ground cinnamon
½–1 stock cube (I use Morga or Hügli
**   vegetable stock cubes)**
salt and pepper

Throw the cabbage into a large pan of salted water with a dash of the vinegar and blanch for 2–3 minutes. Drain well.

Take a heavy pan and gently fry the shallot in the butter with the cloves and allspice. When the shallot has softened, add the drained cabbage with the remaining vinegar, sultanas, carraway and cinnamon. Crumble the stock cube into the juices at the bottom and stir well. Season lightly if you used a salty stock cube (Morga make a non-salted or a sea-salted vegetable cube which is good) and simmer, covered, for 10–15 minutes until crisply tender. Boil fast uncovered if there is too much juice, then serve—preferably at once.

* *Good Food from Farthinghoe*

Ŧ ✳✳   **Braised Celery**

Crunchy and spicy flavoured celery straight from the fields after a few sharp frosts is at its best for serving raw in sticks to eat with cheese. But it also makes a good braised vegetable, and is especially nice when cooked in some good stock, reduced to practically nothing.

Ingredients
4–6 people

2–3 heads celery
1 small diced carrot
1 small finely chopped onion
1 rasher bacon and any spare bacon rinds
1¼–1½ pt (750–900ml) approx good beef
   or chicken stock
1–2 tbs fat from the stock or good
   dripping (or use rather fatty stock)
salt and pepper

Remove the outer stalks of the celery heads, trim the bases and cut off the tops, leaving 5″–6″ (12cm–15cm). Wash them very well under running water, then cut in halves lengthways, or in quarters if the heads are very large. Throw into plenty of boiling salted water, boil for about 8–10 minutes and drain.

Choose a heavy, wide-bottomed casserole or gratin dish, preferably one in which they fit tightly in one layer, from which they can be served, and one that can cook on the top of the stove if necessary. Butter it generously and scatter with carrot, onion and diced bacon. Use any bacon rinds you have, tied into a bundle, because the gelatine they give off improves the sauce. Lay the drained celery on this bed, season lightly and pour over enough stock barely to cover, adding the dripping. Cover with a butter paper and lid and cook in a moderate oven (350°F/180°C/Gas 4) for 1½–2 hours, removing the lid after the first half hour, until the celery is very tender and the juice is reduced and lightly browned. Boil away excess juice on the top of the stove if necessary. Remove the bacon rinds before serving and season as necessary.

This will reheat well in a covered casserole.

* Chicory and Apple Salad with Walnut Dressing

Chicory can be grown during the summer, then de-capitated, dug up and forced in the cellar or a dark cupboard during the winter. It is very useful for winter salads, though the heads are never as perfect as those in the shops. Even though I grow the variety *Pain de Sucre* and it is blanched in the dark, this vegetable is always a little bitter, and appeals to some people more than others. I like to include something sweet like apple in the salad and give it quite a lavish dressing.

Ingredients
4–6 people

2 heads chicory
3 red-skinned apples
2 oz (50g) walnut halves

Dressing
1 finely chopped shallot
4–6 fresh-chopped mint leaves or good
  pinch dried mint (or use mint vinegar)
1 teasp Dijon mustard
1 tbs wine or rosepetal vinegar
2–3 tbs walnut oil
2 tbs light oil such as sunflower
salt and pepper

25 people

6–8 heads chicory
10 red-skinned apples
4–6 oz (100–175g) walnut halves

Dressing
2–3 tbs finely chopped shallot
handful chopped mint leaves or ½ teasp
  dried mint (or use mint vinegar)
1 tbs Dijon mustard
3–4 tbs wine or rosepetal vinegar
8–10 tbs walnut oil
6–8 tbs light oil such as sunflower
½ teasp salt
pepper

Dressing. Place the chopped shallot and mint in a salad bowl with the salt, pepper, mustard and vinegar. Stir to dissolve the salt, then vigorously stir in the oils to make a dressing, or shake together in a well-sealed jar.

Quarter, core and cut up the apples and toss in the dressing. Slice in the chicory and add the walnuts. Toss and serve.

* **Christmas Salad**

We often need salads at Christmas to go with cold meats and pies. This one is easy to prepare, is nice and crunchy and keeps well, so I usually make a big batch. You can also add hard-boiled eggs, diced turkey or ham if you want to make it into a main course salad.

Ingredients

25 people

1–2 eating apples	4–6 eating apples
6 oz (175g) potatoes boiled in their skins	1¼ lb (500g) potatoes boiled in their skins
6–12 oz (175–350g) cooked beetroot	1½ lb (675g) cooked beetroot
2 dill cucumbers (optional)	4–6 dill cucumbers
1 shallot or ½ very small onion	2 shallots or 1 very small onion
2–4 sticks celery or ½ head Florence fennel	1 head celery or 2 heads Florence fennel
6 oz (175g) thinly-sliced white cabbage	1¼ lb (500g) thinly-sliced white cabbage
1–2 oz (25–50g) walnut halves	3 oz (75g) walnut halves
1–2 tbs vinegar	6 tbs vinegar
salt, pepper and sugar	1 tbs sugar
	salt and pepper

Dressing

Dressing

8 fl oz (225ml) mayonnaise	1½ pts (900ml) mayonnaise (approx)
1 teasp paprika	1–2 tbs paprika
1 teasp Dijon mustard	1–1½ tbs Dijon mustard
½ clove garlic	1–2 cloves garlic
¼ teasp dried dill or dill seed	1 teasp dried dill or dill seed
little vinegar to taste	vinegar to taste
1 small beetroot (optional)	1 small beetroot (optional)
salt and pepper	salt and pepper

Core the apple. Dice the potatoes, beetroot, dill cucumbers and apple. Finely chop the onion and slice the celery or fennel. Turn with the sliced cabbage into a bowl and sprinkle with salt, pepper, a little sugar and the vinegar. Add the dressing and toss well. Serve scattered with the walnut halves.

Hard-boiled eggs, diced turkey or ham can all be added to this salad.

Dressing. Combine the mayonnaise with the paprika, mustard, pressed garlic and dill or dill seed. Add vinegar to taste and correct the seasoning.

If you wish, you can process a small beetroot in with the mayonnaise for a rose pink dressing, but don't over do it or it can be very lurid!

Puddings

𝒯 ∗∗　Christmas Honours Tart

I call this Christmas Honours Tart because the topping is roughly the same as that used for Maids of Honour, those elegant and delicious little tartlets with jam in the bottom and an almond sponge topping. It's rather a nice and different way of using mincemeat, and the segments of orange and lemon stop it from being too sweet.

Ingredients
4–6 people

Pastry
6 oz (175g) plain flour
2 tbs icing sugar
3½ oz (85g) chilled butter
1 egg yolk
1–2 tbs cold water
pinch salt

Filling
12 oz (350g) mincemeat
2 oranges
1 lemon

Topping
2 oz (50g) butter
4 oz (100g) castor sugar
1 egg
3 oz (75g) ground rice
4 tbs ground almonds
few drops almond essence
12 whole almonds, blanched

Pastry. Sieve the flour, salt and icing sugar into a bowl or the food processor. Add the firm butter cut up into hazelnut-sized pieces and rub in or process to the breadcrumb stage. Bind with the yolk and a very little cold water. Form into a flat disc and rest for 1–2 hours in the fridge in a plastic bag. Roll the pastry to fit a 9″ (24cm) removable base flan tin. Prick the pastry, line with tinfoil and baking beans and bake in a hot oven (400°F/200°C/Gas 6) for 6–8 minutes until the pastry is set. Remove the tinfoil and cook a few minutes more.

Filling. Cut the peel, pith and skin from the oranges and lemons and cut out the segments without any skin. Cut up the segments and mix with the mincemeat. Spread over the base of the pastry and remove the tart from the flan ring.

Topping. Cream the butter, beat in the sugar and cream well. Gradually add the whisked egg and fold in the ground rice, ground almonds and essence. Spread over the mincemeat filling and decorate with the whole almonds.

Bake in a moderately hot oven (375°F/190°C/Gas 5) for 20 minutes, then turn down to moderate (350°F/180°C/Gas 4) and continue to bake for 50–60 minutes until firm, golden brown and cooked right through. Cover lightly with tinfoil towards the end of the cooking time if necessary. Serve hot, warm or cold.

F ***   Superlative Mincemeat Pies

Having given my mincepie* recipe before I should like to include a real old fashioned recipe here.

Puff pastry was most often used for Christmas mincepies and it is extremely good. They should rise from the patty pans like little vol-au-vents, and the paste underneath should be rolled a little thinner than the top paste. They can be frozen uncooked, then cooked straight from the freezer. Of course, only home-made puff pastry has that real buttery flavour.

Ingredients
36 pies (approx)

Puff Pastry
8 oz (225g) 'strong' flour
8 oz (225g) best unsalted or lightly salted butter
6 fl oz (175ml) iced water (approx)

squeeze lemon juice
pinch salt
egg wash
¾–1 lb (350–450g) Lemon Mincemeat
(see page 275)

Puff Pastry. Sift the flour and salt into a bowl and add a quarter of the butter, diced, and a squeeze of lemon juice. Rub in the butter, then add the water to make a medium firm dough, known as *la détrempe*. Knead a little but do not overwork the dough, or it will become too elastic. The remaining butter should be of the same consistency as *la détrempe*, firm but spreadable. Make it into a square flat cake. Roll the pastry into a rectangle, place the butter on one half and fold the other over to encase the butter, sealing the edges. Roll carefully to a rectangle (stop at once if the butter shows signs of coming through), then fold up the bottom third of the pastry and fold down the top third over it. Press the edges together and rest for 20 minutes in a plastic bag in the fridge.

Replace on the floured board, with the folded edge to your left, and roll out into a neat rectangle. Fold in thirds as before and give the pastry a half-turn to the right so that the folded edge is again on your left. Roll again, fold, and rest for 20 minutes. Repeat two more 'rolls' and 'turns', rolling only in a lengthwise direction as slantwise rolling will produce an uneven rise, and rest again for 20 minutes.

Repeat this process once more so that the pastry has seven 'turns' and four 'rests' in all. The pastry is now ready to be kept until needed. Five turns would be adequate for these pies.

Mincemeat Pies. Roll the pastry very thinly and with a fluted cutter cut out 36 × 3" (7–8cm) rounds for the tops. Roll the remaining pastry a little thinner and cut 36 × 3" (7–8cm) rounds for the bases; any re-rolled pastry should be used for bases only. Lay the rounds in pie tins, prick the bases lightly and place a spoonful of mincemeat in the middle of each. Moisten the edges with cold water and cover with a top round of pastry. Seal the edges well and slash or prick the tops. Paint with egg wash and cook in a hot oven (400°F/200°C/Gas 7) for about 15–20 minutes until well risen and golden brown. Serve hot, or rewarm on serving.

$\mathcal{F}$ ✳✳✳   Mocca Roulade with Praline Cream

There is a great vogue for those rich chocolate roulades, and I am always being asked for recipes. This one has a touch of coffee and a light praline filling. If you prefer not to roll the roulade you may cut it into two equal pieces and sandwich them together with the cream, or bake the mixture in two round tins.

Ingredients
6–8 people

6 oz (150g) dark eating chocolate,
   Meunier, Bournville or the like
1½ teasp powdered coffee
2 tbs warm water
5 eggs
4 oz (100g) vanilla castor sugar or sugar
   and a few drops of vanilla essence
8 fl oz (225ml) whipping cream
icing sugar

Praline Powder
½–1 oz (12–25g) browned almonds or
   hazelnuts
2½ oz (65g) castor sugar

Place the broken chocolate, powdered coffee and warm water in a bowl over warm water to melt. Separate the eggs. Whisk the yolks and vanilla sugar until thick and pale, and fold in the melted chocolate. Whisk the egg whites until they just hold a peak, fold into the mixture and turn into a Swiss roll or roasting tin approx size 13″ × 10″ (33cm × 25cm) lined with Bakewell paper. Cook in a moderately hot oven (375°F/190°C/Gas 5) for about 20 minutes until just firm to the touch. Leave to cool for several minutes, then turn out on to another sheet of Bakewell or greaseproof paper or a clean cloth. Trim the hard edges from the long sides so that it can roll easily, and leave to get cold.

Whip the cream and fold in the praline powder. Spread the cream all over the roulade, then, using the paper or cloth underneath to help, carefully roll the roulade up. Turn on to a serving dish and serve sprinkled with icing sugar.

Praline Powder. Sprinkle the sugar in a thin layer in the bottom of a heavy saucepan or frying pan to heat until the sugar melts and turns a good caramel brown. Pour over the browned nuts on a sheet of greased tinfoil and leave to cool and harden. Pound to a rough powder and store in an air-tight jar.

P **   **Plum Pudding**

Make your Christmas pudding as far ahead as you like. Even 1–2 years is not too much, and it gives the pudding time to mature in flavour and become a fine dark colour. But should you be making it only a week before Christmas, don't worry; boil it for 6–8 hours on two separate occasions (if you have time), then give it another four hours on Christmas day, and it will be dark and succulent. Scrubbed silver coins or trinkets can be inserted with the point of a knife just before serving.

Ingredients
plenty for 6–8 people

4 oz (100g) plain flour	8 oz (225g) sultanas
¼ teasp salt	4 oz (100g) grated carrots
½ teasp mixed spice	4 oz (100g) grated peeled apples
½ teasp grated nutmeg	2 oz (50g) flaked almonds
8 oz (225g) fresh white breadcrumbs	grated rind and juice ½ lemon
8 oz (225g) grated or chopped suet	2 tbs brandy, rum or whisky
8 oz (225g) soft dark brown sugar	3 eggs
8 oz (225g) currants	1 tbs black treacle (optional)
8 oz (225g) raisins	

Sift the flour with the salt and spices into a large mixing bowl, then add all the dry ingredients and mix well together. Add the lemon juice, brandy, rum or whisky, beaten eggs and treacle, and stir and beat thoroughly with a wooden spoon (don't forget that everyone should have a stir and make a wish). Pack into a greased 3 pt (1.7l) pyrex, china or plastic bowl, cover first with a butter paper or buttered greaseproof paper, then with a double layer of tinfoil or a floured cloth. Tie on tightly and give yourself a loop of string as a handle (or knot the corners of the cloth together in the middle of the top of the bowl), because otherwise it can be very difficult to lift the bowl from the steamer or saucepan.

Bring a large saucepan of water to the boil. Put a steamer (with a close-fitting lid) containing the pudding over the saucepan (it must fit tightly so that the steam really surrounds the pudding). Alternatively, stand the pudding in the pan of boiling water, preferably on a rack or two skewers or even a folded cloth, so that the bowl is not actually touching the bottom of the pan, and with the water reaching halfway up the pudding bowl (too much water and it will all boil into the pudding, making it soggy). Cover closely and keep at a steady boil for 6–8 hours.

Keep the water replenished with boiling water when it gets low (if you pop a marble into the saucepan you can hear when the water is getting low). Never let the water boil dry, because a plastic bowl will melt with disastrous results, and in a glass or china bowl the pudding will burn.

When cooked, cool and leave to mature on the shelf for a year or more!

On Christmas Day. Re-boil or steam for 4 hours, then remove from the pan and take off the cover. Run a flexible knife carefully round between the bowl and the pudding and put a warmed plate upside down on top of the bowl. Turn over the plate and bowl together and give a good shake, and it should come out easily. Stick a nice sprig of berried holly in the middle of the pudding. Warm a little brandy (or brandy and vodka mixed for a really good flame). Pour it over the pudding, light at once with a match and rush it to the table.

Serve with Brandy Butter (*see page 272*).

Chestnut Yule Log

This rich chestnut-chocolate log is wonderful at Christmas. Try making it with fresh chestnut purée (see Nesselrode Pudding overleaf) instead of cheating with a tin! A little goes a long way, and it will last well in the fridge or can be frozen. Double the quantity will be enough for a party of 25, especially if you have a fruit pudding as an alternative.

Ingredients
8–10 people

1 lb (450g) chestnut purée made from
    fresh chestnuts *(see page 266)* or a tin of
    unsweetened purée
5 oz (125g) plain eating chocolate,
    Meunier, Bournville or the like
6 oz (175g) soft unsalted butter
4 oz (100g) vanilla sugar
½ teasp vanilla essence
1 teasp brandy
little icing sugar

Crème Chantilly
¼ pt (150ml) whipping cream
vanilla sugar to taste or castor sugar and
    vanilla essence
½ whipped egg white

25 people

Double all the quantities

Break up the chocolate and place it in a bowl over hot water to soften. Beat in the soft butter in flakes until blended, then beat in the sugar, chestnut purée, vanilla essence and brandy. When cool and thickening turn on to oiled cling film or tinfoil and form into a log. Chill in the fridge, then turn out and mark as a log. Sift over icing sugar and serve in thin slices with Crème Chantilly. It will keep for up to a week well wrapped in the fridge, or can be frozen.

Crème Chantilly. Whip the cream with sugar to taste until holding its shape. Whisk the egg whites to a peak and fold in.

✳✳✳   Nesselrode Pudding

I have my great-great-grandmother's recipe for this classic moulded chestnut pudding. From my delvings through old books, I suspect that she took the recipe from Eliza Acton, for the quantities and turn of phrase are so similar. Much as I enjoy it, especially made with fresh chestnuts in November, I think it is a little heavy for our present-day taste, now that fancy moulded shapes, creams and blancmanges have rather lost favour. So, rather hesitatingly, I have lightened the mixture; you can even add two whisked egg whites and serve it as a soufflé. As Malaga, the sweet wine recommended for this version, is not readily available, I have turned to rum or marsala. Serve it decorated with Crème Chantilly (*see page 265*) and marrons glacés or Preserved Chestnuts in Syrup (which, by the way, will keep for a year), and I think you will like it.

Ingredients
8–10 people

24 fine chestnuts or 1 lb (450g) tin
    unsweetened purée and only 7 fl oz
    (200ml) water
2 oz (50g) glacé cherries
2 oz (50g) candied citron peel
3 tbs sweet Malaga wine or rum or
    marsala
18 fl oz (525ml) water
1 vanilla pod
5 oz (125g) vanilla or castor sugar

1 tbs gelatine
17 fl oz (500ml) whipping cream
thin strips lemon rind
2 egg whites (optional)
good pinch salt

To Decorate (optional)
some Crème Chantilly, marrons glacés or
    Preserved Chestnuts in Syrup

Dice the cherries and peel and macerate in the Malaga, rum or marsala.

To Skin Chestnuts. I think I have finally found the ultimate in easy chestnut peeling. The trick is carefully to cut halfway round the circumference of each nut, midway on the rounded side between tip and base, and just through the shell and skin. Drop the nuts, a few at a time, into boiling water for 2–3 minutes, then remove them one at a time with a slotted spoon; take them in a kitchen cloth in your hands and push off the top half of the shell and skin (like the top of a boiled egg); then squeeze from the bottom and out should pop the whole nut, leaving the inner skin and shell behind.

Chestnut Purée. Simmer the chestnuts in 15 fl oz (450ml) water with the vanilla pod until beginning to soften; then add 3 oz (75g) of the vanilla or castor sugar and stew gently until very tender. Drain, remove the vanilla pod and reserve the liquid. Purée the chestnuts, adding a pinch of salt and enough of liquid to make a soft purée, sieve if necessary.

Sprinkle the gelatine on to the remaining cold water and soak for a few minutes.

Place 7 fl oz (200ml) cream in a saucepan with the vanilla pod split, 2 strips of thinly pared lemon rind and the remaining sugar and heat. Add the soaked gelatine and bring gently to the boil. Boil for 1 minute only, then keep hot, covered, to infuse for a good flavour until ready to use. Strain into the chestnut purée and cool until beginning to thicken (so that the cherries and peel do not sink once folded in). Whip the remaining 10 fl oz (300ml) cream until just holding its shape, whisking in any liquid from the cherries and peel. Fold into the chestnut with the chopped fruit. Turn into an oiled mould or bowl and chill. Turn out once set, or serve from the bowl. Decorate with whipped Crème Chantilly and the chestnuts or grated chocolate.

If you decide to use the egg whites, whisk until just holding a peak and fold in. Then turn into a 3 pt (1.7l) serving bowl.

P **   Prune and Whisky Mousse with Whisky Snow Cream

Don't you believe prunes are nursery food! They make a marvellous mousse with whisky, and I like to top them with this whisky-flavoured Snow Cream variation.

Ingredients
4–6 people

1 lb (450g) prunes
3 oz (75g) sugar or to taste
½ stick cinnamon
4 fl oz (100ml) whisky
1 tbs gelatine
2 tbs cold water
4 egg whites

Whisky Snow Cream
15 fl oz (150ml) whipping cream
1 tbs whisky
rind and juice ½ lemon
1 egg white
1 tbs vanilla or castor sugar to taste

25 people

3 lb (1.35kg) prunes
9 oz (250g) sugar or to taste
1½ sticks cinnamon
12 fl oz (350ml) whisky
3 tbs gelatine
6 tbs cold water
12 egg whites

Whisky Snow Cream
15 fl oz (450ml) whipping cream
3 tbs whisky
rind and juice of 2 lemons
2–3 egg whites
3 tbs vanilla or castor sugar

Soak the prunes overnight in just enough water to cover, then add sugar and the cinnamon stick and simmer until tender. Add the whisky and continue to simmer for a little until the juice is rich and syrupy.

Sprinkle the gelatine on to the cold water in a small bowl, soak for several minutes, then stand the bowl in a pan of hot water to melt.

De-stone, purée and sieve the prunes, adding in the juice to make a soft dropping purée, then stir in the melted gelatine. Whisk the egg whites until just holding a peak and fold into the cold prune mixture. Turn into a 2 pt (1.2l) soufflé dish and leave to set. Pipe or swirl the whisky snow cream over the mousse before serving.

Whisky Snow Cream. Mix the cream, whisky, lemon juice and grated lemon rind, and whisk till nearly stiff. Whip the egg white until just holding a peak and beat in the sugar. Gradually whisk into the cream mixture and pile on top of the prune mousse.

Variation for 25 people. You will need 3 × 2 pt (1.2l) soufflé dishes.

F ✱✱   Christmas Ice with Hot Mincemeat Sauce

Nutmeg is generally used very discreetly, but sometimes, at the right moment, it's nice to use it more lavishly. It seems to go rather well with the crème de cacao in this refreshing dish, perhaps because nutmeg and cocoa beans grow side by side in Grenada. This is not a true ice cream but a frozen dessert and, like all frozen dishes, benefits from a little mellowing before you eat it. The fresh mincemeat sauce, which would be enough for 10–12 people, will keep in the fridge or freezer, and can be used with pancakes or with bought vanilla ice cream.

Ingredients

4–6 people	*25 people*
8 fl oz (225ml) double cream	1¼ pts (750ml) double cream
2–3 tbs crème de cacao or rum	6–8 tbs crème de cacao or rum
6 fl oz (175ml) natural yoghurt	18 fl oz (550ml) natural yoghurt
6–8 meringue shells	20 or so meringue shells (made from 3 egg whites and 6 oz (175g) castor sugar)
1 teasp freshly grated nutmeg or to taste	2–3 teasp freshly grated nutmeg to taste

Mincemeat Sauce	*Mincemeat Sauce*
1 large or 2 medium apples (Cox for choice)	2 large or 3 smaller apples (Cox for choice)
2 oz (50g) raisins	4 oz (100g) raisins
2 oz (50g) currants	4 oz (100g) currants
2 oz (50g) sultanas	4 oz (100g) sultanas
2 oz (50g) flaked almonds	4 oz (100g) flaked almonds
1 oz (25g) candied peel	2 oz (50g) candied peel
2 oz (50g) soft dark brown sugar	4 oz (100g) soft dark brown sugar
½ teasp mixed spice	1 teasp mixed spice
grated rind and juice ½ lemon	grated rind and juice 1 lemon
grated rind and juice 1 orange	grated rind and juice 1 orange
segments of 1 orange (optional)	segments of 2 oranges (optional)
2oz (50g) diced fresh pineapple (optional)	4 oz (100g) diced fresh pineapple (optional)
2 oz (50g) skinned, halved and pipped grapes (optional)	4 oz (100g) skinned, halved and pipped grapes
4 tbs crème de cacao or rum	8–10 tbs crème de cacao or rum

Whip the cream until stiff. Whisk in the crème de cacao or rum before folding in the yoghurt and crumbled meringues with plenty of grated nutmeg. Turn into a serving bowl or individual oiled cocotte dishes with a disc of Bakewell paper placed in the bottom. Freeze until firm.

Mincemeat Sauce. Peel and core the apples and dice the flesh finely or process in a food processor before adding in all the remaining ingredients and stirring together or processing briefly. If you have added the fresh fruit and wish to keep the mixture, it is best kept in the freezer.

To Assemble. Mellow the ice cream in a fridge until not too firm. Heat the mincemeat sauce in a saucepan. Run a knife round the rim of each cocotte and turn out the ices, peeling off the Bakewell paper, or serve from the bowl. Hand the piping hot sauce round separately.

*   Apricot and Banana Flambé

How useful a quick last-minute pudding can be. I always like to have a tin of nice apricots in my store cupboard so that I can whistle this up when I want it. It also makes a tasty sauce to go with ice cream.

Ingredients
4–6 people

15 oz (400g) tin apricots
2–3 bananas
1 oz (25g) butter
2–3 tbs light brown sugar
¼ teasp mixed spice
grated rind ½ orange or lemon
2–3 tbs apricot syrup
2–3 tbs Grand Marnier, orange or apricot
    brandy
good squeeze lemon juice

Melt the butter in a wide frying pan. Drain the apricots. Peel and cut the bananas into 1" (2–2cm) lengths. When the butter is hot, add the apricot halves and banana pieces and sprinkle with the sugar, spice and grated rind. Toss and sauté over high heat for several minutes until the banana is just cooked and the juices are syrupy. Add the apricot syrup and heat through before pouring over the Grand Marnier. Have a match ready or, if you cook on gas, just tip the pan to ignite once the Grand Marnier has warmed. Shake until the flames extinguish, add a good squeeze of lemon juice and serve at once.

𝓕 *   Brandy Wine Sorbet

Try this sorbet when something light and refreshing is called for to counter-act a heavy meal but you still wish to keep the Christmas theme. It's very refreshing and makes a delicious end (or entr'acte) to a meal.

Ingredients
4–6 people

11 oz (300g) granulated sugar
1 pt (600ml) water
1½ lemons
2 oranges
8 fl oz (225ml) white wine
3 fl oz (75ml) brandy

Place the sugar and the water in a saucepan and heat gently, stirring until the sugar has dissolved. Then turn up the heat, stop stirring and boil fast for 4 minutes. Cool and chill. Add the grated rind of half an orange and half a lemon to the syrup. Stir in all the orange and lemon juice, which should come to about 8 fl oz (225ml). Add the wine and brandy, then strain and freeze to a firm mush, stirring the frozen sides to the middle once or twice.

When just about to set, turn into a food processor with metal blade or liquidiser and process until smooth and pale, or freeze in an ice cream maker for approx 30 minutes. Turn into a bowl or container and freeze.

Mellow in the fridge for ¼ hour or so before serving if too firm. It can then be scooped into individual chilled glasses, if you wish.

Miscellaneous

𝐹 ✳✳   Special Turkey Stuffing

A rather special stuffing with fruit and nuts, and excellent with turkey.

Ingredients
approx. 2 lb (1kg)

1 lb (450g) pork sausage meat
8 oz (225g) white breadcrumbs
3 oz (75g) large raisins
2 oz (50g) dried apricots or stoned prunes
4 oz (100g) whole hazelnuts
1 oz (25g) butter
1 finely chopped onion

the turkey liver (this can be added later)
2 eggs
1 tbs fresh chopped parsley and a little
    thyme or ½ teasp dried mixed herbs
grated rind 1 lemon
salt and pepper

Soak the raisins and apricots or prunes in a little water for ½–1 hour. Toast the hazelnuts in a hot oven or under the grill until an even golden brown, then rub off their skins in a kitchen cloth. Fry the onion gently in the butter until soft. Pick over the turkey liver, removing any green-tinged flesh which might taste very bitter from the bile. Cut it into small dice and sauté with the onion until just firm. Combine the sausage meat, breadcrumbs, eggs and herbs and beat well. Stir in the liver, onion and remaining ingredients. Stuff the cavity of the turkey with this and sew up the opening with strong button thread.

If making the stuffing ahead, leave out the liver, dice, sauté, and add when you stuff the bird.

✳   Bread Sauce

This is one of the oldest of English sauces, and is still traditionally served with turkey and chicken. The classic way is to boil the whole onion in the milk and then discard it. I prefer to cook chopped onion and include it in the sauce.

Ingredients

1 small onion
½ pint (300ml) milk
3–4 cloves

4 oz (100g) white breadcumbs
1–2 oz (25–50g) butter
salt and pepper

Finely chop the onion and put it in a small saucepan with the milk and cloves. Cover, and simmer gently until the onion is tender (about ½ hour). You can do this the day before, if you like, and have the breadcrumbs ready in a bag or from the freezer.

Shortly before serving, fish out the cloves, then sprinkle in enough breadcrumbs to make a fairly thick sauce. Don't forget that they swell up so that the sauce gets thicker after a while, and it should not be too solid. Season with salt and pepper and stir in a little butter in small pieces. Keep warm, turn into a sauceboat and hand with the turkey.

**   Cumberland Sauce

This recipe for this famous sauce comes from my great-great-grandmother. It's lovely with cold ham, tongue, or game pies and terrines. It seems to get better and better as you keep it, so make it well ahead.

Ingredients
approx ¾ pt (450ml)

6 shallots
5 tbs white wine vinegar
2 oranges
2 lemons
3 sugar lumps
1 teasp potato flour or arrowroot

5 tbs sherry
1–2 teasp made English mustard
2 teasp ground ginger or grated fresh
   root ginger
½ lb (225g) red currant jelly
2 tbs Grand Marnier or orange brandy

Dice the shallots finely and simmer gently, covered, in vinegar with a pinch of salt until softened.

Rub the sugar lumps on the lemons for zest and take julienne strips from the oranges and lemons. Blanch in plenty of water for 15 minutes until tender. Drain and refresh under the cold tap to set the colour. Squeeze ½ a lemon and ½ an orange. Mix the potato flour with 1 tbs sherry. Add everything to the shallots, whisking the red currant jelly well first because, if bought, it can be difficult to melt. Bring to the boil and simmer for 3–4 minutes. Pour into a jar and keep tightly stoppered when it should keep for months.

ℱ *   Brandy Butter

A light, well creamed brandy butter, holding its brandy well, finishes the Christmas puddings or mince pies properly.

Ingredients
Makes approx 11oz (300g)

4 oz (100g) soft, lightly salted butter
4 oz (100g) castor sugar
3–5 tbs brandy or to taste

Have the butter really soft so that it will cream easily. Cream the butter well, then gradually add the sugar, beating well. When all the sugar is added and the mixture is very soft and creamy, drip in the brandy, a little at a time beating all the time (if you warm it a little, it will be absorbed more easily). When complete, pile into a dish, preferably your serving dish for, once hardened, it cannot be re-creamed or moved easily. Cover closely and keep in the fridge (for a week or so) or in the freezer.

✳✳   Gingerbread Christmas Tree Decorations

It's rather fun to make some eatable decorations for the Christmas tree, and it's a nice change from plastic and glitter. Of course, if you think they won't get eaten then you can leave out all the goodies such as almonds, peel and currants, and make them with syrup rather than honey.

Ingredients
3 dozen small shapes

6 oz (175g) honey or syrup
1 oz (25g) butter
5 oz (125g) castor sugar
8 oz (225g) plain flour
½ teasp baking powder
2 oz (50g) cornflour
2–3 teasp ground ginger
¼ teasp ground cardamom
4 oz (100g) flaked almonds
1½ oz (35g) candied peel
¾ oz (20g) currants (optional)
½ egg, whisked
good pinch salt

Icing
½ egg white
2 oz (50g) icing sugar
1 teasp lemon juice

Place the honey, butter and sugar in a saucepan and warm until the sugar has melted; then cool. Sift the flour, baking powder and cornflour with the ground ginger, cardamom and salt into a bowl and add the almonds, crunched small with your hands, the peel and currants. Pour on the cooled honey and the egg and mix to a smooth dough. Knead and set aside in a plastic bag in the fridge for 1–2 hours or overnight.

Roll the mixture on a floured board to ⅛″ (3mm) thickness, then cut out diamonds, hearts and other shapes with biscuit cutters, or use your own large heart shapes cut out from cardboard. Make a good hole for a thread to hang them from, then place on greased baking trays and cook in a moderate oven (350°F/180°C/Gas 4) for 15–20 minutes until pale golden and cooked. Remove to cool and crisp on a rack, and make sure the hole is still there. While still warm, paint with icing if desired. Work decorative thread or fine ribbon through the decorations to hang up.

Icing. Beat the egg white and mix with the icing sugar and lemon juice to make a mixture with a good coating consistency.

P ✳✳   Christmas Cake

We should start to think about making this cake in the last week of October, preferably even earlier, to give it time to mature before digesting the brandy dosage. I have to admit, though, that it has been made as late as the week before Christmas, when it was still rather sticky and brandified (though it only got one dosage), but was still voted a great cake. I always bake it in an oblong tin to make the cutting easier.

Ingredients
5½ lb (2.5kg) approx

5 eggs
9 oz (250g) self-raising flour
½ teasp salt
1½ teasp mixed spice
¾ teasp freshly grated nutmeg
¾ teasp ground cinnamon
¼ teasp ground cloves
12 oz (350g) stoned raisins
12 oz (350g) currants
12 oz (350g) sultanas
6 oz (175g) glacé cherries
3 oz (75g) chopped almonds
3 oz (75g) ground almonds
6 oz (175g) mixed peel
9 oz (250g) softened butter

8 oz (225g) soft dark brown sugar
grated rind 1 lemon
½ teasp almond essence
4 tbs brandy
3–6 tbs milk

To Finish
10 tbs brandy
3–4 tbs apricot jam
1½ lb (675g) almond paste (*see page 110*)

Royal Icing
3 egg whites
good squeeze lemon juice
1½ lb (675g) sifted icing sugar

To Prepare the Tin. Line a 8″ × 9½″ (20cm–24cm) oblong tin or a 10″ (25cm) diameter circular tin, about 3″ (8cm) deep, with two thicknesses of greaseproof or Bakewell paper to come above the rim. Paint greaseproof (not Bakewell) paper with melted butter and tie a double layer of brown paper round the outside, also coming well above the top.

Break the eggs into a bowl and stand the bowl over a pan of lukewarm water for 5–10 minutes for the eggs to warm. Sift the flour with the salt and all the spices. Quarter and wash the cherries, dry well and roll in a little of the flour. Mix all the fruit, nuts and peel together and toss with a little flour. Cream the butter until pale and creamy, beat in the grated lemon rind and sugar. Cream really well.

Whisk the eggs until frothy, then gradually beat into the creamed butter and sugar (if the butter and sugar have been really well creamed, they should hold all the egg without curdling, but add 1 tbs flour if the mixture does look like curdling). When all the egg is added, stir in the fruit and the flour mixtures. Stir well and add the brandy, almond essence and enough milk for the mixture just to drop off the spoon.

Turn into the prepared tin, make a good dip in the middle and bake in a slow oven (300°F/150°C/Gas2) for the first 1½ hours, then in a very slow oven (250°F/130°C/Gas 1) for about another 3 hours. It's cooked when a skewer comes out clean. Do not overbake. Cool in the tin, then turn out on to a rack. When absolutely cold, wrap in tinfoil and seal in a container or tin until 6 weeks before using.

To finish. In early November unwrap and, from the base, carefully skewer the cake all over, but without going through the top crust. Spoon over 5 tbs brandy and repack the cake for another month or so. About 10 days before using, repeat brandy dosage, paint with warmed apricot jam and cover with almond paste. Leave for 3–4 days before icing and decorating.

Royal Icing. Put the egg whites in a bowl or the food processor with a good squeeze of lemon juice. Beat for a moment to break them up, then gradually work in the icing sugar, using enough to make the mixture stiff enough to stand in peaks. Use at once or—better for fine icing—leave overnight (scrape the mixture down and pop the bowl inside a plastic bag so that the icing cannot dry out). Cover the cake in a generous layer of icing, then mark in swirls and peaks with a wet palette knife before sticking in a sprig of holly or your decorations.

✳✳ An Excellent Lemon Mincemeat

From my great-great-grandmother's book I have yet another recipe, this time for a mincemeat that includes cooked lemon and baked apples. On delving further, I find many recipes along these lines, either called lemon mincemeat or perhaps excellent or superlative mincemeat. In all these old recipes, I find the proportion of suet a bit too much for today's taste, especially when cooked in puff pastry, so I have diminished it a bit.

Ingredients
6 lb (2.7kg) approx

3 thin-skinned lemons
6 cooking apples
1 lb (450g) raisins
1 lb (450g) currants
¾ lb (350g) suet
1 lb (450g) soft dark brown sugar
3 oz (75g) mixed peel
4 fl oz (100ml) brandy
2 tbs orange marmalade
1 teasp ground ginger
1 teasp ground allspice
1 teasp crushed coriander seeds } *or* **1½ tbs mixed spices**
½ teasp ground nutmeg
¼ teasp ground cloves
a little ground black pepper
½ teasp salt

Grate the rind and squeeze the juice from the lemons, then boil the shells for about 1 hour until tender enough to beat to pulp. Core and bake the apples. Drain and pulp the lemon shells, making sure no pips get in (food processor nowadays!), and scrape the baked apples from their skins. Add all the remaining ingredients, stirring well. Turn into a jar, cover closely and keep for two weeks before using.

*** Praline Truffles

The price of good chocolates is so high that the effort of making these quite wicked and utterly delicious truffles is well justified. They are superb for presents and for Christmas, and the children love helping to make them.

Ingredients
25 approx

4 oz (100g) good plain chocolate such as Bournville, Terry's or Meunier
4 oz (100g) unsalted or lightly salted soft butter
3 fl oz (75ml) double cream
4 oz (100g) praline powder
1–2 drops natural bitter almond essence
1 oz (25g) sifted icing sugar

1½ oz (35g) sifted cocoa and a little more for rolling the truffles
petit four cases

Praline Powder
2 oz (50g) mixed whole blanched almonds and hazelnuts
4 oz (100g) granulated sugar
4 tbs water

Break up the chocolate and melt it gently in a bowl set over warm water. Leave to cool but not to re-set. Cream the well-softened butter and beat in the praline powder. Whisk the cream, gradually adding the cool but flowing chocolate. Combine the butter and praline mixture with the cream and chocolate mixture, gradually working in the almond essence, icing sugar and cocoa. Leave in the fridge to firm a little before forming into balls. Roll these in extra cocoa and set into petit four cases or on greaseproof paper to firm up. Keep cool and eat within a week or so.

Praline Powder. Brown the almonds and hazelnuts in a hot oven (400°F/200°C/Gas 6) until light golden brown, watching that they don't burn. Place the hazelnuts on a sheet of kitchen paper inside a kitchen cloth, pull into a tight bundle and rub vigorously to remove the skins. Open and pick out the nuts, leaving behind the flakes of brown skin.

Place the sugar and water in a saucepan and stir over gentle heat until the sugar has completely dissolved. Once dissolved, turn up the heat and boil fast, without stirring, until the syrup is golden brown. Add the nuts and continue to cook until the syrup is a good brown. Have a sheet of oiled tinfoil ready and quickly pour out the praline into a thin layer. Leave to cool and harden. Break up the praline and process to a fine powder in the food processor. Alternatively, turn into a heavy duty polythene bag and bash to a powder with a rolling pin. Turn the praline powder into a tightly stoppered jar and it will keep for a week or two, and can also be used to sprinkle over puddings and cakes or added to icings.

*** Preserved Chestnuts in Syrup

The exorbitant price of marrons glacés has prompted me to try to perfect this recipe. The marrons will keep for a year and can be eaten on their own, drained, as a sweetmeat, used to decorate puddings, or served with their syrup in little glasses, topped with a cap of Crème Chantilly. There are, however, a few pitfalls. If the chestnuts are not cooked enough first, they tend not to absorb the sugar (which must happen very slowly anyway), but will go hard; if you cook them too much, they tend to break into pieces; they taste as good but are not so elegant. Buy the largest, shiniest, hardest chestnuts you can find, preferably in November when the crop first comes into the shops, and make them then because, later on, they shrivel inside the shell, are harder to peel and are not nearly so good.

Ingredients

1 lb (450g) peeled chestnuts *(see page 266)*	8 fl oz (225ml) water
12 oz (350g) granulated sugar	1–2 vanilla pods or vanilla essence to
12 oz (350g) glucose or dextrose	taste

Place the peeled chestnuts in a pan with the vanilla pods and just cover with water. Cook *very* gently until *nearly* tender, then drain carefully.

Place the sugar, glucose and water in a pan and heat gently, stirring, until the sugar has completely dissolved before bringing the syrup to the boil. Add the chestnuts, vanilla pods or about ½ teasp essence and bring back to the boil once. Leave the chestnuts and syrup in the covered pan, in a warm place (near the stove or a radiator) until the next day. Then uncover and bring gently to the boil. Boil for 2–3 minutes only, then cover and leave again in a warm place for another day.

On the third day, boil up as on the previous day and have some jars washed and warmed. Remove the chestnuts from the syrup and pack in the jars. Boil the syrup down until quite heavy. Pour over the chestnuts, cover and seal.

**   Crystallised Grapefruit

Crystallised fruit and other Christmas goodies are so expensive that it is well worth making these delicious and very cheap home-made preserved grapefruit. The pastry chef at the Troisgros restaurant in Roanne showed me how to do them.

Ingredients

4 grapefruit	2½ lb (1.15kg) granulated sugar

Place the wiped but unpeeled grapefruit on the table in front of you stalk end up. Cut off all four sides generously, leaving a small square middle core which you discard. Cut the pieces into ½" (1cm) segments. Place in a pan, cover generously with cold water and bring to the boil. Boil for one minute, then drain. Repeat twice more, starting each time with cold water. The third time drain them but not too thoroughly, and turn into a heavy pan with the sugar. Stir and heat very gently until the sugar melts completely, then simmer very slowly for 1–1½ hours until the grapefruit is tender and the remaining syrup is very thick. Drain well, and roll the pieces in granulated sugar.

Lay on greaseproof or kitchen paper on racks to dry. Once dry, pack into tins or boxes and it will keep for 6 months or more.

CONVERSION TABLES

Weights		Liquid Measures	
Imperial	**Recommended Metric Conversion**	**Imperial**	**Recommended Metric Conversion**
¼ oz	6g	1 fl oz	25ml
½ oz	12g	2 fl oz	50ml
¾ oz	20g	3 fl oz	75ml
1 oz	25g	4 fl oz	100ml
1½ oz	35g	5 fl oz (¼pt/1 gill)	150ml
2 oz	50g		
3 oz	75g	6 fl oz	175ml
4 oz (¼ lb)	100g	7 fl oz (⅓ pt)	200ml
		8 fl oz	225ml
5 oz	125g	9 fl oz	250ml
6 oz	175g	10 fl oz (½ pt)	300ml
7 oz	200g		
8 oz (½ lb)	225g	11 fl oz	325ml
		12 fl oz	350ml
9 oz	250g	13 fl oz	400ml
10 oz	275g	14 fl oz	425ml
11 oz	300g	15 fl oz (¾ pt)	450ml
12 oz (¾ lb)	350g		
13 oz	375g	16 fl oz	475ml
14 oz	400g	17 fl oz	500ml
15 oz	425g	18 fl oz	550ml
16 oz (1 lb)	450g	19 fl oz	575ml
		20 fl oz (1 pt)	600ml
1½ lb	675g		
2 lb	900g	1½ pts	900ml
2½ lb	1.15kg	1¾ pts	1l
3 lb	1.35kg	2 pts	1.2l
3½ lb	1.6kg	2½ pts	1.5l
4 lb	1.8kg	3 pts	1.7l
5 lb	2.25kg	4 pts	2.25l
6 lb	2.7kg	5 pts	2.8l
7 lb	3.2 kg		
8 lb	3.6kg		
9 lb	4.0kg		
10 lb	4.5 kg		

Oven Temperature Chart			
Very Slow	225°F	110°C	Gas ½
Very Slow	250°F	130°C	Gas 1
Slow	300°F	150°C	Gas 2
Very Moderate	325°F	170°C	Gas 3
Moderate	350°F	180°C	Gas 4
Moderately Hot	375°F	190°C	Gas 5
Hot	400°F	200°C	Gas 6
Hot	425°F	220°C	Gas 7
Very Hot	450°F	230°C	Gas 8
Very Hot	475°F	240°C	Gas 9

Approximate Meat Roasting Thermometer Readings		
140°F	60°C	Very Rare
150°F	65°C	Beef
160°F	70°C	Lamb
170°F	75°C	Duck and Pâté
180°F	80°C	Pork and Chicken
190°F	85°C	Well done
200°F	90°C	Very well done

The reading will usually rise by 5°F after removing the meat from the oven.

ADDRESSES OF SUPPLIERS

Suttons, Torquay, Devon—seed catalogues
Thompson & Morgan, London Road, Ipswich, Suffolk—unusual and worthwhile seeds
John and Caroline Stevens, Suffolk Herbs, Sawyers Farm, Little Cornard, Sudbury,
  Suffolk—out of the ordinary herbs, vegetable and wild flower seeds
Henry Doubleday Research Association, Convent Lane, Bocking, Braintree, Essex—
  booklets and advice on organic gardening
MacDonald Fraser, 17 Caledonian Road, Perth—hill mutton
F. Heinemann Ltd., 11 West Smithfield, London, E.C.1—suppliers of sausage skins
Orvis Ltd., Nether Wallop Mill, Stockbridge, Hampshire—suppliers of Wild Rice

INDEX

References to recipes are indicated by bold type